*Franz Joseph I
of Austria
and His Empire*

Franz Joseph I
of Austria
and His Empire

by Anatol Murad

TWAYNE PUBLISHERS, NEW YORK

To Broadus and Louise Mitchell
in appreciation of
many years of inspiring friendship

Preface

In this book, I have tried to sketch the life and reign of Franz Joseph I, to revise some widely accepted estimates of his character and personality, and to appraise his role in the disintegration and eventual collapse of his Empire. As the preservation of the Empire was the guiding rule of Franz Joseph's life, it would be impossible to understand the great events in this Emperor's life and reign without knowing something also about the character and problems of his multinational, multilingual Austro-Hungarian Empire. The book, therefore, deals not only with Franz Joseph himself, but also with his Empire. Hence the title: *Franz Joseph I of Austria and His Empire.*

The present brief essay makes no pretense of being an exhaustive biography of the Emperor or a full history of his reign. It is intended as an introduction, with a maximum of facts packed into limited space. I hope that, despite its brevity, the book gives a rounded description of Franz Joseph and his empire for readers not familiar with them, and that it may also have something to offer—some different views and interpretations—to those who already know much about the subject. To this latter group the presentation may at times appear too sketchy, to the former group too detailed. On balance, the treatment will probably be found to be too brief, as it must be in such a short book. Those who want to delve deeper into the subject may find the Selected Bibliography on pp. 245-250 a convenient take-off point. The literature on Franz Joseph and on the history of the Austro-Hungarian Empire during his reign is immense and is still continually being added to. It would be beyond the scope of the present volume to list all that has been written about these subjects; but the Selected Bibliography includes most of the significant works in the field.

The information on which *Franz Joseph I of Austria and His Empire* is based was gathered almost entirely in Austria—the State Archive, the Austrian National Library, the Universities of Vienna and Graz. In all these institutions I received patient and courteous assistance, for which I herewith express my thanks.

Spending a year's sabbatical leave from the University of Puerto Rico in Austria to prepare this book, I recaptured the spirit and flavor of the age of Franz Joseph in the midst of the monuments of his reign and of my own youthful memories. Born and raised in Vienna, the first years of my life coincided in time and place with the last of Franz Joseph's. He was the revered old Emperor of my schooldays and of my parental home; the occasions on which I saw him, and then his majestic funeral, are vividly remembered boyhood experiences. Now, fifty years later, conversations with many Austrians—students, professors, librarians, retired officers and officials, princes and janitors—have impressed me with the reverence still manifested for the old Emperor in many circles of Austrian society, and with the tenacity of the Franz Joseph legend.

Much of what has been written about Franz Joseph is partisan, ranging from adulation to denigration. One author (Spitzmüller) finds it difficult to discover the least shadow in the picture of this paragon of virtue.[1] Another (Gopčevič) can find no words strong enough to condemn Franz Joseph's scandalous baseness and lack of character.[2] The same accusation of partisanship can undoubtedly be leveled against my own book. Though I was careful to desist from dispensing praise or blame, and intended to let the facts speak for themselves, I could not escape, any more than can any biographer and historian, having to select the facts with which to construct the portrait of my subject. This selection inevitably introduced some conscious or unconscious bias. It cannot be helped. In endeavoring to be objective, I had to dismiss defamatory but unsubstantiated allegations against the Emperor's conduct. On the other hand, I had to strip Franz Joseph of some of the virtues with which the pious fables of Byzantine admirers bedecked him and which I myself had previously believed, and to focus (especially in chapters 6, 7, and 8) on some less widely known aspects of his life and personality, which tend to dim his luster. Of Franz Joseph the reverse may be said of what Mark Antony observed at Caesar's burial: The evil that Franz Joseph did was interred with his bones, while the good that he did—or that he is credited with—lives after him. And since, unlike Mark Antony, I have come not to bury Caesar, but to resurrect him, it is incumbent upon me also to resurrect some of the facts buried with him or at least respectfully overlooked in popular portraits of this venerated ruler.

Regina, Canada, 1968

NOTE ON NAMES

Personal Names

The subject of this book is called by his German name, *Franz Joseph*, and not *Francis Joseph*. The English form makes two distinct names of what in German sounds like one single name, pronounced *fransyosef*. In German, the name is often spelled *Franz Josef*, but here the alternative German spelling *Franz Joseph* is adhered to because (1) the "f" in place of the "ph" would inject into the name a note of modernism totally foreign to its bearer and, more importantly, (2) the Emperor himself spelled his name *Franz Joseph*—with a "ph."

Names of members of the Imperial family and of other personages are similarly rendered in the form of their own language in order to avoid possible confusion and also to preserve the essential flavor of the names. On the other hand, the names of historical figures whose names are well-known in their English form, have been rendered in that form, and not in the original German. Thus: Empress *Maria Theresa* (1740-80), not *Maria Theresia*; *Charles V* (1519-56), not *Karl V*; *Frederick II* (Hohenstaufen Emperor 1215-50), not *Friedrich II*; but, the Emperor *Friedrich III*, not *Frederick III*, the first Habsburg Emperor (1452-93).

This method of treating names may be inconsistent, but it seemed to offer a solution to a minor, though vexing, problem.

Place Names

Places are given the names and spellings used in *Webster's Geographical Dictionary* (Revised Edition, 1963). Many cities and towns in the non-German parts of the Austro-Hungarian Empire used to be better known by their German names. For example, *Kroměříž*, a town in Czechoslovakia, was generally known as *Kremsier*, its German name. *Timisoara*, a city in Romania, used to be better known by its Hungarian name, *Temesvár*. In these and similar cases the present name is used, and the former name is added in parentheses.

Contents

CHAPTER

Preface   vii

Notes on Names   ix

1   Introduction: Emperor Franz Joseph I
of Austria   1

2   How Franz Joseph Became Emperor   6

3   Franz Joseph's Lands and Peoples   10

4   The Revolution of 1848   23

5   By the Grace of the Czar   34

6   Franz Joseph's Character and Personality   45

7   The Soldier Emperor   60

8   Franz Joseph's Simplicity   72

9   The House of Austria   85

10   Franz Joseph's Parents and His Education   96

11   Empress Elisabeth   105

12   Troublesome Relatives   118

13   Franz Joseph and His Constitutions   130

14   The Struggle for German Hegemony   149

15   The Hungarian Settlement   169

16   The "Mission" of the Habsburg Empire   180

17   The Economy of Franz Joseph's Empire   187

18   The Making of World War I   203

19   The Peace Emperor   212

APPENDIX

A   Titles and Territories of Franz Joseph
on His Accession to the Throne   223

B   Franz Joseph's Chief Ministers   226

C   Habsburg Rulers   229

Notes   232

Genealogical Chart   238/239

Chronology of Events in the Life and Reign
of the Emperor Franz Joseph   241

Selected Bibliography   245

Index   251

CHAPTER 1

Introduction: Emperor Franz Joseph I of Austria

Hardly a year goes by without some newspaper or magazine in the United States commemorating some event in the life of Franz Joseph with an article, often with pictures of the Emperor as an old man with bald head, "Emperor beard"—white mustache, side whiskers, clean-shaven chin—a benevolent expression in his tired eyes, yet majestic, unapproachable. Most readers of this book, therefore, are likely to have at least some slight acquaintance with this famous monarch.

He was born on August 18, 1830, at Schönbrunn, the summer palace of the Habsburg Emperors in a Vienna suburb; he died there on November 21, 1916. He reigned sixty-eight years—longer than any European monarch in all history except his contemporary, Prince Johann II of Liechtenstein, who outlasted Franz Joseph by reigning seventy years, from 1858 to 1929.*

Franz Joseph cannot be called a "great" ruler. He won no great wars, conquered no empires, was no reformer, and unlike the Habsburg Emperors of the baroque, he had no interest in

---

* Louis XIV of France was king for seventy-two years, from 1643 to 1715. But as Louis was four years old when he became king, his mother acted as Regent in his stead. His personal reign did not begin until 1661, and therefore lasted only fifty-four years.

art, built no Schönbrunn, founded no Prado. He was pedantic
and without any streak of genius. What distinguished him was
an unique air of majesty which set him apart from all others,
even members of his immediate family. His presence was awe-
inspiring. Theodore Roosevelt, who visited Franz Joseph in 1910,
was impressed by the Emperor's dignity. "You see in me," Franz
Joseph told Roosevelt, "the last European monarch of the old
school."

Franz Joseph was born to be Emperor, and he was endowed
with regal qualities that enabled him to live up to his destiny.
His personality stood completely in the service of his Imperial
office; the man was subordinated to the monarch. He was per-
vaded by the sense of being Emperor by the Grace of God, and
he never doubted his own and his officials' authority. The preservation of his Imperial power, the strengthening of his Empire
as a Great Power, was the law of life which Divine Providence
had prescribed for him. Liberal and democratic ideas of government he rejected as reprehensible and false. He remained all his
life a believer in autocracy.

Despite his aversion to democratic ideas, Franz Joseph in time
became "the very model of a modern constitutional monarch."
Reversing the usual development from well-meaning young ruler
to black old tyrant, Franz Joseph started as a detested tyrant and
became the "old Emperor." Resented, hated at first, Franz Joseph,
with the passage of the years, became respected, even revered,
by the broad masses of his subjects. As an old man he enjoyed a
genuine popularity. This was partly a tribute to his age, partly
admiration of his impressive fitness even in old age, gratitude for
the prolonged peace he had granted his subjects and for the
tolerance of his regime, troubled and imperfect though it was;
but it was also compassion with the man for the blows fate had
struck him: defeat in war, loss of provinces, and a series of personal tragedies—his first child dead in infancy, his brother executed, his only son a suicide, his wife murdered, his nephew and
heir-apparent assassinated. The Emperor bore these misfortunes
with fortitude, and the people respected and admired him for it.

Franz Joseph lived in the epoch ending with the First World

War—which he unleashed and which destroyed his Empire—but he did not belong to his time. Even in that vanished world of more than fifty years ago, Franz Joseph was an anachronism. He was a dyed-in-the-wool reactionary who not only resisted modern trends but wanted to turn back to earlier ways. He was a medieval man at heart, and he probably would have felt more at home in the medieval world; his ideas and values were medieval. Opposed to innovation in most things, he also distrusted modern technology. He refused to use a telephone or an elevator; he insisted on documents being submitted to him in longhand and was annoyed when he had to read typescript; he reluctantly rode in an automobile once or twice in his life. He did, however, use telegraph and railroad, the technological achievements of his youth. Paradoxically, his frequent travels, though by railroad, gave his reign a medieval stamp. His court, always on the move, was reminiscent of the time when feudal kings had no fixed residence, but had to travel with their retinues from manor to manor to collect, and consume, their revenue in kind. Franz Joseph took his entire court establishment with him when he traveled to Budapest or Gödöllö (his castle near Budapest) or Ischl (his summer villa near Salzburg). Even when he traveled abroad he was accompanied by several high-ranking aides and a number of secretaries.[1]

Though Franz Joseph belongs to a now distant past, the half century which has elapsed since his death has not erased him and his times from the memory of the Austrian people. Not only the elderly, who were born in the time of Franz Joseph and perhaps saw the old Emperor now and then, driving along Mariahilfer-strasse on his way between Schönbrunn and the Hofburg (the Imperial palace in the center of Vienna), but also younger people are familiar with the figure of Franz Joseph. Books about him are displayed in the show windows of nearly every bookstore in Austria; newspaper and magazine articles about him abound. You see Franz Joseph everywhere—in statues, on gold and silver coins, now minted for hoarding and for use as jewelry. Visit the Museum of Art History in Vienna and you are confronted by a bust of Franz Joseph. At the head of the festive stair in the

University—Franz Joseph. Commemorative tablets inform you
that this or that building was constructed in the reign of Franz
Joseph. The State Theaters, also built under Franz Joseph, display his initials, topped by the Imperial crown, on doors, on
mirror frames, and wherever loyal imagination could find an
excuse to put them. These daily reminders perpetuate the presence of Franz Joseph. Austrian promoters of tourism, by under-
lining the historical attractions of their country, have helped
to stir interest in Franz Joseph. Nostalgically, Austrians look
back to the time of their past glory, when Vienna was the hub
of an empire, one of the great world centers with a brilliant
intellectual and artistic life, and full of Imperial splendor. Over
this vision of a vanished golden age floats the father image of the
"old Emperor": the symbol, the personification of the good old
days.

There was, to be sure, a seamy side to this glittering life. There
was poverty and protest aplenty. But it is also true that even the

Franz Joseph's time was the time of the "gay Vienna" of story
and film; the Vienna of the *Heurigen* (this year's wine), of
coffee houses, elegant balls, of marvelous theaters and one of
the world's great operas. Vienna was the music capital of the
world: It was the Vienna of the Strausses—Johann Strauss, father
and son, Richard Strauss, Oscar Straus—of Mahler, Bruckner,
Hugo Wolf, Brahms. Austrian literature, too, shone brightly in
Franz Joseph's time, with Adalbert Stifter, Grillparzer, Hugo
von Hofmannsthal, Arthur Schnitzler, and a host of other great
names. Franz Joseph's Vienna was also a great scientific center.
Especially in many fields of medicine, Vienna led the world up
to the time of World War I. Theodor Billroth in surgery, Sigmund Freud in psychology, Karl Landsteiner in pathology, Julius
Wagner-Jauregg in neurology, and dozens more, made Vienna
the Mecca of physicians and surgeons from all over the world.
Though concentrated in Vienna, the cultural life of the monarchy
flourished in Budapest, Prague, and other cities as well. Kafka,
Rilke, Dvořák, Smetana, among many other non-Viennese con-
tributors to artistic and cultural life, belong to the age of Franz
Joseph.

There was, to be sure, a seamy side to this glittering life. There
was poverty and protest aplenty. But it is also true that even the

lowest classes of society shared to some extent the gaiety and joyfulness of "gay Vienna."

To what extent, if any, Franz Joseph contributed to the atmosphere of well-being, of euphoria, in his Empire, will be revealed in the subsequent chapters. But whether or not he had anything to do with it, his name and image are inextricably woven into the memory of this great period in Austrian life.

CHAPTER 2

How Franz Joseph
Became Emperor

On Saturday, December 2, 1848, Archduke Franz, as he had been called until then, ascended the throne of the Austrian Empire as Franz Joseph I. The event had been prepared in strictest secrecy and took place in the Moravian city of Olomouc (Olmütz, now in Czechoslovakia), the temporary residence of the Imperial family, in a subdued spirit of somber solemnity, with little pomp or fanfare. It consisted of a series of legal transactions: Emperor Ferdinand I "The Kindhearted" abdicated; Franz Joseph, then eighteen years old, was declared to have attained majority; Archduke Franz Carl, brother of Ferdinand and father of Franz Joseph, renounced his claim to the throne; Franz Joseph was proclaimed Emperor.

The new Emperor had intended to bear the name Franz II, after his grandfather Franz I,* whom he had loved as a child and whom he admired. But only the day before his elevation, it had been decided that he should call himself Franz Joseph. This would symbolize a new era in government, combining the conservatism of Franz I with the progressive reformism of the popular Joseph II (1765-90). As his motto Franz Joseph chose *viribus unitis*— expressing his aim to make his Empire strong by unifying and centralizing it.

The reason for the subdued spirit pervading the historic event

---

* The first Emperor of Austria, 1804-35; the last of the Holy Roman Emperors, as Franz II, 1792-1806.

was that the Empire was engulfed by revolution. "Perhaps never before did a monarch ascend the throne in similar moments," wrote the Vienna correspondent of the Augsburg *Allgemeine Zeitung*,[1] "moments which indeed call for the full vigor of youth . . . the full ingenuousness of youth." Habsburg rule was in grave danger of collapsing. Twice that year the Revolution in Vienna had put the Imperial family to flight, first to Innsbruck, the second time to Olomouc, a fortress city. Never, until its end in 1918, had the dynasty been harder pressed than in 1848. Franz Joseph was conscious of the gravity of the situation, of the heavy responsibility placed upon his young shoulders. After the ceremony, he knelt before his uncle who whispered: "God bless you, be good, God will protect you." All eyes were moist. Then, giving way to emotion, Franz Joseph threw himself into his mother's arms to hide his tears.[2]

It was Franz Joseph's mother, Archduchess Sophie, who had arranged the changing of Emperors. She was ambitious, domineering, and she had become the power behind the throne—"the only man at court," as the people said when they did not speak of her in less complimentary terms. When Emperor Franz I died in 1835, she had expected her husband Franz Carl to become Emperor instead of his elder brother, the epileptic, mentally deficient, childless Ferdinand. Franz Carl was himself of probably less than average intelligence, and without any ambition, but he was not feeble-minded, and with the help of his capable wife could have made an acceptable emperor. But Prince Metternich, the then all-powerful Chancellor, perhaps in order to perpetuate his own control of Empire affairs, had persuaded Franz I not to deviate from the established law of succession, and to let Ferdinand be Emperor.

Thwarted in her ambition to be Empress, Sophie was determined at least to put her son on the throne and to make herself "Empress-Mother" without waiting for the death of the "*Trottel*" (idiot) on the throne. Events proved her right, for as it turned out, waiting would have been disappointing: despite illness, Ferdinand lived longer than any previous Habsburg Emperor; he did not die until 1875, at the age of eighty-two, three years after her own death! Sophie had schemed to push her incompetent brother-in-law off the throne and put her son in his place, as soon as young Franz reached majority. The "changing of the heads" in the House of Austria had originally been planned for August 18, 1848, when Franz would be eighteen years old. The revolution intervened and made a smooth transference of power at that time impossible. But in another way the Revolution furthered Sophie's plans. Ferdinand—in his goodness of heart which proved his unfitness to be a ruler—had compromised the dynasty by promising the people he would meet all their demands. Now that the Revolution was being beaten down, a way had to be found to get out of honoring Ferdinand's promises. A new monarch would not be bound by his predecessor's commitments, and so the shift of throne occupants was decided upon. Difficulties arose at the last moment when Ferdinand had second thoughts about abdicating and Franz Carl discovered he might like to be Emperor after all, at least for a short time. It took the ingenuity of the two brothers' wives to talk them out of their obstinacy.

When they saw the posters proclaiming the change of Emperors, the people could not believe their eyes; the news took them completely by surprise. There was much speculation about the meaning of the event, and there were different reactions to it. Conservatives, aristocrats, and army officers were enthusiastic, confident that the young, dashing, imposing, self-assured Franz Joseph would be the savior of the Monarchy. The Parliament, meeting at Kroměříž (Kremsier, now Czechoslovakia), was stunned into unbelieving silence by the announcement. In Vienna, some of the people rejoiced, believing that now at last good times would return, the price of meat would go down, the new Emperor would prove benevolent and merciful like his uncle. But most people were in no mood to acclaim the new ruler, sensing the true purpose of his elevation to the throne at this juncture. The people had nothing against the Emperor Ferdinand who was kind and sympathetic to their demands, but they feared Franz Joseph because he would be ruled by his mother. Under her regime, all gains made by the Revolution would be lost. True, Franz Joseph proclaimed himself a "constitutional" Emperor, who promised "to share Our Rights with the representatives of Our Peoples." What this promise was worth when Sophie had the power—through her devoted son—the future was to show.

The unpopularity of the change of Emperors, the hatred and mistrust of the lower classes for the house of Habsburg as a whole, excepting the kindly Ferdinand and the popular Archduke Johann, had been the reason for keeping the plans for the Emperor switch secret lest previous announcement add fuel to the flames of revolution; and for springing it on the people as a surprise and a *fait accompli*. Resentment was widespread. The rebellious Viennese sneered at the young "Fratz"—by substituting a *t* for the *n* in "Franz" on the proclamations posted in the city, they had renamed the new Emperor "brat." There were meetings of armed bands; the army was again called out.

In Hungary resentment was stronger still. Hungarian leaders and press spoke of Franz Joseph as the "impudent royal youngster," the "unripe fruit of a rotten tree." People joked about Franz Joseph being no more King of Hungary than he was King of Jerusalem, both of which titles he claimed[3] (see list of titles in next chapter). The Hungarian government declared Franz Joseph's accession illegal, and even deposed the Habsburg dynasty. Franz Joseph had to prove his right to his Empire by the might of his army.

The course of the Revolution, and how Franz Joseph conquered it, will be the subjects of subsequent chapters. But an account of these stirring events will have added meaning after a brief survey of the extent, composition, and character of the Empire which Franz Joseph laid claim to on that memorable December 2, 1848, at Olomouc.

CHAPTER 3

Franz Joseph's Lands and Peoples

TITLES AND TERRITORIES. "We, Franz Joseph the First, by the Grace of God Emperor of Austria; King of Hungary and Bohemia, King of Lombardy and Venetia, of Dalmatia, Croatia, Slavonia, Galicia, Lodomeria and Illyria; King of Jerusalem &c; Archduke of Austria; Grand Duke of Tuscany; Duke of Lorraine, of Salzburg, Styria, Carinthia, Carniola; Grand Duke of Transylvania; Margrave of Moravia; Duke of Upper- and Lower-Silesia, of Modena, Parma, Piacenza and Guastalla, of Oświecim and Zator, of Teschen, Friuli, Dubrovnik and Zadar; Count, with princely rank, of Habsburg, of Tirol, of Kyburg, Gorizia and Gradisca; Prince of Trento and Bressanone; Margrave of Upper- and Lower-Lusatia and in Istria; Count of Hohenembs, Feldkirch, Bregenz, Sonnenberg &c; Lord of Trieste, of Kotor and in the Windish March . . ."

With this recitation of his titles, the new Emperor started a Proclamation to the peoples of his Empire on December 2, 1848, the day he ascended the Habsburg throne. Present-day readers may be more struck with the air of Graustarkian comedy, than with the ruler's exalted station, suggested by this fanciful-sounding list of titles. Some were in fact imaginary, yet most of them corresponded to lands which Franz Joseph claimed as his. (Discrepancies between titles and territories are analyzed in Appendix I.)

What were the territories claimed by Franz Joseph and constituting the Austrian Empire? The answer is summarized in Table 1, which lists the names of the territories included in the Habsburg Empire at the time of Franz Joseph's accession, in the order of the time at which these territories were acquired by the house of Habsburg, together with their areas and the names of their capital cities. The total area of Franz Joseph's Empire in 1848 was 257,478 square miles—after Russia, the largest country in Europe. It was a little larger than the combined areas of New England, New York, New Jersey, Delaware, Pennsylvania, Ohio, and Indiana; only 10,000 square miles smaller than Texas!

Size and Nationalities of Population. The new Emperor's proclamation was addressed to "My" peoples. Who were "his" peoples? How many of them were there? What was their nationality? What language did they speak? The answers to these questions are summarized in Table 2.

The total population of the Empire was about 37½ million, larger than that of any other European country at the time—again excepting Russia. But unlike that of most "nation-states," the population of the Habsburg Empire was not composed of one single, or at least predominant, national group, but was made up of many different nationalities, none with a preponderance. In this respect, the Habsburg Empire was unique among European states. There was no Austrian "nation." France was French, Piedmont (the nucleus of the emerging Kingdom of Italy) was Italian. Great Britain, it is true, included Scots, and Welsh, and Irish, as well as English people, often at loggerheads with one another, but the English were in a decisive and dominant majority; and there was no language problem as there was in the Austrian Empire: even the rebellious Irish spoke English and had largely forgotten their own Gaelic language. Russia may have counted as many or more nationalities than the Habsburg Empire, but here again, the Russians were dominant, the non-Russians were conquered minorities on the periphery of the Russian Empire. In the Habsburg Empire, on the other hand, there were no dominant racial, national, or language groups.

Table 2 lists in the order of their numerical strength the language groups—essentially corresponding to ethnic, or national groups—in the Empire in 1848: there were 8 million Germans,

TABLE 1

Lands of the Austrian Empire in 1848

Column 1 Date of First Acquisition	Column 2 Name of Land	Column 3 Area in Square Miles	Column 4 Capital City	Column 5 Date of Last Restoration
1282	Archduchy of Lower Austria	7,658	Vienna	
"	Archduchy of Upper Austria	4,625	Linz	1816
"	Duchy of Styria	8,662	Graz	
"	Duchy of Carniola	3,845	Ljubliana (Laibach)	1815
1335	Duchy of Carinthia	3,989	Klagenfurt	1815
1363	County (ranked as principality) of Tirol and Vorarlberg	11,311	Innsbruck	
1374	County (ranked as principality) of Gorizia and Gradisca with Margraviate of Istria and the City of Trieste with its Territory	3,078	Trieste	1815
1526	Lands of the Bohemian Crown:			
"	Kingdom of Bohemia	20,065	Prague	
"	Margraviate of Moravia	8,583	Brno (Brünn)	
"	Duchy of Upper- and Lower Silesia	1,988	Opava (Troppau)	
"	Lands of the Hungarian Crown:			
"	Kingdom of Hungary	82,799	Budapest	
"	Kingdom of Croatia and Slavonia with the City of Fiume and its territory	8,889	Zagreb (Agram)	1815
"	Grand Duchy of Transylvania	21,209	Sibiu (Hermannstadt)	
"	Croatian-Slavonian and Servian-Hungarian Military Frontier	11,175		1815
1714	Kingdom of Lombardy	8,337	Milan	1815

TABLE 1–*Lands of the Austrian Empire in 1848* (cont'd.)

1772	Kingdom of Galicia and Lodomeria with the Duchies of Zator and Oświecim and the Grand Duchy of Cracow	30,320	Lvov (Lemberg)	1846
1774	Duchy of Bucovina	4,033	Chernovtsy (Czernowitz)	
1797	Kingdom of Venetia	9,224	Venice	1815
"	Kingdom of Dalmatia	4,925	Zadar (Zara)	1815
1805	Duchy of Salzburg	2,763	Salzburg	1816
	Total area	257,478		

Source: Based on Schmitt, F., *Statistik des österreichischen Kaiserstaates. Nach "Hain's Handbuch der Statistik."* Wien, Verlag von Tendler & Co., 1858.

Column 1 indicates the year in which the first part, not necessarily the whole, of a territory came under Habsburg rule. Tirol and Vorarlberg, for instance, were acquired piecemeal through inheritance, marriage, purchase, and conquest; but the first part of it came to the Habsburgs in 1363. The dates in Column 5 indicate later restorations of all or part of a territory after it had been temporarily lost. The Austrian Empire lost many possessions in the Napoleonic period, but recovered most of them in 1815 or 1816, after the defeat of Napoleon. The areas of the several lands shown in Column 3 are of the parts of the indicated country still in possession of the Emperor in 1848. In the case of Silesia this was only a small part of the whole Duchy of Silesia, most of which had been lost to Prussia in 1742. Of course there were also many possessions that had come to the Habsburgs and had been lost again in their entirety, such as Burgundy, the Netherlands, Spain, and Portugal. Here only those are listed which were still part of the Empire in 1848.

5½ million Magyars, 5 million Italians, 4 million Czechs, and so on. The Germans were the largest contingent, but far from a majority. If all the Slavs were grouped together, they would add up to over 15 million, almost twice the number of Germans, though still not a majority of the population. But the Slavs formed two quite distinct groups: Southern and Northern. The group of Southern Slav nations—Serbians, Croatians, Slovenes, totaling 4 million people—were close enough to be counted as one, at

TABLE 2

Population of the Austrian Monarchy in 1848, According to Language Groups

	Total Population	Germans	Magyars	Italians	Czechs	Ruthenians	Romanians	Poles	Slovaks
Lower Austria	1,494,399	1,474,067			11,803				
Upper Austria & Salzburg	856,694	856,694							
Styria	1,003,074	650,200							
Carinthia & Carniola	784,786	260,821							
Littoral (Istria, etc.)	500,201	9,385		116,860			1,555		
Tirol & Vorarlberg	859,250	529,419		320,211					
Bohemia	4,347,962	1,727,950			2,549,975				
Moravia & Silesia	2,250,594	751,325			1,327,120			131,422	
Galicia, Bucovina, & Cracow	5,253,621	133,000	5,446		2,182	2,616,799		2,001,143	
Dalmatia	404,640			28,500					
Lombardy	2,670,833			2,667,868					
Venetia	2,257,200	12,036		1,873,002					
Hungary (approx.)	11,000,000	1,156,400	4,708,260	4,000		475,310	1,029,680		1,822,730
Transylvania	2,182,700	250,000	566,500				1,290,000		
Military Frontier (without frontier armies)	1,226,408	41,337	106,067	434	9,590		203,931		
Imperial-Royal Military (incl. frontier armies)	491,786	128,286	32,500	52,700	96,300	50,100	20,700	37,700	
Totals	37,584,148	7,980,920	5,418,773	5,063,575	3,996,970	3,142,209	2,545,866	2,170,265	1,822,730

Source: Based on Historisch-ethnographisch-statistische Notizen über die Nationalitäten Österreichs, ihre Zahlen und Sprachverhältnisse. Nebst einer kurzen Darstellung der politischen Angelegenheiten der Serben und ihrer Privilegien . . . Zusammengestellt von EINEM BESCHAULICHEN REISENDEN. Wien, Verlag der Buchhandlung von Albert A. Wenedikt, 1849. pp. 66 ff.

	Ser-vians	Croats	Slo-venes	Jews	Friu-lians*	Molda-vians	Gyp-sies	Arme-nians	Bul-garians	Greeks	Ladi-ners*	Rus-sians	Alba-nians
Lower Austria	4,233			4,296									
Upper Austria & Salzburg													
Styria			352,874										
Carinthia & Carniola		17,697	506,266	2									
Littoral (Istria, etc.)		134,545	185,757	3,530	48,569								
Tirol & Vorarlberg				978							8,642		
Bohemia				70,037									
Moravia & Silesia		663		40,064									
Galicia, Bucovina, & Cracow				346,702		140,626		5,384				2,339	
Dalmatia	374,725			410									1,005
Lombardy			26,317	2,965									
Venetia	739,240	689,580		4,760	341,085								
Hungary (approx.)			49,600	265,620			33,000	3,000	13,580	10,000			
Transylvania				7,000			60,000	9,000	200				
Military Frontier (without frontier armies)	339,176	524,048		537									1,288
Imperial-Royal Military (incl. frontier armies)	19,000	27,600	22,000		4,300		600						
Totals	1,472,141	1,398,366	1,142,814	746,901	393,954	140,626	93,600	17,384	13,780	10,000	8,642	2,339	2,293

Note: Though the figures in this table give the appearance of exactness, they are not exact, partly because the Hungarian and military figures are estimates, partly because there are errors in additions in the sources from which the figures were derived.

* Friulians and Ladiners are possibly of Celtic origin. Their idioms belong to the Raeto-Romanic, Neo-Latin dialects. Friulian is spoken in the region around Udine in Northeastern Italy (in 1848 still under Habsburg rule); Ladin in South Tirol (now also part of Italy)—around Bolzano (Bozen) and in the Dolomites.

least in their national aspirations, and today all these nations live within the boundaries of Yugoslavia. The Northern Slavs—Czechs, Slovaks, Poles, Ruthenians (also called Ukrainians)—were less united among themselves except in their common aspiration to national independence. Today these peoples live in Czechoslovakia, Poland, and in the U.S.S.R.

Not only were there many different nationalities, or language groups, but to complicate matters further, they cut across the boundary lines of the several crownlands (provinces). Almost 2 million Germans lived in predominantly Czech Bohemia, more than 1 million Germans lived in Hungary. Of the more than 5 million inhabitants of Galicia and Bucovina, half were Ruthenians (Ukrainians), 2 million were Poles. Hungary comprised fourteen different language groups; Galicia and Bucovina nine. In only three of the crownlands did all the inhabitants speak the same language: Lower Austria and Upper Austria (at that time including Salzburg) were inhabited by Germans; Lombardy by Italians. Language minorities in these provinces were negligible. But all the other provinces had more or less substantial minorities. Table 2 shows where the members of the several language groups lived.

A TOWER OF BABEL. There was no single language in which all the peoples of this many-tongued Empire could communicate. Attempts had been made, especially by the Emperor Joseph II, to make German the lingua franca of all Habsburg lands, but with little success. Although most educated persons in the several parts of the Empire understood and spoke German, the great masses of the people understood and spoke only their native language. It is not difficult to imagine the complexities of administration in this Tower of Babel.

NATIONALISM TABOOED. It is not surprising that in this multinational Empire, where no single national group predominated, the nationalistic aspirations of any were tabooed; and these nationalistic aspirations became increasingly strong and persistent during the reign of Franz Joseph. To aim at national independence meant to aim at restricting if not altogether abolishing Imperial power; it was therefore inimical to Habsburg interests. People were expected to be loyal to the Imperial house, not to their respective countries. It was the policy of the Habsburgs never to identify themselves with nationalism of any sort. In Germany and in Italy, when these countries emerged as nation-states, even in Russia, the monarch could be leader and symbol of the nation; the soldier could be asked to die for his country —for Italy, for the *Vaterland*, for Mother Russia. Not so in Austria. The Habsburg ruler was non-national. Franz I is credited with the famous remark when someone was referred to as an Austrian patriot: "Is he a patriot for me?" The Emperor's soldiers died for the Emperor, not for their country. If they wanted to die for their country—Hungary or Italy, for instance—as many of them were ready to do, they were as likely to do so before Imperial firing squads or on the gallows as on the battlefield. A patriot was a traitor—unless he was a patriot for the Emperor.

NAMING AN EMPIRE. This unique feature of the Habsburg Empire as non-national in a nationalistic age was also mirrored in its name. At the time of Franz Joseph's accession it was called the Austrian Empire. The true meaning of this name was that the Emperor was of the Habsburg family—the "House of Austria"; but it was often interpreted to mean that the people living in the Empire were "Austrians." They were so in the sense that they were subjects of the Habsburg ruler, but not in the sense that they were of Austrian nationality. The population of Austrian nationality (inhabiting Lower Austria, Upper Austria, Salzburg, Tirol, Vorarlberg, Styria, Carinthia) itself constituted only some 10 per cent of the total Empire population. The 90 per cent non-Austrians mostly resented being called "Austrians."

After Franz Joseph's "Settlement" with Hungary in 1867 (see Chapter 15), the Empire was called Austria-Hungary, or the Austro-Hungarian Empire, or the Dual Monarchy. In fact, of course, it was neither Austrian, nor Hungarian, nor Austro-Hungarian. The Austrian part, or rather the non-Hungarian part, of Austria-Hungary was officially called: The Kingdoms and Provinces Represented in the Empire Council. This got around the delicate problem of naming, or not naming, any particular nation forming part of this conglomerate. The Hungarian part of the Empire, officially called the Kingdom of Hungary, also contained

several non-Hungarian nations, but at least there was no doubt
that the Hungarians were the "master race,"* while all the other
peoples living in the Kingdom of Hungary were subject races,
though outnumbering the Hungarians.

In 1908, the problem of naming the Empire was further complicated by the annexation of Bosnia and Hercegovina. These
two Balkan provinces were assigned neither to Austria nor to
Hungary but were administered by a military governor under
the joint authority of Austria-Hungary. The Empire then consisted of three parts: (1) The Kingdoms and Provinces represented in the Empire Council; (2) The Kingdom of Hungary;
(3) Bosnia and Hercegovina. How was the Empire as a whole
to be named?

To avoid hurting national feelings by calling the Empire
Austrian or Hungarian or Austro-Hungarian, it was often called,
even officially, simply "The Monarchy." This designation was
used not only in its strict sense of a form of government, but
meant also all the lands and peoples under the Habsburg scepter.
One spoke of France, Germany, Italy, and so on, and the
Monarchy.

CHANGES IN TERRITORY AND POPULATION, 1848-1914. Franz
Joseph lost his two flourishing Italian provinces to the emerging
Kingdom of Italy—Lombardy in 1859, Venetia in 1866. This
reduced the area of his domain, and temporarily also the population of his Empire. But the natural growth of population tended
to offset the departure of the Italians from the Monarchy; and
the loss of territory was compensated by the seizure of Bosnia
and Hercegovina (occupied 1878, annexed 1908) from the crumbling Turkish Empire, so that at the end of his reign Franz Joseph
had some 4,000 square miles more than he started with.

Table 3 shows the extent of territory included in the Monarchy
at the end of Franz Joseph's reign. It also shows the Empire's

---

* A sympathetic reader suggested that "the phrase 'master race' has con-
notations to our generation which may not be intended." The connotation,
though not intended by the author of this book, was certainly intended by
those who coined the expression long before Hitler. The phrase "master
race" (German: *Herrenvolk*) expressed not only domination of other
peoples, but implied racial superiority of the ruling people and contempt
for the inferior subject races.

TABLE 3

Area and Population of
Austro-Hungarian Monarchy, 1869-1914

	Area in Square Miles	Population in 1,000 1869	1914
Lower Austria	7,658	1,990.7	3,635.0
Upper Austria	4,625	736.6	864.0
Salzburg	2,763	153.2	221.3
Styria	8,662	1,138.0	1,467.8
Carinthia	3,989	337.7	406.2
Tirol	10,306	776.3	979.7
Vorarlberg	1,005	102.6	150.8
Bohemia	20,065	5,140.5	6,860.0
Moravia	8,583	2,017.3	2,666.6
Silesia	1,988	513.4	776.0
Galicia	30,320	5,444.7	8,211.8
Bucovina	4,033	523.4	818.3
Carniola	3,845	466.3	530.2
Littoral, with Trieste	3,078	582.1	938.0
Dalmatia	4,925	457.0	667.6
Austria (Cisleithania)	115,840	20,379.8	29,193.3
Hungary (Transleithania)	125,689	15,530.4	21,480.8
Bosnia-Hercegovina	19,776	—	2,075.8
Austro-Hungarian Monarchy	261,305	35,910.2	52,749.9

Source: Based on *Der Grosse Brockhaus,* Wiesbaden, F. A. Brockhaus, 1955, Vol. VIII. p. 642.

population in 1869, soon after the "Settlement" with Hungary, and in 1914, near the end of Franz Joseph's reign. In 1869, total Empire population was somewhat smaller than it had been in 1848, owing to the loss of the Italian provinces. Without these, the population of the Monarchy amounted to 32½ million in 1848, and had increased by about 10 per cent to 35.9 million by 1869. From then on population growth by natural increase was considerably larger, so that despite a large emigration, primarily to the United States, the population of Austria-Hungary grew by 41 per cent to 50.7 million in the forty-five years from 1869 to 1914. The capture of Bosnia and Hercegovina added another two million souls to the Empire.

Table 3 also shows the relative areas and populations of the two parts of the Monarchy after the Empire was broken up by the "Settlement" of 1867. Hungary had 52 per cent of the territory, but only 43 per cent of the population of the Austro-Hungarian Empire.

CHANGES IN NATIONAL COMPOSITION OF EMPIRE POPULATION. The changes in the national composition of the Empire population are shown in Table 4. The first place, in the order of numbers, was occupied by the Germans from the beginning to the end of Franz Joseph's reign. The Italians went from second place in 1848 to ninth in 1910, because of the surrender to Italy of Lombardy and Venetia. This put the Magyars, who had been third in 1848, in second place in 1910. Unfortunately, however, the population figures for the Hungarian part of the Monarchy must be suspect. In its desire not only to "Magyarize" the non-Magyar population of the Kingdom of Hungary, but to create an impression that the Magyar population was larger than it really was, the better to justify Magyar domination of the multinational Kingdom of Hungary, the Hungarian government manipulated the census figures, counting non-Magyars as Magyars. This explains the virtual doubling of the Magyar population in the sixty-two years between 1848 and 1910, and also the slow growth in the Romanian and Slovak groups, as well as the actual decline in "other" populations (see also note [1] in Table 4). The remarkable increase of the Poles may perhaps be in part explained by a similar "Polonization" of the Ruthenian (Ukrainian) population, which showed a much smaller growth rate. In the Polish-Ruthenian territories it was the Poles who were the "master race." Generally the less "developed" nations increased at a faster pace than the "developed" nations—the South Slavs and Poles faster than the Czechs, the Slavs as a whole faster than the Germans. This is another instance of the now widely recognized fact that birth rates tend to vary inversely with levels of living and education.

TABLE 4

*Composition of Empire Population According to
Language Groups, 1848 and 1910*

Language Group	Rank in 1848	Numbers in 1,000 1848	Numbers in 1,000 1910	Percentage of Total Empire Population 1910	Percentage of Total Empire Population 1848	Rank in 1910
Germans	1	7,981	11,988	21.26	23.54	1
Italians (incl. Ladiners & Friulians)	2	5,466	768	14.56	1.50	9
Magyars	3	5,419	10,062[1]	14.43	19.86[1]	2
South Slavs	4	4,027	7,145	10.73	14.01[1]	3
Czechs	5	3,997	6,436	10.65	12.63	4
Ruthenians (Ukrainians)	6	3,142	3,991	8.37	7.82	6
Romanians	7	2,546	3,224	6.79	6.32[1]	7
Poles	8	2,170	4,968	5.73	9.75	5
Slovaks	9	1,823	2,032	4.81	3.97[1]	8
Others	10	1,013	312	2.67	.60[1]	10
Total		37,584	50,926	100.00	100.00	

Source: 1910 figures based on Census of 1910, and *Statistische Rückblicke
aus Österreich*, Vienna, k.k. Statistische Zentralkommission, 1913, p. 3.
Figures for 1848, from Table 2.

[1] This figure does not reflect the true size of the Magyar population. In its
attempt to "Magyarize" the non-Magyar population of the Kingdom of
Hungary, the Hungarian government counted not only Jews and Gypsies
but also many of the Slav and Romanian inhabitants as Magyars. The number of real Magyars was probably in the neighborhood of 7 million. The
figures for non-Magyar groups living in Hungary should be correspondingly increased.

RELIGIONS OF EMPIRE PEOPLES. While the peoples of the
Empire were at each others' throats to promote their respective
national interests, they did not quarrel about religion, as their
ancestors of 300 years before had done. Ever since the reign of
Ferdinand II (1619-37), whose motto was "better a desert than
a country inhabited by heretics," Habsburg lands had been
cleansed of Protestants. In 1910, 79 per cent of the Empire population were Roman Catholic, another 12 per cent were Greek

Catholic, and 2½ per cent were Greek Orthodox. The rest belonged to insignificant religious minorities.

The one discordant religious note in Franz Joseph's reign was his Concordat with the Pope (August 18, 1855), which gave the Church vast powers, especially over education, in the Empire. This surrender of state powers to Rome, bearing the stamp of Archduchess Sophie's piety and her ecclesiastical friends' influence, caused grave resentment even in Catholic circles. Liberal trends eventually forced Franz Joseph to repeal the Concordat (March 21, 1868)——an event celebrated in Vienna with festive illumination. From that time onward religious or church questions were not of decisive importance in the Monarchy.

From this somewhat anatomical and statistical introduction of Franz Joseph's Empire, its territories and peoples, let me turn to the turbulent events immediately before and after Franz Joseph was "called to put the Crowns of the Empire upon our Head."

CHAPTER 4

The Revolution of 1848

THE ERA OF METTERNICH. The Revolution of 1848, in the midst of which Franz Joseph ascended the throne, was the harvest of decades of reaction and repression during the era of Metternich. Count (later Prince) Klemens Lothar von Metternich und Winneburg (1773-1859) had become the chief Minister of the Emperor Franz I just when Habsburg fortunes in the struggle with Napoleon had reached a low point with the defeat of the Austrians at Wagram (July 6, 1809). Metternich managed to save the hard-pressed Empire by playing along with Napoleon, arranging Napoleon's marriage with the Emperor's daughter, Archduchess Marie Louise, in 1810, and even making an alliance with him in 1812. When Napoleon's fortunes declined, Metternich switched sides and emerged as the leader of the coalition that finally conquered Napoleon. Metternich—the "coachman of Europe"—was in the driver's seat at the Congress of Vienna (November 1814 to June 1815), distributing the spoils of victory and initiating a new era of reaction in Europe. This new era was epitomized by the Holy Alliance, formed in 1815 by Russia, Prussia, and Austria, and the subsequent agreements between the European powers to crush popular uprisings wherever and whenever they might occur. Austrian troops repeatedly assisted foreign monarchs in beating down revolutions and restoring autocracy, as in Modena, Parma, and the Papal States in 1830.

Equally or more urgent than putting down uprisings abroad was the stifling of revolutionary stirrings and ideas within the Monarchy. This was done by a complex system of supervision, censorship, and repression. There was need for such repression, as the old order of absolutist rule in the interest of the reigning house and its aristocratic and clerical supporters was being challenged by the rising liberalism and nationalism kindled by the French Revolution and fed by the Industrial Revolution. Metternich kept these growing movements gagged and bound, but in doing so he also strengthened them. By 1848, dissatisfaction with Metternich and his "system" had spread through all classes of society, including even the Imperial family, which enjoyed no exemption from Metternich's police spies. There was of course scant possibility for organized and articulate opposition; but revolution was in the air all over the Empire, with varying accents on demands for national independence, popular government, economic freedom, and liberation from feudal fetters.

In Italy, Galicia, and especially in Hungary under the ultra-Chauvinist Lajos (Louis) Kossuth, opposition to the regime took a primarily nationalistic turn; Italians, Poles, and Hungarians clamored for national independence.* In Bohemia, Germans and Czechs joined in demanding an independent Bohemia, but nationalism there was strongly supported by liberal aspirations. In Austria proper all classes, including the aristocracy, demanded greater participation in government, relaxation of censorship and police supervision, and freedom from bureaucratic chicane. Also in the German provinces of the Monarchy, nationalism was an element in the general dissatisfaction, with many German Austrians favoring an all-German state (i.e., a union of all the then thirty-eight German states), as well as expansion of German influence over the other nationalities in the Monarchy. In addition to demands for national liberation, and to bourgeois demands for liberal reforms, the workers and peasants added their dissatisfactions to the revolutionary ferment. Industrialization, though retarded, had made enough progress in several parts of the Monarchy to create a substantial proletarian working class with all its familiar poverty, insecurity, unemployment, child labor, horri-

---

* Independence was then mostly understood, by the peoples of the Monarchy, to mean self-government within the Monarchy, rather than separation from the Monarchy; though the Italian provinces and, after the initial phases of the Revolution, also Hungary wanted to cut loose entirely from Habsburg rule.

ble housing, and degradation. As earlier the English workers in the "Luddite" riots (1811-16), so now the Austrian workers turned against the machines as the supposed authors of their miseries. In 1846 and 1848, rioting workers smashed machines in Vienna, Prague, and several other industrial cities. The army had to be called out. Peasants were restive in many parts of the Empire. Serfdom, abolished in the reign of Emperor Joseph II, had been restored under his successors. This was the chief complaint. In Galicia, the peasants, mostly Ruthenians, had risen against the Polish nobility in 1846 while the nobles themselves were in open revolt against the Habsburg government, and the government played each side against the other. In Lower Austria, a bad harvest in 1847 drove the miserable peasants to refuse to meet the feudal exactions of their landlords, and to face the soldiers, sent to subdue them, with scythes and flails.

Such were conditions in the Habsburg Monarchy in the beginning of 1848. Nation was pitted against nation, class against class, army and police against everybody, in a witches' cauldron of conflicting tensions. At any moment the lid would blow off and the revolutionary kettle boil over.

THE STORM OF 1848.   The Revolution of 1848 was not confined to Austria. All Europe, with the exception of Spain, Russia, and Scandinavia, rose against the reaction which had been enthroned in 1815. Starting with a local uprising in Sicily in January, the Revolution quickly spread to France. News of the Paris Revolution in February electrified the capitals of the Habsburg Monarchy—Vienna, Budapest, Prague, and Milan. People sensed that the day of liberation had come, and they rose spontaneously. But being without leadership, without preparation, and consequently without a clear understanding of the nature of the Revolution, their struggle was confused. Alignments shifted constantly. Groups that at one moment made common cause against Habsburg oppression fought each other in the next as hostile classes or nations. This benefited the equally planless and leaderless counterrevolutionary forces, which in addition had the advantage of superior armed force.

Hungary.   The first outbreak came in Hungary. In February, Kossuth's motion for the appointment of an independent ministry

for Hungary was approved by the Hungarian Parliament and—
after initial hesitation—by the Emperor, who appointed Count
Lajos Batthyány to head a ministry including Kossuth as Minister
of Finance. In March a series of laws enacted by the Hungarian
legislature made Hungary a virtually independent country within
the Habsburg Monarchy. These "March laws" were approved
by Emperor Ferdinand on April 10, 1848.

But the Vienna government, while ostensibly recognizing the
Hungarian government, prepared to overthrow it. Josip (later
Count) Jelačić, in whose anti-Hungarian and pro-Habsburg sentiments the court put great hope, was appointed Ban (governor)
of Croatia, a Hungarian crownland. Jelačić defied the Hungarian
government, kicked out Hungarian officials, and declared he
would take orders only from the Emperor. Batthyány demanded
Jelačić's dismissal. The Emperor, having himself appointed the
Batthyány government, acceded to Batthyány's request in return
for the promise of Hungarian support against the rebellious
Italians. New frictions arose between the Imperial government
and Budapest when the Hungarians established their own national
army and General Count Lamberg, sent by the court to take command of the Hungarian troops, was lynched in Budapest by defi-
ant patriots. In the see-saw of concessions and retractions which
marked Imperial policy (or rather the lack of one) in 1848,
Jelačić was reappointed Ban and invaded Hungary on September 11, 1848. The Imperial Minister of War, Count Latour,
ordered officers serving in the Hungarian Army, previously
directed by him to obey only the Hungarian government, now
to accept orders from Jelačić—a switch which left many of them
confused and eventually brought them before the firing squad
as traitors to one side or the other.

The Hungarian Army was now in open war with Imperial
troops. At the same time a civil war was raging in Transylvania.
Under Hungarian pressure, the Transylvanian Diet had voted for
union with Hungary. But the Germans and Romanians in that
country wanted independence. Not willing to grant to others
what they demanded for themselves, the Hungarians put down
the rebellion with merciless cruelty.

Bohemia. In Prague, the Czechs formulated demands for revolutionary reforms on March 11; and on March 29 they petitioned the "King of Bohemia" (the Emperor Ferdinand I, who was Ferdinand V as King of Bohemia) to unify all lands of the Bohemian Crown as a separate unit within the Empire, with popular representation and a central government in Prague. Prague was to be equal to Vienna and Budapest. On April 8, the Emperor agreed to these demands. This concession to the Czechs brought enraged protests from the Germans, who feared Slav domination of the Empire. Thereupon the Vienna government promulgated an Empire Constitution which made no provision for an independent Kingdom of Bohemia. Now the Czechs were infuriated. They convened a Slav Congress at Prague on June 2, 1848, presided over by the Czech historian František Palacký. The Slav Congress drafted a constitution making the Empire a federation of states with equal rights for all nations and their languages. Rejection of this constitution by the Emperor led to riots in Prague. After five days of clashes with the people in the streets of the city, the guns of Imperial troops under Prince Alfred Windisch-Grätz prevailed on June 17, 1848. German and Hungarian liberals and democrats, instead of coming to the aid of their Czech fellow revolutionists, applauded Windisch-Grätz's victory. National antagonisms were stronger than revolutionary solidarity.

The crushing of the Revolution in Prague by military force was not the first success of the counterrevolution. Some weeks before, rebellion had been silenced by guns in Lvov (Lemberg), the capital of Galicia, and the entire province had been placed under martial law. But the victory of Windisch-Grätz over the people of Prague was a decisive turning point in the Revolution.

Italy. In the Italian provinces, increasing rebelliousness broke out into open revolution on March 18, when Milanese crowds clamored for separation of Lombardy from the Austrian Empire. The demand was of course rejected by the Austrian Governor. Five days of street fighting forced Field Marshal Count Johann Josef Radetzky to withdraw his weak garrison to Verona. Thereupon King Charles Albert of Sardinia,* seeing a chance to seize

---

* The island kingdom of Sardinia included Savoy and Piedmont on the mainland. Its capital city was Turin.

Lombardy, assumed the role of liberator of the oppressed Milanese, declared war against Austria, and invaded Lombardy with 80,000 soldiers. Pope Pius IX preached a crusade and sent an army against Austria, as did Tuscany and Naples. Charles Albert won victories. A rising in Venice liberated that city from Austrian rule on March 26.

All seemed to favor the Italians, when suddenly the fortunes of war turned. Facing revolution in Rome and fearing an Austrian and German schism, Pope Pius reversed himself on April 29 and declared he had no intention of waging war against a Christian nation. This brought dissension to the Italian ranks. The inhabitants of Lombardy mistrusted Charles Albert and were hostile to his Piedmontese soldiers. The King of Naples recalled his army to crush revolution at home. Most important, Radetzky started to win victories against heavy odds. On May 6, with only 19,000 men, he defeated 41,000 Piedmontese at Santa Lucia near Verona, a feat all the more remarkable in view of the hostility of the Veronese population which immobilized a large portion of Radetzky's forces. In July, a series of victories by Radetzky around Custoza forced Charles Albert to surrender Milan and to conclude an armistice on August 9. Toward the end of the year, Austrian troops had also reoccupied all of Venetia, except Venice itself.

The first stage of the Italian Revolution, which had taken the form of a war of national liberation from Austria and national unification under the King of Sardinia, had been put down; the war had been won by the Imperial forces. After the defeat of Charles Albert, the Revolution went into a second stage, taking a more republican turn. Venice had proclaimed itself a Republic; Tuscany and Rome followed. The Pope fled in disguise and called for armed assistance to force his Romans into obedience. In Bologna, the Austrian garrison was driven out by revolutionists. All Italy was rebellious. The Emperor's Italian troubles were far from over.

Vienna. In Vienna, the Revolution came on March 13. Students gathered around the Landhaus, where the Diet of Lower Austria was meeting, and demanded popular representation, and freedom of speech, press, religion, and teaching. They were supported in these demands by craftsmen and factory workers. Factories were closed by strikes; workers armed with iron bars converged on the city from the suburbs.

Archduke Albrecht, the military commander of Vienna, rode through the excited crowd and was hit by a piece of wood thrown at him. This enraged the Archduke; he ordered the artillery, posted at a nearby gate to the Hofburg, to shoot into the crowd. Today, a commemorative tablet near this spot honors the courage of Sergeant Johann Pollet who at the risk of his own life refused to fire the guns into the populace. His brave refusal could not avert bloodshed. Italian grenadiers, pushed into attack by Archduke Albrecht, wrought carnage with butt and bayonet in front of the Landhaus. Emperor Ferdinand "the Kind-hearted" was outraged. He would not permit the soldiers to shoot at his people, he said. This humane reaction attested the Emperor's incapacity to rule; perhaps it was not his insufficient mind, but his abounding heart which made him unfit to be Emperor.

Metternich had brushed the disturbance aside as a mere brawl. Before the day ended, he had been driven from office and from Vienna. People of all classes demanded his resignation if not his death; the Imperial family insisted that he be sacrificed to save them. Forgotten were the decades in which he had restored Habsburg power after its near-extinction by Napoleon. Metternich resigned that same night and fled to England, with no help from the court, but with 1,000 ducats lent him by the grateful Salomon Rothschild.* He stopped at the castle of Feldsberg, which had been put at his disposal by its owner (a Prince of Liechtenstein), but was ordered by the village council to be off within twenty-four hours, for fear of riots. At Olomouc, the military commander and the archbishop refused to let him into the city.

The next day, March 14, censorship was abolished. On March

---

* Rothschild had been made a baron in 1822 and had been supported by Metternich in many business ventures, as well as in his efforts to emancipate the Jews of Europe.

Metternich, though rich, needed cash at once and apparently had no way of getting it except by borrowing.

15, a constitution was promised; and on that day Emperor Ferdinand, riding through the streets of Vienna, was cheered by the people, who knew him for a harmless, good-natured man. The promised constitution was promulgated on April 25. This constitution, however, pleased no one but the archdukes and the landed aristocrats to whom it gave all power. New and more drastic demands and more riots were the consequences. On May 15, hard pressed by armed students and workers, Ferdinand promised them everything, then fled secretly to loyal Innsbruck.

On July 22, a newly elected Reichstag (parliament) met in Vienna to draft another constitution. A few days later, the youngest delegate, Hans Kudlich from Silesia, introduced the only reform that survived the eventual defeat of the Revolution: abolition of all feudal obligations of peasants. Once this measure had been approved, the peasants went home and abandoned the Revolution. Kudlich later fled to the United States and became a respected physician in Hoboken, New Jersey, where he died in 1917.[1]

With tempers apparently quieted in Vienna, and with victories won in Prague and in Italy, the Emperor returned to Vienna on August 12. But the city had not yet done with revolution, though the people were as foggy and unclear regarding its nature and aims as they had been from the start. Karl Marx went to Vienna on August 28, tried to explain to the workers the real issues in the Revolution and to convince them that petitions to the Emperor were useless.[2] A principal opponent of Marx's interpretation was the journalist Hermann Jellinek, who was soon to pay with his head for his revolutionary articles. He was executed— with many others—in November. Marx was not among the victims; he had left the city in ample time, on September 7.

Fresh violence was unleashed by a series of incidents, culminating in a new explosion in early October. On October 5, an Italian regiment marched out of Vienna to fight the Hungarians, as earlier Hungarian troops had helped to defeat Italians. The Viennese were in sympathy with the Hungarian revolutionists and resented military action against them. When a Viennese grenadier battalion was to follow the Italians the next day, October 6, the grenadiers refused. Troops loyal to the government tried to force the grenadiers to their duty, but the grenadiers, with the aid of the people, defeated the government troops. The victorious populace marched to the Ministry of War, where the Cabinet was assembled. Count Latour, the hated Minister of War, tried to hide in civilian clothes, but was found and, though he offered to resign, could not save himself from being lynched. His naked corpse was strung up on a lantern post.

After this new outrage, the Court fled to Olomouc. Vienna was in open rebellion. The army, pillar of Habsburg power, now marched to subdue the city, Windisch-Grätz closing in on it from the North, Jelačić from the South. A Hungarian revolutionary army sent to the aid of the Viennese was beaten by Jelačić. Many of the Viennese wanted to capitulate; others fought to the last. Windisch-Grätz ordered a general assault on the city on October 26. The city's resistance was stubborn. Not until October 31 did a bombardment overcome the last defenses.

During November 1848, execution squads were busy restoring order. Among those executed was Robert Blum, who was a delegate from the German Parliament at Frankfort and had come to Vienna with parliamentary immunity. Commander-in-Chief Prince Windisch-Grätz, however, recognized neither Parliament nor immunity when dealing with revolution. The Vienna City Council humbly thanked His Highness for his mildness.

FRANZ JOSEPH IN 1848.   Nine months had passed from the first outbreak of the Revolution to Franz Joseph's elevation to the throne. Where had Franz Joseph been, and what had he done during this period of gestation leading to his emergence as Emperor? In the first weeks he was with his family at the Vienna Hofburg, faithfully attending to his studies. This dull routine was joyfully terminated by the young Archduke on April 25, when he left Vienna to join Radetzky's army in Italy. His mother had sent him there, not so much to win laurels as to remove him from danger. In Vienna he was exposed to physical danger—one never knew what the revolutionists might do—but also to danger of being implicated in government affairs and of later being held responsible for promises made or acts committed by the government. Sophie expected to put her son on the throne

soon, and she wanted him to start his reign free from all commitments. Prince Windisch-Grätz, now the mightiest man at court,
the confidant of the Imperial family, constantly consulted by
Archduchess Sophie, also urged her to send Franz Joseph away,
so that he could not be identified with the regime of his uncle
and would be free from every obligation on becoming Emperor.
As did all those who were privy to the secret of Franz Joseph's
imminent accession, Windisch-Grätz saw in the change of
monarchs the means of escaping from the obligation to keep
Ferdinand's promises. The time for the switch of Emperors
had not yet arrived, he thought, but he told the court—meaning
the Empress Maria Anna, wife of Ferdinand, and the Archduchess
Sophie—that he would let them know when the right moment
had come.

In Italy, Franz Joseph's dream of seeing military action was
soon realized. On May 6, he took part in the Battle of Santa
Lucia, won by the Austrians (see p. 28). Glowingly he wrote
to his mother about the glorious army and how it was going
to chase the cowardly Piedmontese right into Turin. The news
from Vienna about "constitutional excesses," as he called them,
distressed him. If Vienna would only show the resoluteness of
Radetzky's regime in Italy! "Here, whoever does not do as he
is told, is arrested and severely punished, and be he a prince or
a priest!" (Letter to Archduchess Sophie, Verona, May 13,
1848).[3]*

---

* Reference will often be made in this book to letters by Franz Joseph to
his mother, Archduchess Sophie. He wrote to her frequently, even as a boy.
That there are so many of these letters has several explanations:

(1) Letter writing was much more customary at the time of Franz Joseph
than it is today, when the telephone allows quicker and more directly
personal communication.

(2) Franz Joseph wrote letters easily. He often wrote at length even to
persons (e.g., Frau Schratt) whom he had seen the same day or expected
to see the next day. A readiness to write letters was a mark of the educated
and cultivated.

(3) Franz Joseph was frequently separated from his mother, when he,
or she, were on official or pleasure trips.

(4) That Franz Joseph wrote to his mother, rather than to his father, is
explained by the domineering and demanding character of the mother and
the great attachment of the son to her.

(5) As Franz Joseph had an exalted position, even as a boy, it is not
astonishing that his letters were preserved.

Now that Franz Joseph had had his baptism of fire, his mother recalled him in order to avoid having his person linked to the severe reprisals against the Italian population. Soon he was initiated into the secret plans for his elevation to the throne. He now stayed again with the Imperial family, first in Innsbruck, where the Imperial family had fled from Vienna, then returning to Vienna in August and moving to Olomouc in October, all this time continuing his preparation for the high office he was soon to fill.

In June 1848, Archduchess Sophie appointed Count Karl Grünne, whose piety and uncompromising opposition to all liberal ideas had won her favor, as Franz Joseph's Lord High Steward. Descriptions of Grünne's character show him as dull, narrow-minded, ignorant, old-fashioned, and brutal. Yet this man was to be, as the Emperor's Adjutant General and Chief of the Military Chancery, one of the mightiest men in the Empire in the first decade of Franz Joseph's reign.

Another significant appointment was made on November 21, 1848. Prince Felix Schwarzenberg was named Minister-President on the recommendation of Prince Windisch-Grätz, his brother-in-law. Schwarzenberg was a determined man, ruthless, willing to use any means to gain his ends, and without moral scruples. With such men at his side, the new Emperor was not in danger of falling victim to the mildness hoped for by his subjects. Franz Joseph had met Schwarzenberg in the Italian campaign and had taken an instant liking to the man who was to be his chief minister in the first years of his reign, and who was to guide him in solving the problems he had to face immediately following his accession. What these problems were, and how Franz Joseph dealt with them, will be the subject of the next chapter.

CHAPTER 5

By the Grace of the Czar

On becoming Emperor, Franz Joseph was confronted by three principal problems, three threats to his power: Hungary, Italy, and the Reichstag. These three had to be subdued if the Habsburg Monarchy and Habsburg absolutism were to be preserved.

How Franz Joseph and his Minister, Prince Schwarzenberg, dealt with the Reichstag, and with the constitution it was preparing, is told in Chapter 13. Franz Joseph and Schwarzenberg were great believers in force and no believers in parliaments and constitutions. They acted according to their beliefs: they used force to destroy the parliament; the army disbanded the Reichstag. That was the simple and obvious solution of that problem. The present chapter tells how Franz Joseph met the other two threats: Italy and Hungary.

NEW WAR IN ITALY. On the day of Franz Joseph's accession, December 2, 1848, the situation in Italy was under control for the time being, though the war with Sardinia was not yet over. The first stage of this war of national liberation had ended with a victory of Imperial troops and an armistice in August 1848. On expiration of the armistice, on March 12, 1849, Sardinia resumed the war, taking advantage of the Emperor's heavy military involvement in Hungary. But this time defeat came even more quickly and completely for the Italians than it had in 1848. The war was ended within a few days, with a decisive victory by Radetzky at Novara, and the abdication of King Charles Albert on March 28. Venice still held out, but deprived of Sardinian naval support, it eventually fell to the Austrians five months later. The peace treaty between Austria and Sardinia restored the territorial settlement of 1815, and with this the pacification of Italy seemed completed.

As it turned out, pacification of the Emperor's Italian provinces was only superficial. Austrian reprisals against those who had sided with the enemy were severe: fortunes were confiscated, heavy fines were imposed, many were imprisoned, and many were executed—960, according to one estimate.[1] These reprisals and other manifestations of Austrian oppression intensified hatred of Austria and led to repeated outbreaks. On February 6, 1853, the Milan main guard was stormed by Putschists and many Austrian officers and men were killed. The incident unleashed a new wave of ferocious reprisals, and these in turn fed the flames of rebellion. In the few remaining years of Austrian rule in Italy, the *Carbonari* (a secret society of Italian patriots) and the followers of the Italian nationalist Mazzini were causing incessant trouble to their Austrian oppressors, who retaliated with prison, whip, and scaffold. Imperial visits to Venice and Milan were occasions for hate demonstrations against Franz Joseph. Crowds gaped silently at the foreign despot; at gala performances at the Teatro Fenice in Venice and La Scala in Milan, the boxes of the Italian nobility were either empty, or occupied by servants, or by aristocrats themselves, but dressed in black and ostentatiously ignoring the Monarch.

INVASION OF HUNGARY. By December 2, 1848, Prague and Vienna had been subdued and the war in Italy was temporarily suspended, but the Hungarians were still in open, armed rebellion against the Imperial government. The task of putting down this rebellion was made more difficult by the change of monarchs. The fundamental principle of the ancient Hungarian Constitution* was that only a king crowned with the approval and assistance of the Hungarian Parliament could be the legitimate ruler. Franz Joseph had not been crowned King of Hungary;

---

* This constitution is not to be confused with Kossuth's democratic constitution of 1848. The ancient constitution dates back to the Golden Bull of Andrew II in 1222. It was recognized by the Habsburg rulers and reconfirmed by the "Reichsdekret" of 1791, declaring that Hungary was always to be ruled according to its own customs and constitution.

his accession was not approved by the Hungarian Parliament; he was, therefore, in Hungarian eyes, not the rightful king. On April 14, 1849, Kossuth, who now dominated the Hungarian government, deposed the Habsburg dynasty altogether. Kossuth himself was elected Governor of Hungary.

Franz Joseph and Schwarzenberg relied, of course, on armed might to reassert Habsburg rule in Hungary. Fresh from his victory over the Viennese, Windisch-Grätz, the Commander-in-Chief of the Imperial armies (except Radetzky's in Italy), invaded Hungary "to restore order." Order, as outlined in one of the Field Marshal's many proclamations, this one of December 29, 1848, was to consist in strict obedience to his commands and "immediate execution of anyone taking even the most trifling order from the revolutionary committee . . . any village in which several inhabitants have the temerity to oppose the Imperial army will be leveled to the ground . . . the village leaders will pay with their heads for any disturbance."[2] Apparently this was only a modest beginning of "order," for in a subsequent proclamation (February 11, 1849) Windisch-Grätz expressed amazement at his own mildness with the rebels, and promised ruthlessness.

Windisch-Grätz's terrorism had little success other than to stiffen the Hungarian people's will to resist. Though at first Windisch-Grätz won victories, he soon began to suffer reverses at the hands of the resourceful young Hungarian General, Arthur Görgei. Thereupon Franz Joseph deposed Windisch-Grätz on that same April 14 on which Kossuth deposed Franz Joseph.

DISMISSAL OF WINDISCH-GRÄTZ. His dismissal by the Emperor came as a shock to the old Field Marshal. Only a few months before, immediately after the accession ceremony at Olomouc, Franz Joseph had embraced him and acknowledged that "to you we owe everything that still remains and exists!" Windisch-Grätz had felt secure in his position at court and even regarded himself as the real power behind the throne he had saved for Franz Joseph, demanding that nothing of importance be decided without his advice![3] Now suddenly he was ousted! To express his contempt for Franz Joseph's behavior, the Field

Marshal returned all the honors and decorations he had received from the Imperial house.

Some historians have regarded the Windisch-Grätz episode as demonstrating Franz Joseph's hardheartedness and as another instance of proverbial Habsburg ingratitude. Others have interpreted it as a courageous act on the part of Franz Joseph, necessary for the preservation of Habsburg power. It is probable that Franz Joseph acted at the behest of Schwarzenberg, whose ideas about policy in Hungary conflicted with those of his brother-in-law. Windisch-Grätz did not want to crush Hungary, but to negotiate with the Hungarian nobles with a view to restoring aristocratic rule. Schwarzenberg distrusted aristocrats in general, but more especially Hungarian aristocrats, many of whom were toying with liberalism. He was opposed to aristocratic rule and wanted to establish a bureaucratic centralist government; he wanted to subjugate Hungary completely and rule it from Vienna as merely another province. It may have been this conflict over policy, rather than military defeat, which motivated the dismissal of Windisch-Grätz.[4]

THE CZAR INTERVENES. Windisch-Grätz's successor, General Baron Ludwig Welden, had no better luck against the Hungarians. To inspire his troops, Franz Joseph personally joined the fight against his Hungarian subjects, bravely exposing himself to enemy fire, though also finding time between battles to attend Mass, as he reported to his apprehensive mother. His heroic example not being enough to turn the tide, the Emperor now looked for outside help. Prussia was willing to give it in exchange for Prussian hegemony in Germany—a condition Franz Joseph could not accept, as he was out to recapture the German Imperial Crown for himself (see Chapter 14). But where Prussia offered help at a price, Russia offered it gratis. This generosity was motivated by Czar Nicholas I's fear of revolution in general and of the Hungarian Revolution in particular. Several of the Hungarian leaders were actually Poles, and there was danger that the Revolution would spill over into (then Russian) Poland. The Czar trembled at seeing the Emperor's army beaten by the Hungarian rebels and was anxious to crush them to avert danger to his own throne.

Eagerly responding to Franz Joseph's personal appeal for help, the Czar sent 100,000 soldiers under Prince Paskevich across the Carpathian Mountains into Hungary in June 1849. The superior forces of the joint Austrian and Russian armies soon prevailed over the Hungarians, who were decisively defeated near Timisoara (Temesvár). Kossuth fled to Turkey, as did many other revolutionists, among them Count Gyula (Julius) Andrássy, who was to play a great role in Franz Joseph's life. On August 13, 1849, Görgei surrendered to the Russians at Világos. Paskevich telegraphed the Czar: "Hungary lies at Your Majesty's feet." On receiving the message, the Czar knelt and prayed. He gave Hungary to Franz Joseph.

EXECUTIONS AT ARAD. General Welden had been replaced as commander-in-chief of the Imperial army in Hungary by General Baron Julius von Haynau, notorious for his cruelty and bloodthirstiness. He had made his fame in Italy by bloody retaliation against the rebellious Italian population of Brescia. This had earned him the epithets "Hyena of Brescia" and "Women lasher of Brescia." Having crushed the Hungarian Revolution, or having it crushed for him by Russian soldiers, Haynau had a field day wreaking his wrath on the Hungarians. Contrary to surrender terms, the Hungarian generals were court-martialed and sentenced to death at Arad. The Czar, more inclined to mildness than was Franz Joseph, and opposed to the executions, was able to save only Görgei, but not the others. Thirteen generals were executed at Arad—those who had surrendered to Haynau were shot; those who had surrendered to Paskevich were hanged. During the hangings, the Imperial anthem was played.

Among the hundreds who were executed in Hungary was Count Lájos Batthyány, who had been appointed by Emperor Ferdinand to head the first Hungarian government in 1848. Though Batthyány had joined the Kossuth party, he had consistently advocated restraint and reconciliation with the house of Habsburg, and it was generally expected that his life would be spared. His sentence to death by hanging was approved by Franz Joseph, possibly at the urging of Archduchess Sophie, who is said to have hated the man because she thought he had treated her insolently. On the day before the execution, Batthyány tried unsuccessfully to commit suicide. Near death from self-inflicted wounds, too weak to be dragged to the gallows, he was ordered shot by General Kempen (later Franz Joseph's Chief of Police)—another man distinguished for his mercilessness, but who in this case was reprimanded for not having carried out the hanging as specified in the death sentence. It is said that Batthyány's widow made her little son take an oath on his father's grave to hate Franz Joseph as a poisonous snake. Another lady, Countess Károlyi, whose son was executed, had the following prophetic wish for Franz Joseph: "May heaven and hell destroy his happiness! May his race vanish from the earth and he himself be visited in the persons he loves most! May his life be doomed to destruction and his children perish miserably!"

The executions and terrorism of 1849 reflected the character of the men around Franz Joseph at that time—most of them generals. Men like Schwarzenberg (he, too, was a general and always liked to wear a uniform), Grünne, Windisch-Grätz, Kempen, Radetzky, and Haynau believed in terror because violence was the principle of their lives. Moreover, they had the power and the opportunity to give free rein to vengeance and vindictiveness, though naturally they tried to hide these motives (probably even from themselves) behind the usual lofty pretense of duty—like parents having to punish a loved child. Perhaps they also delighted in cruelty for its own sake, not merely to avenge wrongs. It is fairly clear that Haynau was a pathological case, who seemed to revel in blood, and who was recalled because of what the Imperial government, certainly not distinguished for mildness, considered excessive cruelty. But what of the others? What is one to make of Windisch-Grätz's bloodthirsty proclamations threatening death and destruction? And Schwarzenberg's remark when the wisdom of a milder course was urged: "Yes, yes! Mildness is all right, but first we'll do some more hanging!"[5]

All this should not be interpreted to mean that these men were somehow "bad" or abnormal. Except for Haynau, they were undoubtedly normal, honorable men, loving husbands and fathers, behaving as other normal men with similar cultural backgrounds would—and did—behave in similar circumstances, with power in their hands. All power tends to corrupt, as Lord Acton said, and absolute power corrupts absolutely. At the time, these wielders of absolute power shocked the world by their cruel deeds. They proved once again Edward Gibbon's dictum about the uniformity of the mischiefs of military despotism.

WAS FRANZ JOSEPH RESPONSIBLE FOR TERRORISM? What was Franz Joseph's part in this terror and blood justice? What was his responsibility for the executions in Hungary and Italy? Even his apologists do not deny that a blood bath did take place, that the executions, especially Batthyány's, were judicial murders, and that Franz Joseph approved them; but they excuse Franz Joseph on the ground that the executions were necessary or that he was too young to be an independent agent, that he acted only as the tool of his mother or of the generals around him. These people, as Baron Wessenberg (Foreign Minister for a short time in 1848) wrote, "drove the young Emperor to force his way to power over gallows and scaffold instead of offering him the opportunity to prepare a lasting peace by bearing an olive branch in his hand and a spirit of reconciliation."[6]

That the Emperor was not his own agent in these early days of his reign is not true. He was exceptionally mature and well prepared for his position. Undoubtedly, he listened to his advisers, as all rulers do, young or old; and he listened especially to his mother. But it was he who made the decisions, and he was too jealous of his power to permit anyone else to make them for him.[7] "When I command, it is to be done!" was the way he thundered at the highest dignitaries.[8] There is every reason to believe that he shared the views and sentiments of his mother and other close advisers, who were the people he admired; there is no evidence that he had any scruples or misgivings about the retribution visited on his subjects, that he wanted to stop the executions, as his uncle Ferdinand wanted to forbid the soldiers to shoot at his Viennese. The fact is that Franz Joseph authorized the executions. Colonel Heller, whom no one can accuse of a want of veneration for Franz Joseph, wrote that Franz Joseph approved the hangings and shootings primarily because, regarding himself as an instrument of God, he considered it his duty to avenge the challenge to his legitimate authority and the insults to the majesty of his person.[9] In later years, when he was reminded of his youthful deeds of violence, Franz Joseph said: "Will people never forgive me? I was only a youngster then!"[10] The remark, quoted by a devoted admirer of Franz Joseph and intended to bring out the pathos of the old Emperor, as indeed it does, reveals that Franz Joseph recognized that these bloody deeds were wrongs, otherwise why should they be "forgiven"? —that he was conscious of having committed them; otherwise, why should *he* be forgiven?—that instead of accepting moral responsibility for them, he thought his youthfulness at the time he committed them should exonerate him—and that he resented being reminded of his youthful misdeeds.

THE BACH HUSSARS. With the surrender of Görgei and the execution of the leaders of the Revolution, Hungary's pacification was (supposedly) completed. In accordance with Schwarzenberg's plans, the country was now ruled by non-Magyar officials of the Vienna government, supported by an elite corps of well-drilled gendarmes. The Austrian officials were derisively called "Bach Hussars," after their chief, the Minister of Interior Alexander Bach and his Hussar-like tactics.

Bach was one of the most successful figures of the Revolution. A peasant's son become lawyer, he first sided with the revolutionists. He was one of the men who, pistol in hand, had forced their way into Metternich's presence on March 13, 1848, to demand his resignation. By November 1848, Bach had shifted so far to the right that Schwarzenberg included him in his Cabinet, where he soon became a power. After Schwarzenberg's death in 1852, and until 1859 when he fell from the Emperor's favor, he was Franz Joseph's chief Minister in fact though not in name, and the chief exponent of the monarch's neo-absolutism during that period. The man who had chased the real Metternich, himself emerged as a new, imitation Metternich, with all the "pre-March" police apparatus and oppressive policies. He also inherited the people's hatred of Metternich. The court despised him, but saw in him a useful tool, and rewarded him by making him a Baron. His detested Bach Hussars kept Hungary under control,

though they could not extinguish desire for national independence and hatred of the Habsburg regime.[11]

ASSASSINATION ATTEMPT. An expression of this hatred was the
assassination attempt on Franz Joseph by the young Hungarian
journeyman tailor János Libényi on February 18, 1853. The Emperor had been walking on the Vienna city walls, accompanied
by his Adjutant, Count O'Donnell. As the two stopped to watch
soldiers drilling below, outside the city walls, Libényi rushed
the Emperor from the back, striking at his neck with a knife.
The timely outcry of a woman who had witnessed the scene
made Franz Joseph turn and avoid the full impact of Libényi's
thrust, while O'Donnell pounced on the attacker and subdued
him. Libényi shouted "Eljen Kossuth!" (Hail Kossuth!) as he
was led away; he was hanged a few days later. Franz Joseph
soon recovered from his injury; thanksgiving services were held
throughout the Empire; and a great new church (the Votiv-
kirche) was built in Vienna to commemorate the Emperor's de-
liverance. On learning that the outrage against her son had been
committed by a Hungarian, the Empress-Mother was full of new
bitterness against this nation which, as she thought, had been
so mildly treated by the Emperor!

CONTINUED RESTIVENESS IN HUNGARY. Few Hungarians shared
the Archduchess' estimate of the Emperor's mildness. Thousands
of their countrymen were still languishing in prison. In Budapest
and in the Hungarian countryside people were arrested for
wearing ribbons in the Hungarian colors, toyshop-keepers for
displaying dolls or pictures with the national colors. On May 6,
1852, the *Pester Zeitung* reported another forty-nine verdicts
by military courts, among them forty-two to death by hanging.[12]

There had also been amnesties, but these did not alter the fact
that the country was governed by a ruthless autocracy, and could
not erase the memory of the hangings and severe prison sentences.
Libényi's attempt on Franz Joseph, possibly connected with a
widespread conspiracy,* was the signal for a new series of trials,

---

* According to Baron Weckbecker, an Adjutant of Franz Joseph, Libényi's
assassination attempt was instigated by Hungarian emigrés in London, from
whom Libényi had received money a few days earlier. The truth was suppressed for political reasons.[13]

convictions, hangings, and imprisonments of Hungarian suspects, among them several society ladies.

Hungary was pacified only on the surface. Beneath that surface, revolution and nationalism continued to agitate the Hungarian people, and were to plague Franz Joseph during his entire reign.

TRIUMPH OF COUNTERREVOLUTION. Franz Joseph had met the dangers facing him on becoming Emperor by reliance on armed force. Army and police held down the rebellious populace. By 1853 two-thirds of the Empire, including Vienna, continued to be under martial law. The people were restive; even in reliable Tirol and Styria the spirit of opposition showed itself. But all liberal and democratic stirrings were as effectively suppressed as they had been in Metternich's time.[14] Franz Joseph was now an absolute, autocratic monarch, as he believed God had intended him to be.

The victory of reaction was symbolized by the triumphal return of Metternich to Vienna on September 24, 1851. His estates were restored to him, and until his death in 1859 he remained an honored elder statesman and adviser of Franz Joseph.

Shortly before Franz Joseph's accession, Windisch-Grätz insisted that the phrase "by the Grace of God" be again included in the Emperor's titles, after it had been dropped as a concession to the revolutionists. When told that objections had been raised to this re-inclusion in Vienna, he commented: "Very well, if they do not want to hear about the Grace of God, they will have to hear by the grace of cannon."[15] The Viennese heard the cannons and got the message. But Windisch-Grätz's cannons were not loud enough to make the Hungarians listen. Franz Joseph's appeal to the Czar for help was an open admission that the Empire had not enough strength to restore the old "Grace-of-God" order within its borders. It was the Czar's intervention that saved the Habsburg Monarchy. When Paskevich laid Hungary at the Czar's feet, the Czar could have kept it for himself; or he could have made it an independent country and have the Hungarians offer their Crown to a Russian Grand Duke, as many were ready to do. But Nicholas I, professing a paternal love for Franz Joseph, and motivated perhaps by a feeling of obligation to his fellow sovereign in trouble, presented Hungary to him

as a gift and so put the Habsburgs back on their feet. Franz
Joseph was really no longer Emperor by the Grace of God; he
was Emperor by the Grace of the Czar.

People often resent those from whom they have received
favors, because benefactors and benefactions point up their own
inadequacies: One does not take pride in living on charity. Perhaps Franz Joseph resented Nicholas and his magnanimity.[16]
Perhaps Schwarzenberg understood this and foresaw (or plotted?)
the action which, as he prophetically remarked, would make the
world marvel at Austria's ingratitude. When the Crimean War
offered Franz Joseph an opportunity to return the Czar's favor
by coming to his aid in his conflict with England, France, and
Turkey, Franz Joseph confronted the Czar with an ultimatum
instead (June 3, 1854), and prepared to launch his army against
him. Metternich shook his old head—not about the immorality,
but about the political danger of this course. "One should never
threaten a big beast of prey with a stick," he said. "It could
become enraged and bite us."[17] Franz Joseph did not heed his
old teacher and kept goading the Russian bear until it did bite.
The story of this is told in Chapter 18.

This and the preceding chapters sketched the conditions of
Franz Joseph's Empire when he took it over in 1848—its extent
and its multinational population, the Revolution which convulsed
it at the time, and how Franz Joseph restored Habsburg absolutism with the help of the Czar. Before returning to the account
of the principal features and events of Franz Joseph's reign, I
turn to a description of himself and his family. In the following
three chapters, I shall try to portray Franz Joseph's personality.
Chapter 6 describes the Emperor's character and personality in
general. The two subsequent chapters, 7 and 8, deal with particular characteristics: The former is devoted to Franz Joseph
the soldier—which he really was, the latter to Franz Joseph the
man of simplicity—which he was not, though biographers and
folklore say he was. Chapters 9-12 tell about Franz Joseph's
ancestors, his parents, childhood and education, and his family.

Franz Joseph's Character and Personality

Most men are not the same at twenty as they are at forty or at eighty. A description of their characters and personalities is complicated by the changes they undergo. But the case of Franz Joseph is simple, because he changed little over the many years of his life. This is one of the notable aspects of his personality. Franz Joseph had matured early. The official declaration of his majority on December 2, 1848, was more than a legal fiction. The young Archduke had completed a course of studies and had reached an awareness of responsibilities, such as few men do before they are twenty-one or older. He was really an adult at eighteen. But having developed rapidly before ascending the throne, he stopped growing afterward. His views, beliefs, prejudices, and interests were essentially the same at eighteen as at eighty-six. Only his physical appearance changed, though in some respects he seemed as youthful at eighty-six as he had at eighteen. His step was elastic, his figure slim and straight, except for a slight stoop in his last years. Only his head showed age; he was bald at fifty-four, white soon after, and his face made him look older than he was.

SCHWARZENBERG'S ESTIMATE OF FRANZ JOSEPH. Prince Felix Schwarzenberg, Franz Joseph's first Minister-President, described the Emperor to Prince Metternich in 1850 as follows: "The Emperor's . . . mental powers are acute, his industry is admirable, especially in one so young as he. He works with great application ten hours a day, and no one knows better than I how many reports submitted to him by his ministers he has rejected after having examined them. His bearing is dignified; his demeanor toward people exceedingly polite, but somewhat dry. Sentimentalists . . . say he does not have a warm heart. Of that warm but superficial good-naturedness of some Archdukes there is not a trace. Yet he is approachable, patient, and has the good intention to do justice to all. He has a profound abhorrence of every lie and is completely discreet. The quality, however, which especially in the present times stands him in good stead, is his courage. I have never yet seen him discouraged for even one moment, in the most difficult circumstances, the dangers of which he judged correctly and accurately. He is physically and morally fearless and I believe that the reason why he can face the truth, even the bitterest, is that it does not frighten him . . . The Empire will have in him what it needs most—a master."[1]

Many subsequent ministers and other persons who knew Franz Joseph have confirmed Schwarzenberg's testimony. They agree in praising the Emperor's innate dignity, his courtesy, his noble, handsome appearance, self-assured bearing, courage, pronounced sense of honor and duty, sober judgment—an impressive catalogue of virtues. Other accounts add less attractive features, and even in the praise of adulators one can read censure between the lines: Franz Joseph was unimaginative, somewhat unfeeling and hardhearted; he kept people at a distance; his intellect was mediocre, his interests narrow, and he was prejudiced against progressive ideas. Some critics, including even Schwarzenberg, said Franz Joseph had lost the approval of the Viennese by his forbidding harshness, reserve, and occasional lack of candor.[2]

A closer look at those features of Franz Joseph's personality which have been emphasized by most of his biographers will fill in details in Schwarzenberg's brief protrayal of the monarch.

INTELLIGENCE. Franz Joseph was intelligent in the sense that he could grasp problems quickly and could make what were regarded as sensible decisions. He also had a remarkably good memory. But he lacked imagination, had no spark of genius, never conceived an original plan or idea—his ideas were inherited or suggested to him by his advisers. His intelligence was of a high order when compared with that of his predecessor, Ferdinand I, who was virtually feeble-minded; but not when compared with the eighteenth-century Habsburg rulers, especially Joseph II. Franz Joseph had the mentality of a narrow-minded bureaucrat or army officer, concerned with petty routine matters—"the mentality of a provincial postmaster," as Robert Payne expressed it in an article in the *New York Times Magazine*.[3]

DEVOTION TO DUTY. Franz Joseph's celebrated devotion to duty reflected his type of intelligence. Meticulously he examined all the reports submitted to him, paid attention to all details, made margin comments, and, as Schwarzenberg said, not infrequently returned these documents for redrafting before he would sign them. All documents submitted to him had to be written calligraphically. One marvels at the skill and time that must have been expended on the preparation of these papers; Franz Joseph himself had a pleasing handwriting and demanded perfection in this respect, sometimes even straightening an imperfectly drawn character or correcting a misspelling.

Even as a young man, the Emperor rose early, but with advancing age he made a fetish of starting his day in the middle of the night. In his old age, his valet had to wake him at three-thirty each morning. At four, the monarch was at his desk, doing his duty as administrator of his Empire. He regarded it as his duty personally to choose all his ministers and other high officials and officers. But he did not regard it as his duty to surround himself with persons of high intellectual caliber; on the contrary, he mostly excluded such persons. Over the decades this practice gave the Austrian bureaucracy an imprint of mediocrity. Entire generations were brought up in this atmosphere.[4]

Franz Joseph's duty also included activities which, to him, were pleasurable: He had to review troops and attend the annual maneuvers; he had to participate in festivities, "court balls" and "balls at court,"* which he seemed really to enjoy, especially as

---

* Court balls were mass affairs to which many persons who were not members of court society, e.g., army officers and administrative officials, had access. Balls at court were much smaller, exclusive events to which only members of the Imperial house, other royalty, and the highest aristocracy were invited.

a young man; and he had to take royal guests hunting, which was his favorite occupation.

Duty demanded of Franz Joseph to be severe with all who challenged his power.[5] The test of his devotion to duty in this respect came at the beginning of his reign in dealing with the defeated revolutionists, as described in Chapter 5. In the same way, acts of Franz Joseph often interpreted as showing ingratitude, such as his abrupt firing of dedicated generals and ministers when they seemed no longer useful to him, were justified by himself and his supporters as dictated by duty. Whatever Franz Joseph did, he always seemed to think it was his "duty." In the last analysis, his duty, as he conceived it, was to extend and preserve the power, glory, and honor of his house and of himself as its head, and thus to carry out God's will.[6] To this duty Franz Joseph sacrificed everything and everybody, including his family.

HONOR. Closely akin to Franz Joseph's devotion to duty was his highly developed sense of honor. The honor of his house and of the Empire, the honor of the army, his personal honor, were ever uppermost in his mind and on his lips. Honor was to him the most praiseworthy quality, dishonor the most contemptible. When he went to war, it was to defend the honor of his house. Though sensing that his declaration of war against Serbia in 1914 might bring catastrophe, and warned that it would cause untold suffering to the peoples over whom he ruled, he was willing to "go down honorably." Choosing the peaceful solution which was available to him presumably would have been dishonorable in his view.

"Honor" was a word Franz Joseph used incessantly in proclamations, letters, and conversations. Yet his acts at times seemed to belie his professions of honor, at least in the eyes of observers not steeped in the emperor's particular—or peculiar—code of honor. He reneged on his accession promise to grant a constitution to all Empire peoples, and he scrapped the Hungarian Constitution already granted in April 1848. One of the Hungarian generals executed in 1849 as a rebel and violator of his oath to the King, reminded his judges that "the King has not kept his oath; I have kept mine." Franz Joseph did not think it dishonorable to call on the Czar to help him put down his, Franz Joseph's, own subjects in 1849. It is not surprising that the whole fraternity of kings and emperors shared Franz Joseph's interpretation of honor in this case. But when five years later Franz Joseph sided with the Czar's enemies in the Crimean War (see pp. 203-204), this could not easily pass as "honorable." Czar Nicholas I, Franz Joseph's benefactor, was so shocked by this (in the Czar's view) dishonorable act that he had all objects reminding him of the ungrateful Emperor removed from his sight and, some say, died of grief over Franz Joseph's betrayal. Habsburg's word was worthless after the Crimean War incident, especially since Franz Joseph had managed to break faith not only with the Czar, but also with the Czar's enemies. "L'Autriche triche," one statesman put it (Austria cheats). Franz Joseph himself was aware that his acts might appear dishonorable, but excused himself by appealing to the higher demands of his "duty"; and it was always honorable to do one's duty.[7] The long reign of the Emperor abounds with examples of acts which to most people would appear dishonorable and which were thought so at the time. Yet Franz Joseph thought his honor unimpeachable and managed to build a reputation for honorable and chivalrous conduct.

CHIVALRY. So famed was the Emperor's chivalry that had the Empire survived he may well have come to be known as Franz Joseph "the Chivalrous." He might also have been called "the last knight," if that cognomen had not been pre-empted by his ancestor Maximilian I (Holy Roman Emperor 1493-1519), as the last medieval ruler. Perhaps Franz Joseph had better claim to the title. Though the age of knighthood had died four centuries earlier, he was like a solitary survivor from that age. His ideas were essentially medieval: He regarded his Empire as a private possession, the patrimony of the house of Habsburg (not as a commonwealth of the people); his own social position, and that of all persons, as determined by inherited rank (not by merit, achievement). With these medieval conceptions of society and human relations went the cultivation of chivalrous virtues: courage, nobility, courtesy, fairness, respect for women, protection of the poor, the mastery of chivalrous exercises. Franz Joseph has been praised for his highly developed sense of *noblesse oblige*.

Here again, however, as in respect to duty and honor, Franz Joseph's own interpretation of chivalry sometimes seems strange to those uninitiated in these medieval mysteries. It is understandable that his "protection of the poor" extended only to the few cases of poverty occasionally brought to his attention, while he did nothing to relieve the poverty of the masses of his subjects, but on the contrary protected the rich, that is, the property owners, from encroachments by the workers—the poor, whom Franz Joseph referred to as "Gesindel" (rabble). It is also understandable that his fairness expressed itself mostly in favor of those of higher status, though stories are told of the Emperor being more severe with aristocrats than with ordinary people, precisely because aristocrats have a higher obligation to conduct themselves impeccably.

What is more difficult to reconcile with Franz Joseph's celebrated chivalry is his attitude toward some women—for instance the morganatic wife of the heir apparent to the throne, Archduke Franz Ferdinand, whom he not only refused to elevate to the rank of an Archduchess, as he could have done, but whom he deliberately humiliated (and permitted his Lord High Steward to humiliate) on many occasions,* for no other reason than that he did not consider her an equal of the Habsburgs, though she was a Countess and of old Bohemian nobility. Also remarkable is Franz Joseph's approval of the beating of women by his police army in Hungary and in Italy. These beatings were not unauthorized excesses of overzealous soldiers, but were officially administered in accordance with army regulations and in the presence of officers who supposedly were men of honor. The victims were not women of ill repute (though this would not

---

* At court functions, Franz Ferdinand's wife ranked below the least and youngest of the Archduchesses. Even in death, Franz Joseph or his Lord High Steward, Prince Montenuovo, refused to accord her Archducal honors. Though her coffin was placed next to her husband's as they were lying in state (they were both assassinated at Sarajevo in 1914), it was placed lower than his and had a fan and gloves placed upon it as a mark of her erstwhile position as lady-in-waiting—a person below royal rank.

have altered the merits of the punishment), but otherwise re-
spectable women found guilty of disrespect to the Emperor.
The Emperor knew about these punishments. Nothing, not even
the hangings, filled the Italians with more revulsion against the
Austrian regime than did these bastinadoes of women, carried
out with Franz Joseph's knowledge.

COURTESY. Franz Joseph's chivalry consisted primarily in his
polite, polished, courtly manner. He is usually portrayed as a
man who did not shout, abuse anyone, use unseemly language,
or lose control of his temper. Yet he often showed annoyance
and displeasure; and most descriptions of the Emperor include
references to fits of anger, to outbursts when things did not go
his way, to irritability and frequent bad humors.[8]

Franz Joseph's courtesy was not of the kind which made
people feel at ease in his presence; rather the contrary. Franz
Joseph lacked warmth. He was not haughty, yet his studied,
impassible courtesy underscored his superior rank, his august
station. There was something frightening about this grand seig-
neurial, icy courtesy of the Emperor. In fact, it was a device
for setting himself apart from all others, for emphasizing the
distance between him and them.

ETIQUETTE. The same end was served by the "Spanish etiquette" for which the Vienna court was renowned and which
during the reign of Franz Joseph was rigidly observed. This
etiquette was really of Burgundian, not Spanish, origin and had
been introduced into the Habsburg court through Maria of
Burgundy, the daughter of Charles the Bold, wife of the Emperor Maximilian I, and grandmother of Charles V (Holy Roman Emperor 1519-56), who was also King of Spain. It was
cultivated with great zeal at the Spanish court and was introduced from there into the Vienna court, which had many ties
with Madrid. The court etiquette or ceremonial was a complicated system of rules governing activities and relations between persons at court. Not only courtiers, attendants, and
servants had to abide by the rules of the ceremonial, the Imperial
family, the Emperor himself, were equally enmeshed in it. Their
simplest everyday acts were performed in accordance with
prescribed ritual: They washed, dressed, and ate as if acting

out religious rites. There was a rule for every occasion. Etiquette prescribed who was eligible to attend court functions, the order of precedence at all functions, the dress in which people had to appear, the special way the table had to be set.*

Franz Joseph was a stickler for etiquette. Infractions of it annoyed him. Even his brothers and his own son had to address him as "Majesty"! His ministers had to report to him dressed in tailcoat; except for long conferences, they had to stand at a prescribed distance from him. A story (possibly apocryphal) is told that when his personal physician was got out of bed one night to hurry to the Emperor's bedside with only an overcoat hastily thrown over his nightshirt, the shocked Emperor exclaimed between coughs: "Tailcoat! Tailcoat!" Empress Elisabeth (Franz Joseph's wife), on the other hand, abhorred rigid etiquette and flaunted it frequently. At her first court dinner as Empress she is said to have taken off her gloves to the mute consternation of all present. Her chief lady-in-waiting whispered to her: "Your Majesty deigned to take off the gloves; the ceremonial forbids it." "You don't say!" Elisabeth is said to have replied, "no sensible person eats with gloves on."

The purpose of the rigid ceremonial was to surround the ruler and his court with an aura of grandeur, of sanctity, a constant reminder of his exalted station. Not pomp, not magnificence, but the observance of these innumerable rules applying only to that particular court invested it with that grandness and venerability which inspired people with awe, much as does the ceremony surrounding the Pope in the Vatican. Under Franz Joseph, etiquette did, indeed, assume Vatican proportions.[9]

EXTERNALISM. Franz Joseph's predilection for the external trappings of majesty expressed his preoccupation with appearances in general. He cultivated the outer, not the inner man. He stifled his personal, emotional, spiritual life in order to preserve the outward dignity of the Emperor; he killed his inner self to protect his outward majesty. That is why he did not grow as a

---

* Viewers of the Imperial apartments in the Vienna Hofburg are shown the family dining room with the table set for some thirty persons in the exact way it was done in Franz Joseph's time. All the cutlery is at the right side of the plate, nothing at the left—an arrangement which strikes one as impractical, but which was prescribed by Spanish etiquette.

person from the time he became an adult; he couldn't, because he stopped being a man and was only an emperor. As a child, as a boy, as a young man he was a human being with affection, feeling, gaiety, and humor. As an emperor, and increasingly with advancing age, he was loveless, without feeling, without humor; he was only majestic. His concern was *tenue*—to be correct, to keep up appearances, put up a front, and avoid scandal.

Franz Joseph's relationship with his wife, the Empress Elisabeth, was an example of this externalism. That his entire relationship with her was superficial, based on external things, and not on the harmony of their personalities, is evident from the way the marriage came about: He saw her, a child of fifteen, was overwhelmed by her beauty and charm, and the next day arranged to marry her. He had not even had time for a real conversation with her. It must soon have become apparent to her that she had nothing in common with her husband. In effect she left him in 1860, six years after marrying him, and after that returned to court only occasionally. To keep up appearances, the story was given out that her absence was necessitated by illness. She traveled, read and wrote poetry, rode passionately, and was a diet faddist. Franz Joseph disapproved of all these things, and of the literary people she had around her, but he strove to make it *appear* that he approved of all she did, that they were happily married, that she was away only for reasons of health. He wrote or telegraphed her often, though his messages show that he really had nothing to say to her; he informed her about the weather and about his hunting exploits. On one occasion he said to an aide: "I humbly thank God that he gave me such a helper [the Empress]. The more you spread these words, the more I shall be obliged to you."[10] He had nothing in common with her, shared none of her interests, and possibly felt little grief at the news of her death. But he was anxious that appearances be preserved; the people should be told that it was a happy marriage! He wished this to be known throughout the world.

With his son Rudolf, too, Franz Joseph's relations were entirely external and superficial. The father never took the trouble to know his son. He probably could not have understood the son's advanced, progressive, rebellious ideas, so far away from his own conservatism; but he seems never even to have tried. He gave Rudolf license to pursue his political and amorous whims (always under secret police supervision), if only appearances were preserved. When Rudolf's behavior threatened scandal, Franz Joseph turned into a severe judge.[11] It was not the intrinsic merits of Rudolf's acts, it was their external effects and appearance that mattered to the Emperor. Rudolf's (alleged) suicide must have been a severe shock to Franz Joseph—not because of the loss of a beloved son, but because of the scandal it created. Franz Joseph is reported to have said that his son "died like a tailor." By this he meant that Rudolf's suicide was a shameful act of cowardice. (Tailors, it should be noted, had a reputation for cowardice in German folklore; this is why the valor of the little tailor who proclaims to have killed "seven at one blow" is so remarkable.) The Emperor's remark shows that he was not concerned with the suffering that drove his son to suicide, but with the outer effects of his act, the shame of which outweighed all of Franz Joseph's other feelings.

That Franz Joseph seemed to be little moved by personal grief is attested by accounts of his "self-control" in the face of the tragedy. He did not let it interrupt his routine of "duty" for even one day. Andrássy reports his astonishment when the Emperor, on receiving Andrássy's condolences, at once launched into a discussion of political matters.

Franz Joseph's reaction to Rudolf's death also provides a sidelight on his alleged "profound abhorrence of every lie." The Emperor's first concern was what to tell the world about his son's death. On authorizing the publication of the (partial) truth about Rudolf's death, the Emperor said: "I owe it to my people to let them know the truth." But his first attempt had been to spread a deliberate lie that the Crown Prince had died of a heart attack. Franz Joseph's love of truth in this case asserted itself only when he saw that he could not make the lie stick.

Similar preoccupation with externals was shown by Franz Joseph's objection to the marriage of his nephew Franz Ferdinand to Countess Chotek: He feared that this marriage to a lady of unequal birth would portend the end of the Monarchy![12]

It seems almost incredible that with his Empire threatening to explode under the pressure of nationalism and growing social dissatisfaction, Franz Joseph could believe the survival of Habsburg power depended on the hereditary titles of his (presumptive) successor's wife! And on hearing that Franz Ferdinand and his wife had been murdered, the Emperor's first remark was: "Terrible! The Almighty does not allow himself to be provoked! A Higher Power has restored that order which I, unfortunately, was not able to maintain,"[13] implying that the assassination was God's punishment for Franz Ferdinand's marriage to the aristocratic commoner. Even God, in Franz Joseph's thinking, was concerned with rank and titles, with external attributes rather than with the soul! Next, Franz Joseph asked how the Archduke had died and was relieved when told that he had died "like a soldier." That was the important thing! The outward appearance! *Tenue!*

In everything, Franz Joseph showed the same concern with appearance, with adherence to forms and formality. His devoutness found expression in conscientious attendance to religious observances: going to Mass, receiving the sacraments, keeping fast days, kneeling to pray every day at the appointed hour. His conversation and correspondence was confined within formulas and devoid of spontaneity. His face showed a perpetual benevolent smile, giving him in his latter days the reputation of a kindly old man.

CONSIDERATION. Though often praised for his consideration of others, there are few instances in which he demonstrated it. Because he liked to get up early, he demanded the same of others. Ministers who found half-past seven in the morning too early to make their report could not expect Franz Joseph's approval. (It is said that Baron Beust accepted appointment as Foreign Minister in 1866 on condition that he would not be called to the Emperor before nine in the morning. Possibly some of Franz Joseph's many other ministers enjoyed similar privilege.) Because he liked to eat fast, his guests had to do the same. State dinners were eating races. On certain occasions, these dinners had to be wolfed in half an hour. Even twelve course dinners were consumed in less than an hour. Guests who wanted to eat without getting a

stomach ache did better to have a leisurely meal either before
or after the Imperial dinner. According to Franz Joseph's last
valet, Ketterl, "all the attendants, from the Lord Grand Master
of the Kitchen to the last waiter, sighed with relief when all
had gone smoothly, for His Majesty, however intensely he may
have seemed to be conversing with his guests, noticed every
infraction, the slightest delay in the changing of plates, and heard
. . . even the faintest noise made in putting down a plate."[14]

MILDNESS. Mildness was another character trait for which
Franz Joseph has been much praised. But here again, the facts
do not quite match the reputation. The Emperor's inclination
was to be severe. Disorders, such as strikes or demonstrations,
always had to be dealt with "firmly." On August 10, 1883, for
instance, on hearing of a workers' demonstration at which one
policeman and several workers were hurt and forty-two were
arrested, the Emperor wired from Ischl to his Minister-President:
"Request prompt and severe punishment of arrested persons."[15]
This without knowing whether the arrested persons were guilty
and how serious their crimes could have been, for in the same
telegram he asked for more detailed reports. When students
passed resolutions considered "impertinent" by Franz Joseph, he
demanded that the Minister-President "take firm steps . . . to
restore order." (March 13, 1889.) A telegraphic appeal by the
parents of an eighteen-year-old boy sentenced to death by a
military court remained unanswered and was put "*ad acta*"—
filed away—"by order of the All-Highest." (September 29, 1884.)
It will be remembered—see p. 41—that the All-Highest thought
his own youthfulness should have exonerated him of responsibility
for the blood bath of 1849! Franz Joseph refused appeals by
Czar Nicholas I for the lives of Hungarian generals in 1849. He
refused even his best friend, King Albert of Saxony, who asked
him to be lenient with the manager of the Ringstrassentheater
(which was destroyed in 1881 by a fire causing the deaths of
hundreds of people). Almost every time, "duty" forced Franz
Joseph to be severe.

On the other hand, it is true that he granted amnesties to
thousands of political offenders, previously put in prison by his
orders, in Hungary and Italy in the 1850's. For these amnesties,

however, Elisabeth's influence was largely responsible—and the hope that they would win the support of the subjected people for Habsburg—more than Franz Joseph's mildness and merciful-ness. In his old age the Emperor did show mildness in commuting death sentences. The number of executions declined in the latter decades of his reign, and in several of the last years there were no executions, though the number of death sentences was about fifty a year.

FACING THE TRUTH. One quality of Franz Joseph especially lauded by Schwarzenberg was his ability "to face the truth, even the bitterest . . ." If this was a correct evaluation in 1850, it changed soon thereafter and for the rest of the Emperor's life. Already the young Franz Joseph showed a tendency not to want to hear disagreeable things; they caused him to become quickly impatient, even impolite and brusque. Kempen's (the Police Chief's) diaries show how Grünne (Franz Joseph's Adjutant General until 1859) and others had, for this reason, developed a tactic to keep unpleasant news from Franz Joseph.[16] Near the end of Franz Joseph's reign, Count Stürgkh, Franz Joseph's next to last Austrian Minister-President, kept himself in power by keeping all unpleasantness from the Emperor and by making everything appear in a favorable light. This "hygienic method" of governing had been enforced by the Emperor's physician, Dr. Kerzl, and the Lord High Steward, Prince Montenuovo, ever since 1908 when Franz Joseph had suffered an illness.

INTERESTS. So completely was Franz Joseph immersed in ruling his Empire that he had little time for any other activities or interests. Besides the pleasure of work, especially of military activities, hunting was his only interest and relaxation. He had no intellectual or artistic interests. As a child he had shown a marked talent for drawing, as evidenced by many of his sketches, often with a humorous slant; but he abandoned this interest when he was Emperor. Unlike many of his Habsburg ancestors who were patrons of artists and collectors of works of art—the Prado in Madrid and the Vienna Collection are their great monu-ments—Franz Joseph had no interest in art or in its furtherance.*

---

* Heinrich von Srbik, who elevates everything Franz Joseph did or did not do to a lofty moral plane, shows ingenuity in praising him even for

Literature was even more alien to him. The assertion that the only book the Emperor ever read was the Army Manual is perhaps an exaggeration; but if he did read other books, it was certainly a rare occurrence.† His mother early noted Franz Joseph's aversion to reading and tried unsuccessfully to get him to read novels. His reading consisted of official papers and reports and a cursory glance at the *Fremdenblatt,* the newspaper reflecting the Foreign Office point of view. He went to the theater occasionally, but had no real interest for that either. In a letter to his mother on August 28, 1849, he writes that he must go to the Burgtheater (at that time to Germany what the Comédie Française was to France) to please a visiting cousin, Georg of Saxony, who wanted to see the play by Goethe produced in honor of the poet's one hundredth birthday anniversary. "We could have done without this useless celebration here, we have better things and men to honor. Georg is keen on the play, but it will bore me and I shall go only for a short while, for Georg's sake."[18] After 1886, Franz Joseph went to the theater only to see Frau Schratt—the actress who was his friend in the evening of his life.

Music had no appeal whatever for Franz Joseph; it may have been actually disagreeable to him; he had no ear. As a young man he liked to have one of his aides play the zither on outings from Ischl, but in later life not even that. He rarely went to the opera; there is no mention of his ever having gone to a concert; and there is no mention of court musicales. How different from earlier Habsburg rulers! His grandfather, the Emperor Franz, for instance, played chamber music every evening unless official court functions interfered. The Emperor Leopold I (1658-1705) conducted his own orchestra. Joseph II was a composer.*

---

his complete lack of interest in art and his failure to further art. The Emperor, Srbik says, did not dictate the directions to be taken by art![17]

† The only reference I have found to a book Franz Joseph is supposed to have read is in his letter of November 6, 1888, to Frau Schratt, in which he told her that he was reading the book she had given him—*Bühnenerlebnisse* (*Stage Adventures*) by Karl Sonntag.

* Among many members of the Habsburg family other than emperors, who were musicians themselves and patrons of musicians, the Archduke Rudolf, Franz Joseph's great uncle, deserves mention. It was for this gifted musician that Beethoven wrote his celebrated "Archduke Trio."

All forms of art, in short, were out of Franz Joseph's world; and so were all sciences. It is not recorded that he showed any interest, any curiosity, for any of the innumerable scientific discoveries and inventions which were made during his lifetime. In this respect, too, he shut himself off from his own age and continued to live in the Middle Ages. His interests were those of a medieval ruler: hunting, war, dynastic intrigue (foreign affairs), ceremony. When he relaxed on occasion, as in the company of Frau Schratt, he liked to hear Vienna society gossip.

The Emperor's limited range of interests, especially his vacuity in matters of art and science, could not be without effect on the cultural life of the peoples whom he ruled. The court of Franz Joseph was not one to attract men of talent and brilliance, as had many German courts—Weimar, Munich, Sans Souci—and Vienna in earlier centuries. Instead of surrounding himself with men of art and science, Franz Joseph made sure that no one should be admitted to court who had not at least sixteen noble ancestors, that is, all of whose great-great-grandparents were of the nobility. It was he who formulated this rule—a sort of inverted Nürnberg law. It is a testimony to the vitality of Viennese cultural life that, despite this grotesquely unintellectual and unspiritual atmosphere of the court, art, literature, and science did nevertheless flourish in the Imperial city in the Franz Joseph era.

ALONE AND LONELY.   The picture of Franz Joseph that emerges from even the most sympathetic descriptions shows him as a man with few human ties and as a man insensible to human joys and sufferings. He had little love for anyone. Neither his wife nor his children were really close to him. His brothers made him uneasy. He revered his mother, but was contemptuous of almost all his relatives.[19] "The Emperor has no friend," Crown Prince Rudolf wrote, "his character, his nature do not permit it. He stands alone and lonely on his height . . ." (Letter to Count Latour, December 2, 1881.)[20] Franz Joseph himself referred to his "drab existence." One is tempted to feel sorry for him, and this was what many of his subjects probably did. Except Frau Schratt and King Albert of Saxony (who died in 1902), he had no friends, had little love, but he had his duty, his honor, his army, and his Empire.

CHAPTER 7

The Soldier Emperor

A PASSIONATE SOLDIER. From earliest childhood Franz Joseph showed a love for all military things, exceeding the normal propensity of little boys for playing soldier. This love was carefully nurtured by his parents and his grandfather Franz I, who never failed to admire and praise the little Archduke's strutting and drilling, and who encouraged it by giving him military toys for Christmas and birthdays. On Christmas Eve, 1833, when he was a little over three years old, Franzi (as his family called him) appeared in the uniform of a regiment of Imperial Infantry. He received his first real shooting gun on his sixth birthday anniversary. His favorite music, he said once, was the shooting of guns, and his favorite smell, the smell of powder. "Ever since his childhood," his mother wrote to Field Marshal Radetzky in 1848, "Franz has been passionately devoted to the military profession."[1]

As Franz Joseph grew older, this early love for soldiery grew to be the main interest of his life. "He lives and dies for the army, our good Emperor," said his Adjutant General, Count Paar. "If only he can see soldiers, he feels like newly born."

EMPEROR IN UNIFORM. Quite naturally for a man so deeply attached to his army, Franz Joseph's habitual dress was a military uniform. Even as a child he often donned a uniform, though only for special occasions. As a teen-ager he begged to be allowed to go to the "Ball at Court" in the uniform of a colonel of Hussars, in which he looked so handsome. Of course he wore a uniform whenever he appeared at military functions and when, at the age of seventeen, he joined Radetzky's army in Italy. From the moment he became Emperor he always wore a uniform, except when hunting or on the rare occasions when he traveled incognito in foreign countries. According to his valet, Ketterl, Franz Joseph had "innumerable" uniforms, many of them magnificent foreign ones presented to him by potentates wishing to humor him or to curry favor with him. The Emperor knew exactly what hat, sash, belt, or other accessories had to be worn with each of these. Also, he knew exactly which uniform was the correct one for any particular occasion. Shortly before the Swedish King Gustav V visited Vienna in 1908, Sweden had introduced new uniforms. Franz Joseph, as a Swedish General, immediately had a new uniform made and sent from Stockholm by special courier, so he could meet the King in the proper, new uniform. Gustav was flabbergasted. "For Heaven's sake! Already in the new uniform? And not even *I* have one!"[2] In 1908, the German princes, led by Emperor Wilhelm II, came to congratulate him on the sixtieth anniversary of his accession. After Franz Joseph, dressed in the Austrian Field Marshal's uniform, had accepted their jointly offered respects, he received each in private audience—and in the uniform of each successive visitor's own country! Most of the Emperor's working time on that day must have been taken up with changing uniforms; the valet's day, presumably, with headaches. Franz Joseph was also much concerned that artists who were painting his portrait—in uniform, of course—should make no mistake in showing the details of the uniform, and that ribbons, stars, and medals should be correctly placed; he sent his valet to check on the artist and on the correct progress of the uniform. His own likeness did not seem to concern him much, but an error in a uniform and its decorations would have amounted to lese majesty. Appropriately, Franz Joseph was laid to his last rest in the Austrian Field Marshal's uniform—white tunic with gold; red trousers with gold lampas.

In habitually wearing uniform, Franz Joseph deviated from the custom of previous Habsburg emperors, none of whom, except Joseph II, either wore uniforms or showed any particular interest for military affairs. Nor did the people, used to the unwarlike civilian dress of his predecessors, approve of Franz Joseph's uniforms.[3] On one occasion, in 1867, the Mayor of Vienna requested the Emperor to appear in civilian attire at some function. The Minister-President supported the request, but Franz Joseph refused. The following year, the Mayor tried again. "Don't trouble yourself," the Emperor said, "it is useless." The Mayor gave up.[4]

IMPERIAL DRILLMASTER. Unlike Joseph II, who dreamed of defeating Prussia's Frederick the Great in battle, Franz Joseph probably did not consider himself a great military leader. His one attempt at generalship—in the Battle of Solferino (June 24, 1859) in which his numerically superior forces were defeated by the French and Italians—cost him the province of Lombardy and 22,000 soldiers. Not strategy, but military drill was Franz Joseph's interest and competence. From the age of four, he had received regular instruction in military drill. His mother thought it touching to see how seriously he took these lessons and with what zeal he tried to carry out every command. On his thirteenth birthday he was given a cavalry regiment and a year later paraded it magnificently before his cousin, Archduke Albrecht, who reported with admiration to Franz Joseph's father about the splendid performance of the son in putting his troops through their paces.

Franz Joseph adored reviewing troops or parading them in review before his peers. He rarely missed a chance to participate in maneuvers, whether in his own empire or in foreign countries. His letters to his mother and to his wife are replete with details about parades in which this regiment or that brigade looked magnificent, or performed brilliantly, about the uniforms the troops wore and about the men who led them—information which was perhaps not terribly exciting for the Empress, whose tastes were more for poetry. But Franz Joseph's heart and soul were in drill. He was a real expert at this and would have been a competent company commander or drill sergeant. In 1866, some irreverent Viennese, anticipating by half a century the Emperor's demise, had prepared this epitaph for him:

> Here the Emperor Franz Joseph lies.
> Regrettably, he was not wise.
> Wanderer, do not tarry! Flee!
> Lest he get up to drill with thee!

All these military pursuits—these maneuvers and parades and visits to military establishments—were doubly satisfying, for in addition to giving him pleasure, they were regarded, at least by Franz Joseph himself, as his "duty." As already mentioned, Franz Joseph's devotion to duty was famed; and contributing to this fame was his unfailing and meticulous attention to his military duty. Within limits, a ruler is able to decide for himself what his duties are. Franz Joseph rarely considered it his duty to inspect civilian establishments, such as hospitals or schools (unless military) or scientific institutions—or the living and working conditions of the people. But his demands upon himself to inspect his beloved army were severe. One of his most pressing duties upon becoming Emperor, with his many crowns tottering on his head, was to have his troops parade for him; and he expressed his Imperial displeasure on that occasion because the ranks and files were not quite as straight as he wanted them.

Not only at home, but even when he was unofficially visiting in a foreign country, and reviewing troops could not be counted as "duty," Franz Joseph's pleasure was to watch the soldiers. At Cap Martin, where he had gone in 1894 to visit his wife, the Empress Elisabeth, he hastened to see the French *Chasseurs Alpins* drill. When he visited the supposedly ill Elisabeth in Corfu, he went every morning to watch the British garrison drill, while the Empress was reading Heine and Homer. One can understand why Elisabeth was unhappy in her marriage with this man. She is said to have remarked that Franz Joseph had the soul of a drill sergeant.[5] Even if she did not actually say it, she must have painfully felt the gulf between his parade-ground mentality and her own poetic soul.

BAPTISM OF FIRE.   As a youth, Franz Joseph was eager to play soldier in earnest at last, and to prove himself worthy of the magnificent uniforms he was wearing. His opportunity came when, at seventeen, his mother sent him to Field Marshall Radetzky's army in Italy, where he received his baptism of fire in the Battle of Santa Lucia on May 6, 1848 (see p. 28). He was carefully guarded, but, according to Radetzky's laudatory report, a cannon ball crashed nearby and Franz Joseph never winced. After this incident he was sent back to the reserves on the pretext that these would play a decisive role in the battle. There is, however, no doubt about Franz Joseph's courage and his desire to stay in the thick of the fighting. On the day of the battle he wrote to his mother that "for the first time I heard cannon balls whistling around me and I am overjoyed."[6] So great was his lust for battle that he implored his mother not to end the war through negotiations, because "this would be a disgrace. We owe it to our honor . . . and to our brave army not to rest until we have chased the Piedmontese out of our provinces and planted the double eagle in Turin . . ."[7] Franz Joseph saw action on two subsequent occasions: In 1849 he participated in encounters between his troops and his rebellious Hungarian subjects; and in 1859, as mentioned earlier, he led his army into the disaster of Solferino.

AT EASE WITH MILITARY MEN. Franz Joseph tended to evaluate men on the basis of their soldierliness. He liked people because they had an interest in military things, disliked them because they were unmilitary. When, in 1847, he first met Prince (later King) Albert of Saxony, who was the son of the twin sister of Franz Joseph's mother and who became his best, perhaps his only, friend, Franz Joseph felt drawn to him at once because Albert was "anti-liberal and with heart and soul a soldier." Conversely, Franz Joseph disliked and distrusted Edward VII of England because that monarch was unmilitary as well as intelligent and witty—unsoldierly qualities which made Franz Joseph ill at ease. Similarly objectionable to him were King Albert of the Belgians and his wife, to whom the Emperor referred as the "professorial pair" because they were so highly educated. "If the King were somewhat military, one could perhaps get closer to him," Franz Joseph said to his Adjutant General. "That he is so completely unsoldierly really makes me dislike him."[8] A shock awaited Franz Joseph when former President Ulysses S. Grant, the great hero of the American Civil War, called on him in 1878. The Emperor asked Grant if he had reviewed any troops in Paris. "No," replied Grant, "I am fed up with these things; I always avoid meeting soldiers or generals, because, although I was educated at the Military Academy of West Point, I never developed a taste for this profession."[9] This remark so startled Franz Joseph that it made him laugh.

It was a disappointment to Franz Joseph that his son, Rudolf, lacked interest for military pursuits.

ARMY CEMENTED MONARCHY. Franz Joseph's love of the military, his identification with the army, sprang from a genuine, natural inclination. He was a born soldier. But beyond this, the uniforms and parades were a symbolic expression of his reliance on the army for the continued existence of his regime. The army was the cement that held the shaky and unwilling Empire together. Even the army could not save that Empire from ultimate collapse, but without the army the end would have come much sooner; it would have come in 1848, before the beginning, not after the end, of Franz Joseph's long reign. The regime of Franz Joseph owed its existence to the army. The army put him on the throne (with Russian help), and the army kept him there to his—and the Empire's—dying day.

In the abundant nostalgic literature which describes the Empire of Franz Joseph as a paradise where people lived happily in freedom under a just, benevolent, peace-loving monarch, the army is extolled as a spiritual, unifying force. "In the army the unity of the multination state became reality. The army supported this state in a quite different and much deeper sense than is implied by the simple interpretation of military power as a coercive device."[10] This no doubt reflects the sentiments of many people who lived in the "golden age" of Franz Joseph, whether in or out of the army, and of some elderly persons today, to whom Franz Joseph and pre-World War I days are a memory of a long-past happy youth.

Facts do not quite bear out this idealized dream picture. The peoples of the Empire lived in continuous strife and struggled for "freedom" and "justice," which they eventually imagined to have achieved when they made an end to the Monarchy. It must be remembered that the Habsburg Empire was broken up, not by external force, as was Poland in the eighteenth century or Germany in 1945, but by internal pressures of peoples forced into an unwilling association. The army of Franz Joseph was

indeed the "coercive device" which maintained this unwilling
association. As in other countries, so in the Monarchy the army
was not only for defense of the people against foreign enemies,
but for defense of the ruler against the people. In the Monarchy,
the army was in fact exclusively an instrument of the ruler, not
an instrument for the defense of the people at all. Even foreign
wars were not fought in the interest of "the people," but in the
interest of the Emperor. This was succinctly expressed by an
Archduchess in 1859, when newspapers criticized the conduct
of Franz Joseph's war with France and Sardinia-Piedmont. "I
fail to see," she said, "what business it is of the people that the
Emperor is fighting a war!"[11] When Franz Joseph embarked
on his last war, in 1914, he pleaded that he was forced into it
"for the preservation of the honor of my Monarchy, for the
protection of its prestige and power position"—not a word about
defending "the people." On the contrary, the people were to
defend *him* and his honor. It was no mere figure of speech when
the Emperor referred to "my army," as he invariably did, instead
of calling it the "nation's army" or the "people's army." It was
his, the Emperor's army; it was his instrument of power; the
soldiers and officers had to swear loyalty to him exclusively.
The people had nothing to do with it—except to pay for it and
furnish the soldiers.

The true character of the army as a coercive device to enforce
obedience to the Emperor was most clearly revealed at the time
of Franz Joseph's accession, in the Revolution of 1848 and its
aftermath. "Now we can really say," an army captain (later
Lieutenant Field Marshal, a rank equivalent to Major General
in the United States) Baron Hugo von Weckbecker, wrote in
1848, "our bayonets are the firmest support of the throne, with
our life blood we have cemented the Monarchy."[12] It was evident
at the time, and later undisputed by the most pro-Habsburg
historians, that "thanks to the army alone . . . Empire and throne
had survived all storms."[13] Members of the Imperial family, including Franz Joseph himself, were fully aware that the army
was the sole reliance, the savior, of the Monarchy. "The army
was the only thing in the Monarchy on whose loyalty and devotion the Emperor could count," Archduke Ludwig, great uncle

of Franz Joseph, wrote on December 4, 1848. "This must continue so, and Franzi [Franz Joseph] who has his heart and soul in the army, will contribute most to it. . . ." Archduchess Sophie, Franz Joseph's mother, praised the "three paladins"—the Generals Windisch-Grätz, Radetzky, and Jelačić—"for saving the dynasty."[14] With similar recognition of the role of guns in establishing his regime, Franz Joseph's first proclamation extolled his glorious army as the pillar of the throne. For years after the Revolution, the Monarchy was ruled by a *de facto* military dictatorship; and throughout Franz Joseph's reign, cities and entire provinces were repeatedly put under martial law when the people showed their hostility to the Habsburg regime.

ARMY AGAINST PEOPLE. Franz Joseph well understood what the function of his army, or any other ruler's army, was: It was not to defend the country, in the sense of "the people," but to defend the ruler's regime over the people. Undoubtedly, he thought this just and honorable, in accordance with God's will, as correspondence with his mother reveals. During the Italian campaign of 1848, Franz Joseph saw how Radetzky fought not only the foreign invader (whom the people hailed as liberator), but the Emperor's own subjects as well. On the urging of his aide, Count Mensdorff, Franz Joseph had asked his mother (letter of May 11, 1848) to instruct him what to do "when it came to the burning of cities and similar punishments in Lombardy"—this was punishment of Habsburg subjects, not of foreigners. (Franz Joseph was recalled from the army to keep him from being identified with Radetzky's ruthlessness against the subject population.) On May 15, 1849, Franz Joseph wrote indignantly: "Dear Mama! . . . In Rhenish Bavaria things have come to a pretty pass. The troops defected. In Rastatt the Baden troops have shot their officers. . . . But the Saxon troops have distinguished themselves and will continue reliable for a long time after this fight."[15] It must be remembered that the troops "defected" to their own people; that the Baden troops preferred to shoot the officers when these officers ordered them to shoot their own people; that the Saxon troops "distinguished" themselves by not refusing to shoot at their own people when their officers commanded them to do so and that after this display

of heroism they could be relied upon to do the same on subsequent occasions. From Schönbrunn Franz Joseph wrote on
September 1, 1850: "Here the mood of the people is getting
worse every day, and yet they are too foxy to let it come to
sabre blows." He seemed to resent the people's uncooperativeness
in not affording his army a chance to beat them up—he used the
term *"dreinschlagen,"* which suggests "to hit out blindly." A
few days later he wrote: ". . . it is Sunday . . . Church parade
outside the city walls, to show the dear Viennese that we still
have troops and cannons . . ."—not to defend them, of course,
but to suppress them, to enforce their obedience. The use of
divine services to parade military power underscores the solidarity
of Church and Army. In Austria, as elsewhere, incense mingled
with the smoke of gunpowder.

The Emperor's recognition, and frequent use, of the army as
a coercive device give the lie to romantic phrases about the army
as an "embodiment of unity." Not only Franz Joseph, but the
entire "establishment" of the Monarchy understood the true
situation; though this is not to say that they saw anything but
right and justice in this state of affairs.

ARCHDUKE FRANZ FERDINAND ON THE ARMY. An especially
straightforward statement about the role of the army was made by
the Archduke Franz Ferdinand, the heir apparent to the throne
who was murdered in Sarajevo in 1914, in a memorandum to the
Chief of the General Staff, Count Beck, dated May 6, 1896. "The
army," he said, "is not solely charged with protecting the father-
land against a foreign enemy, its main task is to protect and preserve the throne and to do battle against any and all internal
enemies. . . . The only reliance of the throne is the army. . . ."
But, the Archduke complains, the army is infected with nationalism and may no longer be useful as an instrument to enforce
Habsburg power over the several nations of the Empire. Hungary
is approaching revolution, elsewhere in the Empire nationalism
is rife. In the past, officers of all nationalities felt as Austrians,
but now they feel as Hungarians, Czechs, Poles. "What reliance
can there be on such troops in a showdown, when they are to
protect the throne and, if necessary, to fight against their own
countrymen . . . ?" A second danger, the Archduke pointed

out, is the spread of Socialist ideas among the soldiers. Surprise inspections of barracks yielded impressive collections of Socialist and inflammatory nationalist handbills. "Today the spirit and discipline of the army is still such that, when occasion arises to resort to arms in case of strikes and suchlikes, the soldier will shoot at his fellow countryman or relative; but how long can this last, if the propaganda becomes even more widespread?"[16]

It is noteworthy that in his reply, General Beck said nothing about the Archduke's analysis of the conflict between government and people and of the role of the army as the only support of the throne against the people. The General seemed to take this interpretation for granted and saw no need to comment on it.

WHAT KEPT THE ARMY LOYAL? If the people of the multilingual Empire were really "disloyal" to the dynasty, how could the Emperor put any reliance in an army recruited from such unreliable, if not openly hostile subjects? Why was this army willing to be "the only support of the throne"? Why did it not make common cause with "the people" and turn its arms against the throne? Four factors may supply the answer:

(1) The officers were, on the whole, loyal to the Emperor (though Archduke Franz Ferdinand's memorandum mentions the Hungarian officers' open contempt for the Emperor). Many officers, especially generals, were aristocrats who also in that capacity were supporters of the Imperial system; also, non-aristocratic officers knew that their advantage, advancement, and prestige depended on the survival of the Monarchy.

(2) Indoctrination and the oath of loyalty to the Emperor helped to suppress disloyal sentiments among the officers and enlisted men.

(3) The system of mixing up nationalities within military units, and of stationing units consisting primarily of one nationality in the territory of another nationality, e.g., Czech regiments in Hungary, or Hungarian regiments in Vienna, blunted the desire and lessened the opportunity for disloyal acts.

(4) Most important, the threat of instant severe punishment always tends to keep soldiers in line. The discipline of an army relies on the cowardliness, not on the courage, of its men. For this reason, one well-tried method of making rebels innocuous

is to draft them into the army. Though there they have weapons, they are also under rigid and ruthless discipline. Continuously supervised, they have little opportunity to hatch mutiny. To refuse to obey—singly or as a unit—is to risk execution and therefore requires unusual courage; it is easier to shoot others, as ordered.

FRANZ JOSEPH AND THE POLICE. The army was in effect a police force. But there was of course also a separate police force, to which Franz Joseph attached great importance. In 1853, the supreme command of the police was separated from the Ministry of the Interior and put directly under the Emperor, even as the army. The Chief of Police, Lieutenant Field Marshall Baron Kempen, had seat and voice in the Cabinet and became one of the most intimate collaborators of Franz Joseph. Kempen, as Chief of Police, and General Count Grünne, as the Emperor's Adjutant General and Chief of the Military Chancery (Militärkanzlei, in effect the Ministry of War)—the War Lord and the Police Lord—were the two most powerful men in the government in the first decade of Franz Joseph's reign.

Franz Joseph indefatigably strengthened his police regime and aimed to tighten the meshes of the net spread over the entire population. Kempen had his spies in all government offices. Courts, high dignitaries, even bishops were under his surveillance. Statesmen and foreign diplomats had their correspondence intercepted by his Black Cabinet. Franz Joseph knew this practice to be illegal and immoral, yet tolerated it.[17]

Franz Joseph's trust in the police is expressed in a letter of March 19, 1858, to his brother Maximilian, then Governor General of Lombardy-Venetia. The letter, mentioning among other things that the Black Cabinet of his ever alert police had intercepted a letter from the King of Prussia (sovereign of a friendly power), admonished Maximilian to be severe in suppressing every nationalist-revolutionary movement in Italy, and demanded better organization of the police—"this important branch."[18] In another letter, of December 26, 1858, Franz Joseph again tells Maximilian that "I cannot impress upon you enough the need for vigilance and for the encouragement of the police."[19] These letters show clearly that Franz Joseph regarded the police as the hub of the Administration. "Black-Cabinet" methods continued to be used later, if not to ferret out revolutionists, at any rate to supervise the Empress Elisabeth and Crown Prince Rudolf. It is not certain whether this was done with the knowledge of the Emperor.

FEAR OF REVOLUTION.   Throughout his reign, Franz Joseph was afraid of revolution. Living apart, in splendid isolation, in his world of autocracy and aristocracy, he did not understand the currents which were transforming society. He sensed impending doom, but was unable to avert it by bending to the new realities. Instead, he entrenched himself and his regime behind his army and his police. "Dreinschlagen"—hitting out—was his chief reliance. He was put on the throne by force of arms. In the early years of his reign the saber regime of Grünne and Kempen supported the *blutjunge** Emperor; and to the end of his days, Franz Joseph met all revolutionary aspirations "with police sabres, if necessary reinforced by rifle volleys of the infantry and grape-shot of the artillery."[20]

---

* The word *blutjung* means extremely young, but literally: blood-young. Many of the "blood-young" Emperor's subjects gave the expression a double meaning by accenting the first syllable.

CHAPTER 8

Franz Joseph's Simplicity

A persistent tale about Franz Joseph is that he was a man of simple habits, a Spartan, thrifty, frugal, undemanding in his personal needs, unassuming, unostentatious. The Emperor's wants were so few, declared one of his servants, that it would not have taken five guilders a day to satisfy them! (The guilder, or florin, was the Austrian monetary unit in the nineteenth century. Five guilders were worth two dollars). Franz Joseph's simplicity was proverbial. Nearly every one of his biographers pays homage to it. When Franz Joseph is discussed in books, in lectures, or in casual conversation today, his simplicity is almost certain to be mentioned—as a redeeming quality, a quality showing his greatness and dedication.

Just what, precisely, did this alleged simplicity consist in? Simplicty may have different meanings; in some of these meanings the Emperor was, in others he was emphatically not, a man of simplicity.

UNOSTENTATIOUSNESS. Franz Joseph was simple in the sense that he was unostentatious, unassuming, not pompous or theatrical. The Emperor could be unassuming because it was taken for granted by himself and by all those around him that he was way above them. He never let himself or anyone else forget who he was; but he was so sure of deference paid him that he did not need to compel it by putting on airs. He walked on an imperial stage, surrounded by imperial pomp and ceremony, but he did not have to be stagy because it was his nature to bear himself like an emperor. He played his part all the more effectively for not playing a part. His simplicity, in this sense, consisted in being completely sure of his own majesty.

COMMON TOUCH. If by simplicity one understands the common touch, the desire to associate with ordinary people and the ability to deal with them as equals, Franz Joseph was not a simple man. There were some Habsburgs who did have the common touch: Franz Joseph's great-uncle, the Archduke Johann (one of the gifted brothers of the Emperor Franz I who were systematically kept out of government affairs by their suspicious, narrow-minded brother and his minister Metternich) was a real "man of the people" who married the daughter of a village postmaster, who believed that if the Habsburg dynasty was to survive it must identify itself with the people, and who enjoyed great popularity. Also the Emperor Franz had the common touch: He liked to walk among the people; he spoke their dialect; and he enjoyed making social calls on families of the bourgeoisie and low aristocracy. Franz Joseph never did these things. He did not have the common touch. He never mingled with the people; he did not (except as a child) speak the Viennese dialect; and his social relations, with one exception, were with royalty, the highest aristocracy, and generals. The one exception was Frau Schratt, the Burgtheater actress who, in the last thirty years of his life, was his friend and comfort.

SIMPLE QUARTERS. Franz Joseph's usual residences were the Hofburg in the center of Vienna, and Schönbrunn, the summer residence in Vienna. These two Imperial establishments are perhaps less pompous than, for instance, Versailles, but are certainly grand and magnificent and majestic, not simple. In the summer, the Emperor stayed at his villa in Ischl, in the mountains not far from Salzburg, his favorite resort, as it had been his parents'. The "Emperor villa" in Ischl is less grand than the Hofburg and Schönbrunn and perhaps gives an impression of simplicity because its architecture is "Francisco-Josephinian," that is, Victorian, a style not generally considered as regal as the baroque which flourished in the age of the Grand Monarchy, especially between 1650 and 1750, the period in which Versailles and Schönbrunn and much of the Hofburg were built. Still, the "Emperor villa" at Ischl, too, is an elaborate, luxurious establishment rather than a "modest villa," as Joseph Redlich called it.[1] So are the other palaces at which Franz Joseph occasionally stayed: the Royal Castle at Budapest, the Hradschin at Prague, Castle Laxenburg near Vienna, Gödöllö in Hungary, and a dozen places more. They were certainly not distinguished by their simplicity.

But, the admirers of Franz Joseph's simplicity object, the Emperor used only three rooms at the Hofburg and at Schönbrunn. This is true and not true. Even an Emperor can use only one room at a time, and Franz Joseph spent most of his time in one of three rooms: his office, his bedroom, and a parlor in which he received callers. Each of these was not so much an ordinary room as a hall, about the area of a modern four-room apartment. For special occasions, when more or larger rooms were needed, the Emperor of course had them at his disposal. There were rooms for family dinners, others for state dinners, balls, and other court functions. There were also waiting rooms, rooms for his guards, and rooms for his servants.

The Emperor's rooms were furnished with customary regal magnificence, as can be seen by visitors to these places today. In one respect, however, his apartments did show simplicity: He had a military, iron bedstead and an undistinguished, ordinary washstand. As Franz Joseph had liked to play soldier from early childhood on, the military bedstead and washstand may have been in part his way of continuing the game as an adult, imagining himself a soldier in the midst of his Imperial splendor. It has not been asserted, however, that he chose this bed and this washstand because he wanted to suffer hardship. Presumably the bed was comfortable, the mattress conducive to sound sleep, the bedclothes clean, the washstand supplied with water, soap, towels.*

SIMPLE MODE OF LIFE. "Franz Joseph's mode of life was extremely simple," according to Baron Kray, one of his staff of secretaries in the last two years of his life.[2] This assertion is made

---

* A perceptive commentator, on reading this paragraph, suggested that the reason for the iron bed may have been the bedbugs which notoriously infested the Hofburg and which would have been hard to dislodge from a wooden bedstead.

admiringly, though it carries unintended sarcasm, coming as it does immediately after a description of the Emperor's retinue, which consisted of: the First Lord High Steward, the Lord Chamberlain, the Lord Marshal of the Court, the Second Lord High Steward, and a dozen more such functionaries with medieval titles; the Captains of the several units of (ceremonial) Body Guards; two Adjutants General; four Adjutants; a bevy of high officials functioning as secretaries; and the Emperor's personal physician, who was always in attendance and who saw the Emperor every day. This staff was not for the entire Imperial family; it was exclusively for the Emperor. The Empress had her own retinue of Lord High Steward and so on, and so had every adult Archduke.*

The Emperor's three rooms and personal needs were taken care of by sixteen persons: a chief valet, two other valets, two doorkeepers, four attendants, two lackeys, three chambermaids, a bath attendant, and a barber. This does not include the kitchen staff, coachmen, and a variety of other menials who served Franz Joseph's personal needs.

It is difficult to discover how and where the alleged simplicity of Franz Joseph's mode of life could have manifested itself. Whereas his grandfather Franz I took walks in public parks, pushing the baby carriage of his infant grandson Franz Joseph amidst the Viennese population, Franz Joseph himself walked

---

* Some idea of the duties performed by these high court officials may be gleaned from the following document preserved, among hundreds of others of its type, in the Haus, Hof, und Staatsarchiv in Vienna:

"Office of the Lord High Steward of His Imperial and Royal Highness, the Most Illustrious Archduke Franz Salvator [husband of Franz Joseph's daughter, Archduchess Marie Valerie]. Castle Wallsee, April 14, 1913.

"To the Office of the Lord High Steward of his Imperial and Royal Apostolic Majesty at Vienna.

"The undersigned Office of the Lord High Steward takes the liberty to remit by Postal Money Order the sum of Kr. 16.45 [about $3.29] as compensation for table service items, specified in the enclosed statements, which disappeared in the course of the recent Illustrious Sojourn at Schönbrunn of Their Imperial and Royal Highnesses, the Most Illustrious Archduke Franz Salvator and the Most Illustrious Archduchess Marie Valerie, with the request kindly to cause a proper receipt to be issued.

"Signed: the Lord High Steward" (seven additional signatures or initials, with comments. Some of these signatures are by officials of the Court Paymaster's Office and of the Court Household Office).

only in his private gardens. As a young man he had walked, if not in the city streets, at least on the city walls—and this was where Libényi tried to assassinate him. After that he seems not to have taken walks in the city. When he stayed at the Hofburg in Vienna as an old man, he used to drive to Schönbrunn (a drive of about half an hour each way) after lunch for a short walk with Frau Schratt in the *Kammergarten* reserved exclusively for his own use, though he had a beautiful garden, now open to the public, adjoining the Hofburg where he could have strolled in complete seclusion. In Budapest he missed his daily walks which he could not take there—because the garden of the Royal Castle was hilly!

Hunting, the Emperor's sport, was the most extravagant imaginable: It required the maintenance of extensive hunting preserves, a staff of foresters, hunters, loaders, and hundreds of beaters who had to see to it that the game presented itself to him while they stayed out of sight. When he traveled—and he traveled a lot—the Emperor usually took his whole retinue with him. This required an entire train. But Franz Joseph did not have just one court train; he had five. Occasionally, when he wanted to travel quite modestly, or "simply," he did not use one of his five court trains, but had only three special cars, including his personal parlor car, attached to a regularly scheduled train. The bath attendant accompanied Franz Joseph only on shorter trips (e.g., to Ischl or Budapest), the barber always.

When the court was at Ischl, horses and carriages were taken there from Vienna: in 1878, for instance, thirty carriages and forty-two horses; in 1890, for the wedding of the Emperor's daughter, Archduchess Valerie, eighty horses and the corresponding carriages! When King Edward VII of England visited Franz Joseph in Ischl in 1908, gobelins and exotic plants were brought from Schönbrunn as decorations for a gala dinner. (Could it perhaps be taken as proof of Franz Joseph's simple way of life that he did not use the gobelins every day at his hunting lodge?) Whenever the Emperor had to appear on horseback outside of Vienna, perhaps to review troops in St. Petersburg or Bucharest, his own horses had to be taken there a few days before by his personal chief trainer. As a young man, the Emperor liked to jump off his yacht for a swim in the Danube; to test the depth of the river at the particular spot, his Adjutant had to jump in first.

To present Franz Joseph as "simple" and averse to personal luxury on the ground that he used no "modern conveniences," such as telephone and automobiles,[3] amounts to a complete distortion of the truth. Telephones and automobiles were not luxuries for Franz Joseph. Indeed, there would have been justification for speaking of the Emperor's simplicity if he had consented to use the telephone instead of summoning those with whom he wished to speak to his presence, or dispatching messages by mounted adjutants; or if he had consented to use the drab automobile instead of elegant carriages drawn by the fabulous Lipizza horses of his Spanish Riding School. In rejecting automobiles and telephones he was really insisting on his accustomed luxury, much like people who reject frozen strawberries and stick to the "simple" old-fashioned way of having them fresh picked. In fact, there is a monstrous finicality and luxuriousness hiding behind the appearance of the simplicity of Franz Joseph with his iron bed that had to be toted along with him so he could be simple, and his servants who had to perform their tasks unseen, and his simple hunter's love of nature which required enormous hunting preserves and battalions of attendants.

SIMPLICITY AT MANEUVERS. At maneuvers, Franz Joseph's valet Ketterl asserts, "the Emperor's simplicity and frugality were almost incredible."[4] But what is really incredible is that the valet should make such an assertion. Here are some of the things he tells about Franz Joseph at maneuvers: Two of the Emperor's horses were taken by the trainer to the maneuver grounds a few days before His Majesty's arrival, to familiarize the animals with the territory. The horses had to have easy, comfortable gaits and had to be immune to noise and to troops marching, so as to be absolutely sure not to shy. A bed—iron, of course—was always taken along for the Emperor ever since on one occasion a bed, not his own, collapsed under him. The Imperial table consisted of boards, but these were covered with white tablecloths. All table ware and other maneuver equipment of the Emperor, as well as the waiters and cooks, had been taken over from the Archduke Albrecht, who had insisted that every-

thing be rich and elegant. (So the Emperor's maneuver equipment could hardly have been "simple.") At meals there was
always white wine and red wine and beer, and everyone could
drink as much as he wanted. Maneuvers cost the Emperor enormous sums of money. On one occasion, in 1894, the Emperor
attended German maneuvers at Stettin. The food was atrocious;
it consisted of undefinable soup, beef cooked too long, and beer.
The valet remonstrated in the name of his master, but the next
day the Emperor was served the same mess. Thereafter the valet
ordered the table d'hôte menu from the hotel for the Emperor.
In this case, if the valet's story is true, Franz Joseph was not
simple and frugal—and courteous—enough to put up with the
food apparently acceptable to the German Emperor and his
officers; and far from subsisting on five guilders (two dollars)
a day, the Emperor paid twenty marks for his lunch alone,
which was more than ten guilders.

VACATIONS. It is frequently asserted that Franz Joseph rarely
allowed himself a vacation. Though he went to his villa in
Ischl every summer, his work routine continued unchanged
even there. Yet he must have managed to find ample time for
hunting (though some of this was counted as "duty.") Corti
reports that between 1848 and 1900 Franz Joseph shot 48,345
head of game.[5] This averages out to nearly 1,000 animals a year.
How many days' hunting does it take to shoot 1,000 deer or
chamois? The Emperor is said to have really hunted each animal
by itself, rather than engage in the mass shootings that his nephew
Franz Ferdinand apparently preferred.*

In his younger years, at least, Franz Joseph did not impress
people as a man who sacrificed his pleasures to his monarchial
duties. On the contrary, there were criticisms by persons around
the Emperor that he devoted too much time to pleasure—rides,
excursions, hunting. Diplomats, too, reported to their governments that the chase was keeping the monarch too much away
from his duties. With advancing age, however, Franz Joseph

---

* According to a story published in *Aufbau und Frieden*, a Prague newspaper, in July 1865, Archduke Franz Ferdinand once shot 2,333 animals in
one day's hunting. Though the article did not specify the weapon used by
the Archduke, it must be presumed to have been a machine gun.

became increasingly addicted to his paper-work routine and correspondingly reduced activities more obviously identified as pleasure.

FRUGAL TABLE. Franz Joseph had breakfast at 5:00 A.M., then nothing until 12:00 or 12:30, when a three-course lunch was served. His valet said Franz Joseph was too modest to ask for some refreshment between meals; he thought the kitchen would not be equipped to give him anything! It strains one's credulity that a man who took the services of so many persons around him for granted, who terrified his kitchen staff at court dinners, would really believe it would be too much trouble for his kitchen to send him a mid-morning sandwich. The Emperor expected his wishes to be anticipated by his servants, and so competent a valet as Eugen Ketterl would have ordered the sandwich on his own authority, if the Emperor had really wanted it. At least the valet could have reassured his master about the ability of the kitchen to produce a sandwich, if wanted. In another connection, Ketterl reveals that during the long morning of work, Franz Joseph sustained the inner man by nibbling biscuits kept on hand in a tin box.

Dinner was at 5:00 P.M. and consisted of four courses, even when the Emperor ate alone. When Frau Schratt came to dine with him, he selected her favorite dishes from the menu card submitted to him. The fare was not elaborate, but carefully prepared and tasty. The Emperor expected and was accustomed to good food, as the German maneuver incident confirms. There was always beer or wine with meals. Franz Joseph preferred Austrian wines—a preference which, far from showing simplicity of taste, is another indication that the Emperor liked high quality, in wines as in other things on his table. Occasionally he took some cognac. The cigars he smoked were always the best.

SPARTAN MODE OF LIFE. The widespread impression that Franz Joseph's mode of life was Spartan is false. He did not deny himself pleasures or comforts; he did not deliberately subject himself to physical hardship. His habits were not the product of self-denial, but merely expressed his likes and preferences. He liked to eat well, though sparingly; he smoked and drank, though here too he was temperate. He did not like drafts and open windows in the winter, and suffered when he went to the apartments of the Empress, who—perhaps to annoy him—had the windows open. According to one account[6] Franz Joseph disliked the Spartan furniture—chairs without backs or arms—which Elisabeth had at her villa in Corfu and wanted to be sure that his own rooms would have comfortable club chairs.

The Emperor used to get up early and retire early because he liked to do so, not because he forced himself to do something unpleasant to himself; it was unpleasant only for those persons around him who preferred more customary hours. Perhaps Franz Joseph's valet enjoyed getting up at 3:00 A.M. to wake the Emperor at 3:30. Most others found this before-dawn routine a trial. One of the bath attendants, who had trouble rousing himself for the Emperor's bath at 3:30, decided to stay up until after the bath. He whiled away the long hours of the night with boon companions and one morning had to lean on the Emperor while he gave him his rubdown. Of course the bath attendant was dismissed.

Another person who did not share Franz Joseph's enthusiasm for early hours was the Prussian King (later German Emperor) Wilhelm I. In 1867 the two monarchs were to meet at a railroad station while Franz Joseph was on his way to the Paris World Exposition. Franz Joseph first suggested 4:00 A.M. as the hour for the encounter. Bismarck advised the King to refuse. In this case, Franz Joseph consented to the late hour of 7:00 A.M., which was acceptable to Wilhelm. Most people connect early hours with virtue and self-denial, late hours with vice and self-indulgence; but there are night owls as well as early birds, each according to his nature. The owl is not less Spartan than the rooster, though it is reputed to be wiser.

CIVIL LIST. Unlike the Prince of Liechtenstein who each year contributes hundreds of thousands of dollars to the public treasury of his tiny principality of sixty-four square miles and 17,000 inhabitants, Franz Joseph relied on the public treasury, that is, on the tax contributions of his subjects, to finance his "simple" mode of life. He was paid a salary, called "civil list." The amount of the civil list naturally changed over the years. In the early part of his reign, it was fl. 3,650,000 ($1,460,000) a year.

By 1901, it had reached Kr. 18,600,000 ($3,720,000) a year. In that year, the Emperor again needed a raise, this time to Kr. 22,600,000 ($4,520,000) a year, which as usual was granted by the Parliament without forcing the Emperor to go on strike (he did not approve of strikes). But a revealing sidelight on public reaction to the size of the Emperor's salary and to the proposed increase is provided by correspondence between the Austrian Minister-President and his Hungarian counterpart about the bill to be submitted to the two Parliaments on the subject. The Austrian Minister-President wrote that his government "cannot conceal from itself that in view of the present political and parliamentary situation, it must count with the possibility that this bill would not be acted upon promptly or at all by Parliament." He recommended getting around this danger by relying on § 14 (providing for rule by decree while Parliament was suspended) or by asking for approval of the higher civil list for only one year instead of for a period of ten years, as had been customary. The Hungarian Minister-President, on the other hand, thought it undesirable to bring up the question year after year. As it turned out, the civil list was set at the higher level for a period of ten years in 1902, and continued at that level until World War I.

Some of the principal items in the annual court budget were the following (in approximate dollar amounts):[7]

I.	Allowances for All-Highest Family		$ 800,000
II.	General Expenses of Court Establishment		2,000,000
	Includes:		
	Salaries of Court Employees	720,000	
	Pensions of Court Employees	200,000	
	Firewood	40,000	
	Medals, Decorations	40,000	
	Guards	240,000	
	Travel	400,000	
III.	Administrative Expenses		1,700,000
	Includes:		
	Court Household	260,000	
	Buildings, Grounds, and Hunting Establishments	680,000	
	Court Music	2,800	
	Court Theaters (Subsidies)	280,000	
	Court Stables	340,000	
		Total	$4,500,000

In addition to his civil list, Franz Joseph had a sizable income
from his private fortune. No official figures are available, but
guesses are that the Emperor's fortune approached or exceeded
$200 million. He was probably the richest sovereign after the
King of the Belgians, who personally owned the Belgian Congo.

In his will, Franz Joseph set up a family Fund of $12 million
and a long list of itemized real estate. This he did, apparently
sensing difficult times ahead for the Habsburg Family, to supple-
ment the future Emperor's possibly insufficient civil list and
"to increase the splendor and prestige of Our House." The
document establishing the Fund is full of clauses emphasizing the
private nature of this family fortune and specifically provides
that "if in the course of events . . . the form of government
of the Austro-Hungarian Monarchy should undergo a change,
which God may prevent . . . ," then this entailed fortune shall
be regarded as private. It also specifically excludes from the
benefits of the Fund all illegitimate descendants or descendants
who, though legitimate, are of unequal birth. Whereas Franz
Joseph's grandfather, the Emperor Franz, had left his love to
"his peoples," Franz Joseph made no testamentary provision for
them.

The Family Fund established by Franz Joseph was in addition
to another such Fund, created long before Franz Joseph and
administered by the successive heads of the house of Habsburg.
The founder of the Habsburg family's private fortune, as distinguished from its "possessions" in the sense of the countries
it ruled over, was Franz I, husband of Maria Theresa. Maria
Theresa was the ruler of the Austrian Monarchy. Franz, as
German Emperor, had no real power and nothing to do. So
he became a financial operator and accumulated an immense
fortune, partly by lending money to his wife, or to the Austrian
State, at stiff rates of interest. He left his fortune to his eldest
son, Joseph II, who supposedly gave it away, though he must
have kept—and left—enough to make his successors rich.

THE MYTH OF FRANZ JOSEPH'S SIMPLICITY. What remains
valid in the allegations of Franz Joseph's simplicity is that he
did not eat or drink much. It is also true that he was not pompous
and that he slept in an iron bed. In no other sense was he a

man of simple habits, was his mode of life simple, or his household simple. On the contrary, he lived on a majestic scale, surrounded by servants and attendants who catered to his every wish.

Why, then, has he been so widely praised for simplicity? Could the iron bed and the moderation in food and drink have been enough to create the simplicity image? The Empress Elisabeth also slept in an iron bed which had to be taken on all her travels; she too ate little; in fact she starved herself nearly to death to keep her famous figure; but she had not the reputation of simplicity.

It is possible that the myth was not entirely spontaneous; that it was, in part, deliberately nurtured. Franz Joseph probably was uninterested in appearing as a simple man. His concern was more with maintaining the Imperial image, the image of the *grand seigneur*. He did not crave popularity, he really despised the common people, and he thought it undignified to curry favor with them. Yet, however reluctantly, the Emperor had to accept that the common people were rising to challenge his power. Perhaps the myth of his simplicity would be a useful lightning rod in the threatening Socialist storm. A passage in the reminiscences of the valet Ketterl suggests this possibility. The Emperor was not opposed to Social Democracy (Marxian Socialism as represented by the Second International), Ketterl says, but considered it superfluous, since he himself aimed for the same goals! "The Emperor could not imagine any man doubting that he, Franz Joseph, could have any other thought but for the welfare of the people. He thought that everyone who knew his, Franz Joseph's, personal frugality and simplicity would have to say to himself that a man who wants so little for himself and who dedicates his whole life exclusively to work, surely could not pursue any selfish ends. For this reason, in his view, every man should be persuaded that no political struggles were needed to get the ruler to do all that is best for the people."[8] Ketterl's accounts are not reliable in every respect, but this passage has the ring of truth. One can imagine the Emperor speaking in this vein to the man who was his valet for nearly a quarter of a century, who woke him up, dressed him, served him at table, put him to bed, day after day, and with whom he must have spoken now and then also about things not pertaining to his duties. A valet becomes a confidant of sorts, even if his master is the Olympian Franz Joseph. What Ketterl here reports may well have been what motivated Franz Joseph to permit his aides to spread the myth of his frugality and simplicity.

CHAPTER 9

The House of Austria

Reverence for his ancestry, for the nobility, honor, and splendor of his ancient House, was a feature of Franz Joseph's personality. A brief sketch of this famous house, therefore, seems called for.

ANTIQUITY AND NOBILITY OF THE HABSBURG FAMILY. Franz Joseph was the head of the oldest and most noble of European dynasties—the Most Illustrious House of Habsburg. There was of course no legal basis for claiming that the Habsburgs out-ranked other reigning houses, but the idea was widely accepted in the Monarchy as well as in Europe generally, and certainly by the Habsburgs themselves. An aura of augustness and sanctity enveloped not only the person of the Emperor himself, but every member of the Imperial family. Also the non-reigning members of the House of Habsburg had for 400 years borne the title of Archduke, a title "unique in the world, older and there-fore more highly esteemed than any title of Grand Duke or Prince Elector," as Archduke Albrecht, a cousin of Franz Joseph, explained. "An Archduke does not, *de jure*, give precedence to any of these . . ." Archduke Albrecht condemned the attempts of liberals and democrats to lower the title "Archduke" to merely "Prince."[1]

Strangely enough, the impression of antiquity attaching to the Habsburg dynasty and the Habsburg throne does not strictly correspond to facts. The Austrian Imperial throne dates only from 1804 (see Appendix A and Appendix C), forty-four years before Franz Joseph's accession. And the dynasty itself was little more than a century old in 1848. Franz Joseph's family bore the name Habsburg-Lorraine, not simply Habsburg. The Habsburg dynasty had in fact ended with the death of the Emperor Karl VI, the last male Habsburg, in 1740. But the continuity of the Habsburg name and of Habsburg rule was secured by two provident measures of this monarch. The first of these was the promulgation of the so-called Pragmatic Sanction in 1713, which secured the succession to his daughters if there were no male heir. This Pragmatic Sanction was ratified by the several Habsburg lands and recognized by foreign rulers (who, however, disregarded their promise after the Emperor's death). The second measure was the choice of a husband for Karl's eldest daughter, Maria Theresa. Had she married a king of France or some other powerful monarch, or even a prince of a powerful family, the Habsburg possessions and name would have been absorbed by that family. Karl VI chose instead the relatively minor Duke of Lorraine, Franz Stephan, to be his daughter's husband. They were married in 1736. To avoid complications with France due to an increase of Habsburg power on the borders of France, Franz Stephan surrendered Lorraine in exchange for Tuscany, a switch that strengthened Habsburg power in Italy. Maria Theresa and Franz Stephan, who as the husband of the Habsburg heiress was duly elected Holy Roman Emperor as Franz I, were the progenitors of a new family, a new dynasty—the House of Habsburg-Lorraine. The name Habsburg was preserved, in fact the name Lorraine was usually dispensed with except in official contexts. For all practical purposes, the Habsburg dynasty was continued by allowing name, titles, and sovereignty rights to be transmitted through Maria Theresa, whose husband had no other function but that of procreation. The couple produced sixteen children (among them Marie Antoinette, the Queen of France who was guillotined in 1793). The Habsburg (really Habsburg-Lorraine) family grew prodigiously and never again was there any danger of its dying out. Franz Joseph was a great-great-grandson of Maria Theresa and Franz Stephan.

THE FOUNDING OF THE HOUSE OF AUSTRIA. The founder of

the Habsburg dynasty was Rudolf, Count of Habsburg, who was elected German King in 1273, as Rudolf I.*

At that time the Habsburg family had no connection with Austria. Rudolf's possessions were in Switzerland, where his ancestral castle of Habsburg stands, in Alsace, and in other parts of southwestern Germany. But he had his eye on Austria from the time he became King, and he soon secured that country for his family.

Austria is a name which first appears in a document of the year 1147 and which means "South land," though it referred to the land known as the "Eastern March" (march meaning border-land) and was a borderland of the German Empire in the south-east. (The German name Österreich means "East land" or "East realm.") This Eastern March, or Austria, first established as a march in the time of Charlemagne, was ruled, from 976 to 1246, by the Margraves (later Dukes) of Babenberg, who had gradually extended their originally small domain to include most of the eastern part of present-day Austria. After the death of the last Babenberg Duke, and taking advantage of the chaotic conditions in Germany during the so-called Interregnum (following the death in 1254 of King Konrad IV and until the election of Rudolf in 1273), King Ottokar II of Bohemia seized the former Babenberg lands. Ottokar, the mightiest of the German princes, and a contender for the German Crown, refused to recognize Rudolf as German King. In an armed showdown between the two, Ottokar was eventually defeated and slain at the Battle of Dürnkrut near Vienna on August 26, 1278. Rudolf claimed Austria for his own family. After settling with various other claimants and making sure of the support of the German princes, he installed his two sons, Albrecht and Rudolf, jointly as Dukes of Austria in 1282. From then on and until 1918, Austria was

---

* Rudolf was not Emperor, because he did not get around to having himself crowned by the Pope in Rome, which in those days was the only way for the German King—or Roman King as he also called himself—to become German Emperor—or Holy Roman Emperor. Later, the German Kings did not have to be crowned in Rome to become emperors, but could be crowned elsewhere by the Pope; and still later, the Emperors were crowned at Frankfort and the Pope was pushed out of the act entirely.

a Habsburg possession and the center of Habsburg power. The family's western possessions, including the ancestral castle Habsburg in Switzerland, were eventually lost to it, but Austria was so much the firm foundation of Habsburg power, and so closely identified with the Habsburgs, that the family came to be known as the "House of Austria." The fateful August 26, 1278, on which the founder of the dynasty won the Austrian lands from Ottokar by armed force, may be taken as the birth date of the "House of Austria."

HABSBURG ANCESTRY. Rudolf I was a powerful and rich noble, whose godfather was the great Hohenstaufen Emperor Frederick II, a circumstance attesting the prominence of his family. But his envious rival Ottokar had belittled Rudolf as an obscure, poor, no-account Count, and succeeded in having this widely believed. The defamation must have rankled in the Habsburg camp all the more as there was some truth to it. The Habsburgs were in fact not among the top families of the Empire; they had no blood relationship with the ancient royal houses; and they could not trace their ancestry as far back as could a number of other families. This defect, magnified by Ottokar's taunts, probably explains why the Habsburgs and their retainers developed a strong desire to discover and proclaim the noble and ancient origins of the family, a pursuit that continued for centuries, long after the need to convince anybody of their exaltedness had disappeared.[2]

Soon after Rudolf had become German King, the Habsburgs discovered that they were descendants of the great Roman family of Colonna, who in turn traced their ancestry to the Julian Emperors—so that the Habsburgs were shown to be really the legitimate heirs of Caesar. But Colonna ancestry turned out not to be too advantageous: On the one hand, several other families discovered that they, too, had Colonnas among their forebears; and on the other hand, Roman genealogists alleged that the Colonnas were originally not Romans at all, but of German descent. Suiting their scholarship to changing circumstances, the Habsburg genealogists discovered that the family of their patrons did not derive from the Colonnas, but from the ancient Roman house of Pierleoni, which had produced a number of great churchmen, including two popes and St. Benedict. This was useful because it gave support to the "sanctity" of the house of Austria. When later researches disclosed that the Pierleoni were Jews in the Middle Ages, the Habsburgs of course dropped the Pierleoni from their list of ancestors.[3]

A thesis developed in the time of Maximilian I (1493-1519), who rejected the Roman descent theory, was that the Habsburgs descended from the Trojan hero, Hector. This version, widely believed, was expounded in a book written for King Charles VIII of France to convince him of the nobility of the house of Austria and to favor the marriage of Charles with the daughter of Maximilian—the marriage of the Most Christian King with the princess of the most noble blood. Another genealogist persuaded Maximilian to claim descent from Noah; and still another traced Habsburg ancestry to the God Osiris.[4] In the Vienna State Archives can be seen a beautifully painted genealogical tree, of 1698, about twenty-five feet tall and therefore only partially displayed, called *arbor monarchica*. This tree outdoes all the others by pushing its roots back to the beginning of the human race—to Adam! It informs us, incidentally, that Adam died in the Year of the World 930 and was buried on Mount Calvary. His wife Eve died in the year 940; the genealogist gives no information about where she is buried.

The genealogists, highly respected scholars, must of course have been aware of the frauds they were perpetrating—frauds which presumably were profitable if the largesse of the patron was proportional to the prominence and antiquity of the discovered ancestors. Of the patrons themselves, some were perhaps taken in by the deception, while others took part in it, depending on their intelligence and sophistication. But even so intelligent a ruler as Maximilian I seems to have at least partly believed the fabrications of his learned genealogists. The people at large mostly accepted these genealogical concoctions uncritically. The entire age was given to swallowing the most outrageous nonsense. People were ignorant, credulous, and superstitious, and they insisted on endowing their kings and princes with heroic ancestry reaching back into the misty age of fable.

In the eighteenth century, the age of reason, Noah and Osiris gave way to more credible, though still fabulous forebears: the Habsburgs were now content to trace their ancestry to one Eticho, an Alsatian duke who died in 690 A.D. and from whom not only the house of Habsburg, but also the house of Lorraine were said to have descended.[5] This facilitated the problem of transferring all the luster of the Habsburg lineage also to the new house of Habsburg-Lorraine; both ancestral families were of equal antiquity.

How the Habsburgs Became Archdukes. Rudolf's son Albrecht was elected German King (in 1298) and so was Albrecht's son, Friedrich, who was, however, elected only by a faction of the German princes, as an anti-king, and who shared his reign with Ludwig "the Bavarian." For more than a century after the death of Friedrich in 1330, no Habsburg was German King until Albrecht II was elected in 1438. During this period the Kings of Bohemia, of the house of Luxemburg, had monopolized the German Crown. The Habsburgs had not quite "made it" yet. They were not yet, what they became later, the unquestioned first family of Germany. At least one Habsburg ruler in that period, Rudolf IV, thought the prestige of his house needed a boost; and he proceeded to provide it in the famous *privilegium maius*. Rudolf, born 1339 and ruler of Austria from 1358 to 1365, was an imaginative man who in his short life added much luster to the Habsburg name. He founded the University of Vienna and caused St. Stephen's cathedral in Vienna to be enlarged to its present size and form. These achievements earned him the cognomen of "The Founder." But judged by the standards of Archduke Albrecht (see page 85), Rudolf probably contributed more to the glory of his house through his *privilegium maius* than through his "foundations."

The *privilegium maius* was a document which this inventive prince ordered his chancery to forge; it purported that on September 17, 1156, the Emperor Frederick I "Barbarossa" had granted all sorts of privileges to the Dukes of Austria, including the right to bear the title of Archduke. Attached to the forged document, preserved in the Vienna *Haus, Hof, und Staatsarchiv,* is a golden bull (seal) of Frederick Barbarossa, which is not a forgery but was probably attached to a genuine document of the same date, really granting certain privileges to the Dukes of Austria. The privileges granted in the genuine document, and which seemed insufficient to Rudolf IV, have come to be known as the *privilegium minus*.[6]

What probably incited Rudolf to order the forgery was the so-called Golden Bull of his father-in-law, the Emperor Charles IV. This "Golden Bull," issued in 1356, established the procedure by which German kings were to be elected: It named seven "electors"—three bishops and four temporal princes—but did not include the Duke of Austria among them. Rudolf resented this and wanted to compensate for the slight to the house of Austria by raising it above all others, by means of his forgery. The Emperor, though his father-in-law, refused to recognize Rudolf's document and forced him to desist from using his phony titles. A century later, however, a Habsburg Emperor, Friedrich III, did recognize the (fraudulent) *privilegium maius* and henceforward the Habsburgs were Archdukes, superior to all others as claimed in the document and as Franz Joseph's cousin Albrecht reminded the family.

HABSBURG COLORS AND EMBLEMS.[7] Habsburg power was symbolized by the double-headed eagle and the black-and-yellow flag. To this day, these symbols are nostalgically cherished by the remaining Habsburg supporters, while the anti-Habsburg Republic of Austria has adopted the red-white-red flag and the single-headed eagle gripping the lowly Socialist hammer and sickle in its claws. The Habsburg eagle held the majestic sword and imperial orb.

The identificiation of black-and-yellow and of the double-headed eagle with the house of Austria is only partly correct—namely in so far as the house of Austria was the Imperial house, for these symbols were Imperial symbols, not Habsburg symbols. The double-headed eagle was the emblem of emperors, of the kings of kings, as far back as the Hittites. The eagle (even with only one head) had of course been a favorite heraldic emblem, since it is the most powerful bird of prey—and only a beast of prey, often a lion or an eagle, can convey the idea of nobility, that is, the idea of force and rapine. A two-headed eagle was presumably twice as noble, that is, rapacious, as a single-headed one, and therefore twice as suitable for an emperor. The Russian Emperors, too, had a double-headed eagle carry their coat of arms. In Germany, the double-headed eagle had existed in the seals of the Holy Roman Emperors since 1361 and continued to be the Imperial emblem thereafter. As the Holy Roman Emperors who came after 1437 were almost all Habsburgs, the Imperial emblem became for all practical purposes a Habsburg emblem.

The black-and-yellow colors, too, were Imperial rather than Habsburg. These Imperial colors may possibly derive from the "Golden Horde" of the Mongol Khans. The "Golden Horde" owed its name to the Khan's splendid golden (or yellow) tent, which displayed a black emblem. The colors of the house of Habsburg were not black-and-yellow, but red-white-red, the Austrian colors, adopted by the Habsburgs after they acquired Austria and had become the "House of Austria."

SUMMITS OF HABSBURG POWER. In the six and a half centuries from the election of Rudolf I to 1918, the "House of Austria" rose in power and glory, though the ascent was by no means steady and uninterrupted. One of the high peaks of Habsburg power came under Maximilian I (1493-1519) and his grandsons Charles V (1519-56) and Ferdinand I (1556-64). Maximilian I was a ruler who enlarged the power and domains of his family through fortunate marriages. It was these marriages which gave rise to the saying: *bella gerant alii, tu felix Austria nube*! (May others wage war, you, happy Austria, marry!) He himself married Maria of Burgundy who brought the rich Netherlands to the Habsburgs. He married his son Philip to Juana the Mad, daughter of Ferdinand of Aragon and Isabela of Castile; this brought Spain and the vast Spanish empire to the Habsburgs. He married his grandson Ferdinand to the daughter, and his granddaughter Maria to the son, of the King of Hungary and Bohemia; through this double connection, Ferdinand could claim the Bohemian and Hungarian Crowns after King Louis II was killed by the Turks in the Battle of Mohács in 1526.

By the Treaty of Brussels in 1522 between the grandsons of

Maximilian, Charles V and Ferdinand I, the house of Austria was divided into a Spanish and an Austrian branch, and it remained divided, though in close connection through many intermarriages, until the death of the last Spanish King of the "Casa de Austria," Carlos II, in 1700. The Austrian Habsburgs thereupon contested the Spanish throne with Louis XIV of France in the War of the Spanish Succession (1701-13). In the Peace of Rastatt, in 1714, the Spanish heritage was divided, the Bourbons carrying off Spain itself, the Habsburgs getting the Netherlands and the extensive Spanish possessions in Italy.

When Karl VI, the last male Habsburg, died in 1740, 457 years had passed since Rudolf I had planted the house of Habsburg in Austria. Thirteen generations had contributed to the building of an empire extending from Brandenburg to Tuscany, from Belgium to the Carpathian Mountains. For a brief time, while Karl VI was also King of Spain as Carlos III, the Habsburg Empire had reached its greatest geographic extent.

After being nearly destroyed by Napoleon, Habsburg power reached a new and last peak in the reign of Franz I of Austria. Under the leadership of Metternich, the house of Austria emerged again as a Great Power, though it had permanently lost possessions in the Netherlands and the Rhineland, and had renounced its claim to the illustrious title of Holy Roman Emperor. Franz Joseph took over the Empire much as it had been geographically reconstituted at the Congress of Vienna in 1815.

HABSBURG MARRIAGES. As with most reigning houses, marriages of the members of the House of Austria were political matters, not affairs of the heart. In fact, as already mentioned, the Habsburgs were especially noted for their use of marriage as an instrument of dynastic policy. Requirements for eligibility as spouses of members of the Habsburg family were essentially two: The candidate had to belong to a reigning family and to the Roman Catholic Church. In the early centuries of the dynasty there was no dearth of eligibles meeting these requirements. Europe was brimful of sovereign families, and they were virtually all Roman Catholic. But with the Reformation, a large number of these families turned Protestant and became ineligible to marry into the house of Habsburg.*

Later, the number of reigning houses, especially Roman Catholic ones, steadily declined. These two circumstances forced the Habsburgs increasingly to marry among themselves and within the dwindling number of Catholic royal families. Inbreeding became the rule. There are numerous cases of first cousins marrying in the house of Habsburg. These marriages between near relatives were contrary to the laws against incest and required a special Papal dispensation, which, however, was always granted without much, if any, protest on the part of the Holy Father. Philip II of Spain, who was a first cousin of the Emperor Maximilian II, was also Maximilian's brother-in-law, and later his son-in-law. Philip III of Spain married an Austrian Habsburg cousin; and his daughter married her first cousin, the Emperor Ferdinand II; the daughter of Ferdinand II, again, married her uncle, King Philip IV. The Emperor Franz I of Austria married one first cousin and, after her death, another first cousin. Franz

---

* The following episode is of historical interest and also supplies an example of how marriages were arranged between dynasties.

In 1559 negotiations had been started between the Emperor Ferdinand I and Queen Elizabeth I of England about the marriage of the Queen with the Emperor's son, Archduke Karl. The intended bride and groom had never met. The Queen wanted Karl to come to England incognito, so she could meet him. Instead of sending his son, the Emperor sent first one, then another emissary, a Count Helfenstein, to whom Elizabeth told she was not interested in marrying. Helfenstein diagnosed this as a game geared to Elizabeth's policy vis-à-vis France, Spain, and Scotland.

The persecutions of Catholics by Elizabeth temporarily put an end to the negotiations. This opportunity was seized by Cardinal Charles of Lorraine to arrange, with the Pope's blessing, the marriage of his niece, Mary Stuart, to Karl of Habsburg. Thereupon Elizabeth, anxious to prevent this proposed marriage, pretended renewed interest in Karl. Negotiations were resumed in 1565 and continued into 1567, despite the fact that her liaison with the Earl of Leicester, as also her aversion to marriage, were known to the Vienna court.

In 1567 Lord Sussex brought the Order of the Garter to the Emperor to press Elizabeth's suit, but at the same time demanded that Karl abandon Roman Catholicism, which Karl of course refused to do. In 1570, when Karl's marriage to a Bavarian princess was being arranged, another English ambassador arrived in Vienna to reopen the question of Karl's marriage to Elizabeth. The ambassador, however, was told that plans for the Archduke's marriage with the Bavarian were definitive, but that the Emperor wished to remain the Queen's friend and brother.[8]

I's second wife, Maria Therese of Sicily (grandmother of Franz Joseph), was in fact her husband's double first cousin: her father (Ferdinand I of Naples-Sicily) was the brother of Franz's mother; and her mother was a sister of Franz's father.[9] Franz Joseph himself married his first cousin, whose parents were also cousins.

CHAPTER 10

Franz Joseph's Parents
and His Education

A SUCCESSOR TO THE THRONE. The Emperor Franz I of Austria was worried about the succession. Not that there was any short-age of male Habsburgs; there were Archdukes galore. But it looked for some years as though there might be no direct descendants of the Emperor to succeed to the throne after his sons. His elder son, Ferdinand, the feeble-minded epileptic, was married, but had no children, and his physical condition made it unlikely that he would ever have any. The other son, Franz Carl, married in 1824, was also childless—for six years—until 1830. In that year, to the great joy and relief of the Imperial family, "on the 18th of August at a quarter past nine o'clock in the morning, Her Imperial Highness, the Most Illustrious Arch-duchess Sophie, consort of His Imperial Highness, the Most Illustrious Archduke Franz Carl, was happily delivered of an Archduke in the Imperial-Royal Palace of Schönbrunn. This most happy news was immediately announced to the inhabitants of the Imperial city by twenty-one cannon shots.

"On August 19, at noon, the baptism took place with tradi-tional pomp in the ceremonial hall at Schönbrunn. The solemn baptismal rites were performed by the Prince-Archbishop of Vienna, Count Firmian, assisted by bishops and mitered prelates. His Majesty the Emperor was godfather and the child received His Majesty's names: Franz Joseph Carl.

"The Apostolic Nuncio [Ambassador], Marchese Spinola, had

arrived with full retinue in three carriages, each drawn by six horses, and witnessed the ceremony in the great hall, as did the diplomatic corps and the court officials in gala."[1]

FRANZ JOSEPH'S FATHER. Archduke Franz Carl (1802-78) was the second son of Franz I by his second wife, Maria Therese of Bourbon-Naples (Sicily) (1772-1807). As previously mentioned, Franz Carl was an man of mediocre gifts and no ambition; a nonentity. For a fleeting moment in 1848, before Franz Joseph's accession, he thought of claiming the throne for himself, but was disqualified by his nominal membership in the discredited "State Conference"—the group of advisers who had guided affairs of state during the reign of the incompetent Ferdinand. Franz Carl had taken no active part in the State Conference, which had been dominated by Metternich, but his mere membership in it identified him with the hated regime.

Like his brother Ferdinand, Franz Carl was good-natured and popular. He had bourgeois tastes, liked simple Austrian food, dressed unostentatiously, and walked among the people. Yet, when he went for his daily drive, he always rode in Imperial style, in coach-and-six, supposedly because coachmen and foot-men got extra pay for this and the Archduke liked to see them get this bonus. He often went to the theater, not because of any literary or Thespian interests, but simply because there was nothing else to do; one of his pleasures was to applaud the actors. He loved Ischl, where he had a really simple villa, long before the allegedly simple, but really elaborate "Kaiservilla" of Franz Joseph. Franz Carl felt at home there; he liked the village people, and they liked him. He was fond of hunting, but as his grandson Rudolf said (perhaps as a dig against some other members of the Imperial family), not in order to murder animals, but out of a true love of nature and of animals.

Franz Joseph seems to have had little communication with his father. It was the mother who ruled the family; the father was pushed into the background. Franz Carl was willing to let his wife manage the education of the children whom he probably did not see any too often and on whom he made little impression.

FRANZ JOSEPH'S MOTHER. In contrast to the ineffectual and insignificant father, Franz Joseph's mother, Archduchess Sophie

(1805-72), was undoubtedly the dominant figure at the Habsburg court in her time. She was beautiful, intelligent, well educated, imperial and imperious, determined to restore, preserve, and increase Habsburg power and prestige.

Sophie was a daughter of Maximilian I Joseph (1765-1825), of the ancient house of Wittelsbach, the first King of Bavaria, and of his second wife, Karoline of Baden. Of Sophie's sisters, one—Karoline Augusta, a half-sister—was the fourth wife of Sophie's father-in-law, Emperor Franz I; of her full sisters one was Queen of Prussia, another was Queen of Saxony (from 1854 to 1873); Sophie's twin sister was another Queen of Saxony (from 1836 to 1854). Sophie herself, ambitious to outrank her queen sisters, had expected to become Empress of Austria when she married Franz Carl. It was one of her deep resentments that she never could realize her ambition to be Empress and had to take second best as "Empress-Mother." On two occasions she had come near to seeing her dream fulfilled: once, in 1832, Ferdinand was so ill that the doctors said he could not live through the next day; and again in 1835, shortly after he had become Emperor, Ferdinand was at death's door, but he again survived. Sophie could not forgive Metternich for putting the *"Trottel"*—the idiot—on the throne after the death of Franz I instead of the better qualified Franz Carl, and for thus depriving her of the chance of being Empress.

As a girl, Sophie was not overly devout and also had some liberal leanings. But later, in the years when she guided the education of Franz Joseph, she was pronouncedly pious and conservative. Vienna's Cardinal Rauscher was in constant attendance upon the Archduchess and was her chief adviser. Sophie firmly believed that hereditary monarchy was a sacred institution, that the people owed homage to the Imperial family, and that the rights of the Emperor were sacrosanct. On one occasion she and her husband had to preside at the formal reception of a new Papal Ambassador. The archducal pair, pinch-hitting for the sick Emperor Ferdinand, were required to be under a canopy. Sophie objected to this on the ground that it was the exclusive privilege of the Emperor; and, she said, she "hated everything that gave even the appearance of encroaching on the rights of the sovereign."[2] She divided people into two classes: good and bad. The good people were those who were submissive and deferential to majesty. The bad people were those who challenged the rights of majesty or who made concessions to liberals and democrats. These bad people were, in her opinion, "ungrateful." Revolution was the most dreadful and shameful thing that could happen. "I could have consoled myself more easily for the loss of my children than for the disgrace of succumbing to student anarchy," she said to General Kempen in 1849.[3] Her hatred for the Revolution and its leaders was uncompromising. She insisted on severity with the revolutionists, wanted them executed. She hated Louis Philippe, the King of France, because in her eyes he was a revolutionary upstart. When the King's sons visited the Vienna court, Sophie treated them disdainfully, so that the princes immediately felt ill at ease and "the voice of the Duke of Orleans was shaking, which pleased me . . . ," as Sophie gleefully wrote to her mother. (The "upstart" princes, incidentally, obviously unprepared for the brand of courtesy practiced by the noble house of Austria, found no other way to retaliate than to maintain their own undiminished courtesy throughout their visit.) Sophie so hated revolution that she wanted God to destroy Paris, this Pandora's box of Revolution (1830) and rejoiced when Paris had a cholera epidemic in 1832.[4] But she did not seem to have minded that her own father had been promoted to the rank of King by the upstart Napoleon.

Kindness and tolerance were not among Sophie's traits. In descriptions of her character and personality, frequent reference is made to her hatred of this and that—revolutionists, especially. She must really have been a hateful person. Yet she has also been described with admiration; and she commanded the loyalty of her entourage. In her own family she was a domineering tyrant. She so craved to be the first lady at court that she made Franz Joseph forbid the Empress Karoline Augusta, Franz Joseph's step-grandmother, to live at the Hofburg. Although Karoline was a kindly, unpretentious lady, loved by her (step) grandchildren, Sophie would not have her around because as an Empress-Widow she would outrank the Archduchess. Sophie's treatment of the Empress Elisabeth, Franz Joseph's wife, undoubtedly was due in large part to that same vanity and jealousy of her position at court. As the Emperor's consort, Elisabeth was the first lady, ahead of the "Empress-Mother." Sophie turned her resentment against the daughter-in-law. Elisabeth, unable to bear the mother-in-law's incessant attacks, left the court—and her family (see Chapter 11).

As Sophie insisted on running her family, so she wanted to run the state. At first she tried to do this through her husband, later through her son. There is much evidence that she had great influence on Franz Joseph's decisions.* Franz Joseph adored his mother and depended on her. He kept her informed about affairs of state and discussed important matters with her. It was to her he wrote faithfully whenever he was away from his family, not to his father, who is rarely even mentioned in Franz Joseph's letters. Even when it came to asking for reinforcements for Radetzky in 1848, and for medals to be sent for the troops, Franz Joseph applied to his mother—another indication that it was she who made decisions in such matters before Franz Joseph's accession.

But especially all decisions affecting Franz Joseph himself, until he became Emperor, were made by his mother; and she continued to run his life after he had become Emperor. Many of Franz Joseph's attitudes, character traits, and ideas, are clearly traceable to his mother: his piety, conservatism, aversion to liberal and democratic ideas, intolerance, belief in aristocratic virtues, devotion to forms and formality, the idea of the legitimacy of dynasties, and of the sanctity of the house of Austria. All these ideas, attitudes, and character traits were strengthened by the influence of Franz Joseph's teachers, who were always chosen

---

* Dr. Franz Schnürer, editor of Franz Joseph's letters to his mother, asserts that Sophie did not interfere in state affairs when Franz Joseph was Emperor; that her influence was only indirect, through the part she had in shaping the Emperor's ideas and personality. In support of this assertion he quotes a letter she wrote to Franz Joseph on April 5, 1852, after the death of Schwarzenberg, in which she said that "only the fear that people might think I want to meddle in the choice of a successor," kept her from returning to Vienna immediately. What this letter shows is that she wanted to avoid the appearance of meddling, but not that she did not actually meddle. In fact, as Dr. Schnürer admits, she did put in her say on that occasion by nominating two candidates for the post.[5]

on the basis of their views coinciding with those of the Archduchess.

FRANZ JOSEPH'S EDUCATION. Immediately after Franz Joseph's birth, the care of the infant Archduke was entrusted to four doctors and to a staff of nine persons serving him exclusively, among them a cook and scullery maid, but not counting coachmen and footmen attending the coach-and-six, which, by the Emperor's order, was to be the conveyance used when the baby was taken for a drive. Head of this cabinet of nine was Baroness Louise von Sturmfeder, who must have been a wonderful old maid who loved her ward dearly and was loved by him. She was his *Aja*, or governess, until he was six years old. Of Prussian origin, she had a strong sense of duty, taught Franz Joseph self-discipline, and saw to it that he would not become conceited as a result of the flatteries of courtiers. As a little boy, Franz Joseph was sweet, sensitive, and appealing, the darling of his grandfather, the Emperor Franz, and a great favorite of his cousin Franz, the Duke of Reichstadt, "*l'Aiglon*," the son of Napoleon and of Emperor Franz's daughter, Marie Louise. (Reichstadt died of tuberculosis in 1832, at the age of twenty-one, but despite his illness was allowed to play with Franz Joseph and had his apartments in Schönbrunn next to Sophie's, who was greatly attached to him.)

When he was six years old, Franz Joseph was tearfully separated from his beloved *Aja*, and his further education was entrusted to men under the guidance of Count Heinrich Bombelles as *Primo Ajo*. Count Bombelles had been selected for the important post by Prince Metternich on the basis of his outstanding qualities. These were, as Metternich said, that Bombelles "thought what I thought, saw what I saw, and wanted what I wanted."[6] His devoutness and conservatism recommended him also to Archduchess Sophie. Count Bombelles was in general charge of the education of Franz Joseph and of his younger brothers, Ferdinand Maximilian (called Max, born 1832), and Karl Ludwig (called Karl, born 1833).* But, in addition, each of the children had a special *Ajo*. The man who was Franz Joseph's real tutor

---

* Another brother, Ludwig Viktor, was born in 1842.

and mentor, who was with him most of the day, and who had a decisive influence on his personality, was Count Johann Baptist Coronini-Cronberg, a narrow-minded, stern military man,[7] a stickler for form and dignity, who taught his young charge pride and self-control. One of the things Coronini impressed upon Franz Joseph was that the true aristocrat must not know the plebeian failing of fatigue, but must be able to overcome every bodily weakness. Coronini, with Sophie, awakened in Franz Joseph the aristocratic tastes and leanings which had largely disappeared from the Vienna court and had given way to bourgeois attitudes in the seventy years preceding the reign of Franz Joseph.[8] The young Archduke's innate love of the military was also greatly encouraged by Coronini, who planted the idea in his pupil's head that the Emperor was to be a warlord—which none of the previous Habsburg Emperors had been.

At the beginning of his formal schooling, Franz Joseph had four to five hours of instruction each day. This was gradually increased to ten and eleven hours a day. The curriculum included French, Hungarian, Czech, dancing, fencing, swimming, music, drawing, and military drill. From the time the boy was nine years old, he also studied Latin, Greek, Italian, and Polish. Franz Joseph had a talent for languages, learned to speak French fluently and well, as also most of the languages of the Empire. He could speak Czech when he was five years old, and at four made good progress in Italian, taught him by his grandfather Franz, who had been brought up in Italy. Franz Joseph never did learn English. Spelling was a problem for him, especially in French.

As a more advanced student, Franz Joseph was instructed in philosophy by Abbot Rauscher, the later Archbishop of Vienna. Archduchess Sophie often sat in on the lessons. In history, Franz Joseph was taught chiefly to climb up and down family trees.[9] Necessarily the interpretations of history presented to him by his teachers had to conform to the views of Metternich and Sophie. Accordingly, everything liberal, and especially everything that had been brought about by revolution, had to be condemned; and the mere word "constitution" was the devil's own.[10] Sciences were largely neglected.

At the age of fifteen, Franz Joseph had finished the equivalent of high school. In the three remaining years of his formal school-ing he had instruction on the university level, mostly in law. Metternich urged Franz Joseph's professors to add what Franz Joseph never did learn: government—not merely signing pro-posals, but initiating them. In 1847, and until March 1848, Metter-nich himself instructed Franz Joseph in diplomacy, politics, and government. Once, when asked what subjects he was presenting to the Archduke, Metternich replied: "You mean what am I trying to teach him? The difficult art of letting people talk!"[11] But this was another lesson Franz Joseph never did learn. He was too impatient to be a good listener, to let people talk, and consequently he was also a poor conversationalist.

MODESTY, SPONTANEITY, TIMIDITY. Count Coronini's views, as Baroness Sturmfeder's before him, coincided with Archduchess Sophie's on the need for a stern upbringing. Many a pleasure was denied; self-importance and haughtiness were forbidden. At Ischl, the Imperial children were occasionally made to serve peasant children, allegedly to teach the little Archdukes respect for the low-born. This concession to the common touch was not, how-ever, carried so far as to allow the Archdukes to play with or-dinary children. Only aristocrats were eligible. The children of the Counts Bombelles and Coronini, of about the same ages as the Imperial children, had been cleared as playmates for Franz Joseph and his brothers. But to preserve distance, the archducal children had to use the familiar *Du* (thou) in addressing their little friends, whereas the latter, because as mere Counts they were not of equal birth, had to use the formal *Sie* (you).[12]

Franz Joseph learned to write admirable letters to his mother and other relatives. Many of these letters are preserved and show remarkable maturity. Though admirers say they are spontaneous, they often sound coached and ungenuine. To his mother he wrote that he remembers with joy "the happy day on which I received Holy Communion with you for the first time." It is difficult to imagine a normal nine-year-old boy writing such a sentence spontaneously. Franz Joseph expressed his love for people and things in prescribed order: first mother, second—but only distantly—father, then nature, God.[13] (Despite her piety, Sophie insisted on ranking ahead of God in the affections of her son.) Franz Joseph also knew exactly the hierarchical scale of greetings: to whom he should send hand-kisses, to whom merely regards, at whose feet he should lay himself, and so on. Such letters, excellent though they are, can hardly be taken as proof that Franz Joseph at that time was "thoroughly natural and healthy, free from phrases and false sentimentality. . . ."[14] Undoubtedly he was that in some respects, for instance in his relationship with his brothers, to whom occasionally, perhaps when he or one of them was ill and quarantined for a few days, he wrote letters full of fun and good humor.

As a boy, Franz Joseph was shy and timid. Horses frightened him, and riding lessons often brought tears.[15] But eventually he conquered his fear and became a good horseman, as he was also a good swimmer and fencer. To be sure, the horses used by Franz Joseph in his riding lessons "were so pious and learned, they could almost read and write," as Corti says;[16] and through all his life, he had to have excellently trained horses which would give him no trouble. Franz Joseph's shyness made it difficult for him to make speeches. He avoided them when he could, and when he did have to make one, he read it, even if it was quite brief. But in other respects he had learned to overcome his shyness, as he had his timidity.

By the time Franz Joseph was eighteen years old, his education had prepared him exceptionally well for the office of a ruler. He had acquired knowledge and had learned to be courteous, courageous, self-assured, dignified, regal—an Emperor.

CHAPTER 11

Empress Elisabeth

Empress Elisabeth, Franz Joseph's wife, has become a legend. Her story has been told, glamorized, and fictionalized in dozens of books, novels, and films. Innumerable portraits record the beauty for which she was famed, though people who knew her have testified that neither brush, nor chisel, nor camera could ever capture her unique charm and loveliness. She was a fairy-tale Empress, tall, slender, graceful, angelic, with magnificent long, dark, reddish hair, and when she galloped through the Prater in her favorite tight-fitting, fur-trimmed, dark blue velvet riding costume, on one of her elegant horses, people simply had to cheer—she was so beautiful! With her physical beauty went a sensitive soul. She wrote moving poems, expressive of her moods; these were mostly nostalgic, somber, and sad. She was unhappy. Her marriage with Franz Joseph was a failure. In the last decade of her life she wore only black—she was called the "Lady in Black"—as an expression of her state of mind. She traveled incessantly, compulsively, a veritable Ahasuerus, seeking and not finding. Like Schubert's "Wanderer," she discovered that happiness was always where she was not.

Love at First Sight. The story of how Franz Joseph and "Sisi," as she was called in the family and also by Franz Joseph, met, became engaged and were married, had all the elements that make a good operetta and a bad marriage. Franz Joseph was looking for a wife, as befitting a young Emperor who had to think of perpetuating his dynasty. It was, of course, his mother who would make the selection. There had been an Archduchess

Elisabeth—a second cousin—in whom Franz Joseph was interested for a while, but Sophie did not approve. A Princess Anna of Prussia also appealed to Franz Joseph, and his mother did try to get her for him, but Anna was already engaged to another man and besides she did not seem inclined to become a Roman Catholic. So the court of Berlin regretfully declined the honor. This probably was no disappointment to Sophie, who had arranged with her youngest sister, Ludovika, married to her cousin Max, Duke in Bavaria,* to have Franz Joseph marry Ludovika's eldest daughter Helene (called Nené). Franz Joseph had met Nené only briefly in 1848, when she was fourteen, but in any case was prepared to obey his mother. A meeting was arranged at Ischl in August 1853. Ludovika arrived with Nené, now nineteen, and her second daughter, Sisi.

Sisi (born December 24, 1837) was then a child of fifteen, a tomboy, the darling of her father whose love for the outdoors, animals, horseback riding, traveling, and versifying she shared. She was also a budding beauty. The mother and aunt were not particularly aware of this and did not think of her as a young lady offered for marriage. But Franz Joseph was smitten at once, paid hardly any attention to Nené who sat next to him at dinner, while Sisi, at the far end of the table, was blushing under his incessant gaze. Next morning, Franz Joseph told his mother how he adored Sisi; he insisted it must be she and no other. Sophie saw how strongly his heart was set on Sisi, that for once he was asserting his own will against hers, and she gave in reluctantly. Two days later, on August 18, the Emperor's birthday, the engagement was formally announced. Sisi cried. Of course she felt flattered, but she was also scared. She did like Franz well enough, she said—and who couldn't like him, he was so handsome and dashing in his trim uniform—"if only he weren't an Emperor!" She could not quite understand what it all meant, what was in store for her; and as for loving him, how could a fifteen-year-old girl know whether she really loved a man after two days of having been stared at by him?

---

* Duke Max belonged to a branch of the house of Wittelsbach whose members had the title of "Duke *in* Bavaria" to distinguish them from the main line Dukes *of* Bavaria.

Duchess Ludovika was tearfully grateful to her sister Sophie for having taken one of her girls—even if it was the wrong one. A telegram sent to Sisi's father, asking his consent, was a mere formality. One did not refuse an Emperor.

THE TRIALS OF SISI. If Sophie wanted her son's happiness, she was right in opposing this marriage or, more correctly, she would have been right in forbidding it. It must have been clear to her that trouble lay ahead. She must dominate her son. This was the only way for her to satisfy her craving for power, not only power over him, as over the rest of her family, but political power. The wife she must choose for Franz Joseph must be submissive to her, docile, not have a will of her own. Nené might have been right, but not Sisi. Sophie recognized that Sisi was not tractable, that she asserted her independence; and she resented the girl for not having been chosen by herself. This would mean friction between Sisi and herself and would make for unhappiness for Franz Joseph. Yet Sisi did try to oblige, to give in to Franz Joseph's, that is, to aunt Sophie's, wishes and demands. But there was trouble from the start between her and Sophie, even before the wedding. Perhaps there would have been trouble between Sophie and any wife of Franz Joseph's. Sophie objected that, in a letter, Sisi addressed her with *Du* instead of the formal *Sie*. Sisi thought it absurd that she should not say *Du* to her own aunt, her mother's sister and her fiancé's mother. It was explained that even the Emperor addressed his mother with *Sie*, and Sisi acquiesced. Sophie criticized Sisi for having yellow teeth. Sisi tried her best to whiten her teeth. Sophie wanted Sisi not to ride so much so as not to endanger her health—knowing how passionate an equestrienne Sisi was. There were constant reproaches and exhortations by the future mother-in-law.

Worse was to come after the magnificent wedding in Vienna on April 24, 1854, which itself was a torture for Sisi, who disliked crowds and pomp. Arriving in Vienna only two days before the wedding, she was in strange surroundings and surrounded by strangers—courtiers and ladies-in-waiting appointed by Sophie to watch, correct, and direct Sisi rather than to serve her. Sisi had not been permitted to bring any attendants with her from her

own home. Tired by all the formalities and receptions and pres-
entations, Sisi was given a book containing the rules of the
ceremonial and was made to study them the night before her
wedding. There was no honeymoon, as Franz Joseph was in
the midst of his Crimean crisis. On the morning after the wedding
night, Franz Joseph, that is, Sophie, demanded that Sisi come to
the family breakfast as though it were just an ordinary day. This
seemed indelicate to Sisi, who thought she should be allowed
her privacy on that morning, but it apparently seemed entirely
proper to her husband and to Mme Mère. Sisi obeyed and suffered
through the breakfast, crimson with self-consciousness and embarrassment. When Sisi, spending her days in loneliness, a virtual
prisoner, while the Emperor was away at his office, tried to
console herself by looking at her beloved parrots, Mme Mère
complained to the Emperor that this may cause the child Sisi
was expecting to resemble a parrot. (This was not said in jest!)
When Sisi's pregnancy was far advanced, Sophie insisted that
she display her condition in public. When the child, a girl,
arrived (March 5, 1855)—not resembling a parrot, thanks to
Sophie's precautions—it was of course named Sophie. Sisi was not
even consulted about the naming of the child. The "wicked
woman," as Sisi called her mother-in-law, took the child from
its mother on the ground that Sisi was not capable of caring for
it. The baby was kept in rooms far away from Sisi's, on a different
floor, and Sisi was allowed to see her child mostly only in the
mother-in-law's presence. It was the same with the next child
(Gisela, July 15, 1856) and with the long-awaited Crown Prince
(Rudolf, August 21, 1858). Her joy in her children soured by
the mother-in-law's incessant presence and interference, Sisi gave
up trying to see them.

   In addition to the "wicked woman," Sisi had two other enemies
at court, both Sophie's creatures: Archbishop Rauscher and
Count Grünne. Rauscher was against her because she wasn't
pious enough to suit him (and Sophie); Grünne, Franz Joseph's
Adjutant General, because he (and Sophie) sniffed the liberal
in her. Together these three with their decisive influence were
able to isolate Sisi and to keep her friendless. Sisi just wanted
her Franzi, not the Emperor entrenched behind paragraphs, rules,

traditions, and ceremonies; but this, too, was impossible. Once he took her with him, and she spent the whole day with him, blissfully sitting near him at his office. When they returned home at night, Archduchess Sophie at once descended upon them and declared it indecent of Sisi to have done such a thing; it was never done again.

Sisi was a child, immature, and necessarily so at sixteen. What was worse was that Franz Joseph was immature. He was so completely dominated by his Mama that he gave in to her on all things, at all times, or virtually so. Though he was twenty-three when he married, he was completely dependent on his mother. He could not free himself from his infantile mother attachment and be a husband. He took his mother's side in her attacks on Sisi and accepted her estimate of Sisi's immaturity and of the need to put her under Sophie's tutelage. He failed Sisi utterly, notwithstanding his gushing protestations of love and adoration of his "angel," etc.; in fact these protestations were another manifestation of his emotional immaturity, as they expressed only his worship of her physical beauty, not any understanding, much less any appreciation, of her personality. Franz Joseph was unaware of his total incompatibility with his wife; he apparently thought that all was well as long as his mother took care of things and approved of him. Sisi would grow up and accommodate herself to Mama's wishes and wisdom.

SISI'S FLIGHT. For some years the incompatibility of the Imperial couple, and the hostility between Sophie and Sisi, were hidden from the outer world. But eventually the inevitable break came. Sisi decided to leave. Toward the end of 1860 she told Franz Joseph that she felt ill and wanted to go to a southern climate. Sophie thought Sisi's going away outrageous, but did not object, as it left her victorious in command of the battlefield —and of the children. The Emperor suggested Merano (Meran, in South Tirol). "No, no," the Empress replied, "I want to go away from this country, far away." She named Madeira. There was no Austrian ship available at the time to take her there, but Sisi could not wait, and so Queen Victoria offered her yacht to the Empress. Sisi stayed away for six months. No sooner had she returned, her health apparently restored, than she had a relapse and had to leave again; this time she went to Corfu for fourteen months. For the rest of her life, she spent most of her time away from Vienna, away from Franz Joseph and his Empire, away from her children and from the "wicked woman." She left fifty-nine times, not counting departures together with Franz Joseph to various parts of the Empire, and she returned only for brief spells. Between her first flight to Madeira in November 1860 and her death on September 10, 1898, a span of 454 months, she was away from Franz Joseph at least 261 months, but of the remaining 193 months, many were spent away from the Vienna court—at Ischl or Gödöllö, for instance.[1]

The official story given out in November 1860 was the usual one in such cases, that the Empress was ill, that she had some pulmonary affliction. Rumors were that the illness was of a different sort, not unrelated to Franz Joseph's infidelities.[2] Jealousy was alleged by some gossips as the motive for Elisabeth's breaking away. But Sisi was not jealous; she did not love the Emperor, and his escapades could at most hurt her pride, but not awaken her jealousy. No, she was not jealous; she was really sick—sick of the "wicked woman," sick of the sham of Vienna court life, of its spiritual drabness amidst its pomp and splendor, of her isolation, and of the hostility surrounding her. She just could not stand it any longer. She wanted no scenes; she wanted to avoid conflict; she had no interest in fighting. She simply left.

FEAR OF INSANITY. Elisabeth's behavior, though understandable enough if one knows the circumstances she had to cope with, impressed people as strange, abnormal. In fact, even Elisabeth herself doubted, and feared for, her sanity. These fears were not unjustified, since insanity had afflicted Sisi's family and Franz Joseph's. On Sisi's father's side, her grandfather, Duke Pius in Bavaria, could not be called quite normal. More ominous, however, was her heritage on her mother's side (which was also Franz Joseph's heritage). Her (and Franz Joseph's) great-grandfather Ludwig IX of Hesse-Darmstadt suffered from hallucinations and saw ghosts. Afraid of ghosts, he spent nights talking with a military chaplain. Sisi's sister Sophie (Duchess of Alençon) had been in a private institution in Graz. Nené (Princess of Thurn Taxis) suffered from religious hallucinations. Alexandra, sister of King

Maximilian II of Bavaria, was incurably insane. Alexandra's nephews (Sisi's and Franz Joseph's second cousins) were King Ludwig II of Bavaria and King Otto of Bavaria. Ludwig II, to whom Elisabeth was strongly attached, and whom she resembled in many ways, was a paranoiac and died insane. Otto, his brother, was insane, and incapable of ruling, through all his twenty-seven years as King. A grand-nephew of Elisabeth's shot himself in an attack of melancholia.[3] In 1889 reports that Elisabeth herself was insane appeared in several newspapers in Berlin and Paris.[4]

Elisabeth lacked balance. When she took up some activity, she went in for it to extremes, as it seemed to others. She loved to walk, and when she walked she walked fast and far, occasionally more than eight hours a day, regular forced marches, leaving her poor ladies-in-waiting panting by the wayside. She rode passionately and would at times ride all day, especially when she went to England to ride to hounds and used up three horses a day, was always ahead of the field, and frightened the gentlemen appointed to "pilot" her by her hair-raising, daring jumps. While all but champion riders came to grief before the end of the chase, Elisabeth was never thrown but once, in France (September 1875), when she rode a horse that was not properly trained. She took lessons in circus riding and became an expert circus equestrienne. In 1885, Elisabeth suddenly developed fears; she was afraid to mount a horse, afraid of horses; she never rode again.

Elisabeth carried to extremes her dieting to keep her marvelous figure. At times she took nothing but a few glasses of raw milk a day, from her favorite Schönbrunn cows, which had to be taken along on her travels; at other times she took only the juice pressed out of raw beef; and once she starved herself so effectively that she developed symptoms of hunger edema. She was inordinately concerned about her hair. Her hairdresser went with her on her voyages; hours were spent daily combing and brushing her hair; and a hairwashing was an all-day affair requiring quantities of eggs and brandy. She was said to have worn, at night, a mask with raw veal in it and to have smeared her face and neck with crushed strawberries in an attempt to preserve her beautiful complexion.[5]

HUNGARY'S QUEEN. Elisabeth returned to Vienna in time to

be with Franz Joseph during his war with Prussia in 1866 and the momentous "Settlement" with Hungary in 1867. In fact it was she who was largely responsible for the reconciliation between the Emperor and the resentful Hungarians, and who arranged for the "Settlement" which recognized Hungary as an independent country with its own government and which created the "Dual Monarchy" of Austria-Hungary. (see Chapter 15).

Elisabeth had a great love for Hungary and the Hungarians. Her first knowledge of them came from a Hungarian count who was engaged by her father to teach her some Austrian history and politics after she had become Franz Joseph's fiancée, and who enraptured her fifteen-year-old romantic heart with Hungarian tales and folklore and literature. Later, at Vienna, Sisi learned Hungarian and favored all that was Hungarian, as a protest against the anti-Hungarian orientation of Archduchess Sophie and the court. Her first visit to Hungary, in May 1857, justified and increased her admiration for that country. Her charm and beauty overwhelmed this chivalrous, romantic people, anti-Habsburg though they were. They adored her, as she loved them. After this first visit she returned to Hungary often and felt at home there. She met and became attached to Count Gyula Andrássy, who had been condemned to death in 1849 by Franz Joseph, escaped, and later returned to become a political leader as Deák's* right-hand man. Elisabeth persuaded Franz Joseph to accept Deák's and Andrássy's proposals for a Hungarian government, and to appoint Andrássy the first Hungarian Minister-President.

Hungary's reconciliation with the Habsburgs was solemnized by Franz Joseph's coronation in Budapest on June 8, 1867. It was really Elisabeth's coronation. The *"Eljens"* were for her, who was the "Fairie Queene" and the good fairy of the Hungarians; and their *"Eljens"* were more frenzied still when the beautiful Queen spoke to them in their own language, which she had learned to speak well. The coronation was Elisabeth's greatest

---

* Ferencz (Francis) Deák (1803-76) was a Hungarian liberal, a figure in the Hungarian Revolution of 1848, but opposed to Kossuth and radical policies. He stood firmly for the restoration of the Hungarian constitution and became the acknowledged leader of Hungary.

triumph. She was a goddess in Hungary. The Hungarian nation gave Gödöllö to their King and Queen—the castle and vast grounds which had pleased the Queen and where from then on she spent much of her time.

On April 22, 1868, Elisabeth's fourth and last child, Marie Valerie, was born in Hungary. It was Sisi's "Hungarian" child and the first of her children she could really have to herself. By this time, Sophie, crushed by the execution of her son Maximilian in 1867 (see Chapter 12), was no longer able to keep up her fight against Sisi. Elisabeth lavished all her love on her last child. Valerie was, as Elisabeth told her once, "the only true joy of my entire married life."

When Elisabeth was at last allowed to choose her own attendants, she surrounded herself with Hungarians. Her Lord High Steward was Hungarian, a Countess Festetics became her confidante and longtime lady-in-waiting; other ladies-in-waiting were Hungarian, too, and her reader and good friend was the Hungarian Ida von Ferenczy. Besides these Hungarian friends, the Empress had one Austrian friend and confidante—her hairdresser Fanny Angerer, who accompanied her on all her travels. When Fanny married a commercial clerk, the Empress had him appointed as her secretary, so she would not have to give up Fanny's services and company.

The Austrians in general, not only the increasingly hostile Vienna court, became less fond of their beautiful Empress as her popularity in Hungary rose. At first they had cheered her wildly, but as she secluded herself from them, and later stayed away for long periods, they resented her, gossiped about her, and this in turn made her turn away from them all the more. Her beauty continued to enrapture people wherever she went, but she was not popular in Austria, or at least in Vienna. The feelings were mutual, as in Hungary.

ELISABETH'S FORGIVENESS. Though she had suffered under the nagging and cruel persecutions of her aunt and mother-in-law, and from the calumnies of Sophie's camarilla, Elisabeth forgave her tormentors in the end. When Sophie lay dying, Elisabeth hurried to her bedside. While other members of the Imperial family interrupted their long vigil, Elisabeth stayed for hours with the dying woman. Corti describes Elisabeth as "touchingly good and kind, as she always is in a great crisis. In the presence of death, all enmity is swept away and forgotten. She thinks of the last few years, when the Archduchess's attitude toward her had been so different from that of earlier times, and she admits to herself that she is not without blame for the misunderstandings between her and the dead woman."[6]

Elisabeth also forgave Count Grünne, that staunch ally of Sophie's in persecuting Elisabeth and in seeing to it that the young Empress was isolated at court. When he thought himself dying, he begged to see the Empress. She came, and he asked her forgiveness for all the evil he had done her. Elisabeth forgave him. Grünne's daughter thanked her so fervently that she could be restrained only with difficulty from throwing herself at Elisabeth's feet.

FRAU SCHRATT. It was Elisabeth's kindness also that brought actress Katharina Schratt into the Emperor's life. Knowing how lonely Franz Joseph was while she was away on her incessant travels, Elisabeth decided to find a woman who could be a friend and companion for him. She would not consider a royal or aristocratic lady, for fear that such a person could too easily be used by ambitious relatives to exact favors from the Emperor. Her choice fell upon the actress whose loveliness, gaiety, and unaffected charm had enchanted Franz Joseph on several occasions. Elisabeth thought to please Franz Joseph by having a portrait of Frau Schratt painted for him. While Frau Schratt was sitting for the portrait, Franz Joseph and Elisabeth paid a surprise visit to the artist's studio—on May 21, 1886—and thus began a friendship lasting to the end of Elisabeth's and Franz Joseph's lives.

Soon Katharina Schratt was the almost daily companion of the Emperor on his walks, or at meals. She had a villa near the Emperor villa in Ischl, so Franz Joseph could enjoy her companionship also in the summer. Regularly, at 6:00 A.M., Franz Joseph walked over to Frau Schratt's villa for breakfast (unaccompanied as it seemed, though detectives were said to be hiding behind hedges and bushes every 300 feet of the way). When Elisabeth was with Franz Joseph, they made a threesome.

Sisi's letters to Franz Joseph usually included greetings to their friend, and Frau Schratt always sent her "handkisses" to her Imperial patroness.

Franz Joseph's relations with Frau Schratt, documented by his many letters to her, published after her death in 1940, showed him at his most human. With her, he could relax, be comfortable, forget court ceremony. He loved the homey atmosphere of her house, the *Gugelhupf* (coffee cake) and comfortable chairs, the gossip and casual conversation about the trifles and trivia of the day.

She was thirty-three years old and he fifty-five when their thirty-year relationship began. What kind of relationship was it? To the outside world it was presented as strictly platonic, but it strains the imagination to accept this official version. Katharina Schratt was separated from her husband, Nikolaus Kiss von Ittebe, because of incompatibility; Franz Joseph was, in effect, separated from Elisabeth for the same reason. But Katharina Schratt and Franz Joseph were highly compatible. They spoke of love and wrote to each other about it—and perhaps this was all there was to it.

The Emperor's first letter to his friend, written two days after the meeting in the portraitist's studio, enclosed an emerald ring, was addressed to the "Gnädige Frau"—a formal address—and was signed: "your devoted admirer." But soon address and signature became more ardent. By December 1888 it was: "My dear, most cherished friend"—"in true love, your affectionate, faithful Franz Joseph." In at least one letter, of February 14, 1888, Franz Joseph poured out his love to Katharina Schratt, but he also told her that he would try to control his ardor though it would be hard to do, and that he wanted to remain her "fatherly friend." Again in 1888: "you are worried lest I regard you as a seductress . . ."[7]

Katharina Schratt was on hand whenever fate struck Franz Joseph. She comforted him after Rudolf's death and when Elisabeth was assassinated, and she came when Franz Joseph himself died. Prince Montenuovo, the First Lord High Steward, had notified her, and when she entered the death chamber, she was received as a member of the family. The new Emperor, Karl I,

offered her his arm to lead her to the deathbed, and Marie
Valerie embraced Katharina Schratt, her father's faithful—only—
friend.

ELISABETH'S EXTRAVAGANCE. Having provided for Franz Joseph
by entrusting him to the care of Frau Schratt, Elisabeth continued
her restless wandering.

Elisabeth's mode of life, even as Franz Joseph's, has occasionally
been described as "simple." And it is true that she lived simply in
certain respects, more so than Franz Joseph. She slept without a
pillow, believing that this would help preserve her beauty. She
ate almost nothing. But she made up for it in other respects. On
her trips to England she took along a whole string of her finest
horses and Hungarian aristocrats—but then touchingly sought to
avoid a hotel bill, as she wrote to Franz Joseph, by not stopping
in London (an unlikely excuse, as she really did not care about
expenses, and would have found any number of palaces open to
her gratis; she simply wanted to avoid having to visit Queen
Victoria, who was a bore to her). Even her frugality occasionally
gave way to sybaritism. She loved fruit ice, wanted it with every
meal (when she did eat at all), and ruined her teeth with it. She
loved lobster and once ran up a lobster bill of fl. 500 ($200). But
these were trifles in comparison with the big expenses—the rent-
ing of chateaux, her train, her yacht. On Corfu, her favorite
retreat, she had an elaborate villa built in the Grecian style, at a
cost of many millions, to gratify her admiration for Greece,
Greek culture, and the Greek language, which she cultivated
assiduously. She named her villa the "Achilleion." As soon as the
Achilleion was finished, she was tired of it, wanted to sell it and
give the money to Valerie who, meanwhile married, presumably
could use the money for her growing family. (Franz Joseph
reassured her that Valerie's family was in no danger of starving.)

Like most royal personages who never earned an income and
never paid their own bills, Elisabeth had no conception of the
meaning and value of money. She often went about with a well-
filled purse to give alms, but she did not pay for her purchases.
Once she went into Kugler's, a famous pastry shop in Budapest,
to buy goodies for Valerie. "Have you any money?" she asked
her lady companion. "Not much, Your Majesty, only about 20

Gulden" ($8). "But that's a lot!" said the Empress and proceeded to make her selections. "Does this come to 20 Gulden now?" she asked. But it came to fl. 150! ($60).[8]

While she traveled, Elisabeth got fl. 46,000 ($18,400) a month. In addition she had $80,000 a year for personal expenses.[9] (The salary of a university professor or of a high government official in Austria at that time was between $800 and $1,200 a year.) But the Empress frequently exceeded her allowance, and Franz Joseph always generously paid her bills.*

ELISABETH'S DEATH. Elisabeth's restlessness, her incessant wandering, was a flight from life itself. Death was her continual preoccupation. Often she remarked that life was a burden to her; occasionally she spoke of suicide. She was saved the trouble by an Italian anarchist, Luigi Lucheni, who murdered her at Geneva on September 10, 1898. Lucheni had no special resentment against Elisabeth; he only wanted to kill some prominent person. He had bought a rusty, pointed file for a few sous, and made it into a dagger by attaching a handle to it. Now that he had the weapon, he needed only a suitable victim. He chanced to read an announcement of Elisabeth's expected visit to Caux and also found out that she was coming to Geneva for a day. Although she traveled incognito, as the Countess of Hohenembs, it was difficult to hide her identity. Even the newspapers reported that the Empress was staying at the Hotel "Beau Rivage." Lucheni waited outside the hotel, near the landing of the steamer the Empress would take to return to Caux. As the Empress, accompanied by her lady-in-waiting, Countess Sztáray, left the hotel and approached the landing, Lucheni rushed at them, struck at Elisabeth, and ran away but was soon captured. The Empress fell under the impact, but was helped up again and continued to walk to the steamer. After she had boarded the ship she collapsed and died, not knowing what had happened to her. Lucheni had plunged the dagger into her heart.

When Franz Joseph received the news, he said: "nothing is spared me in this world."

---

* Ketterl, Franz Joseph's valet, asserts that it was often a battle to get the Emperor to pay the extravagant Empress's bills.[10] But this assertion is not supported by any other witness.

CHAPTER 12

Troublesome Relatives

Franz Joseph considered the family of Habsburg-Lorraine to be exalted above all others, but he disapproved of many of its members. He disapproved of them precisely because he regarded the house of Habsburg as exalted—and these relatives did not behave in a manner which Franz Joseph thought fitting and proper to their high station. Once, for instance, an Archduke (who was for a while regarded as the heir to the throne) nearly caused the wife of an ambassador to faint by suddenly appearing before her in improper dress at the famous Hotel-Restaurant Sacher (scene of "Reunion in Vienna"). The somewhat inebriated Archduke wore nothing but his officer's cap, gloves and a sword. Franz Joseph's justice was swift: The Archduke, though his favorite nephew, was banished for a whole month to a monastery in Upper Austria, where he is said to have left a big hole in the abbot's wine cellar. On another occasion, a young Archduke serving as a naval officer was guilty of misconduct and insubordination so severe as to cause Field Marshal Archduke Albrecht, the grand old man of the family, when he heard of it, to declare he should have been put in irons. The Emperor punished the malefactor by transferring him to the infantry. Later this same Archduke renounced all his titles, honors, and archducal income, took the name Leopold Wölfling, and wrote an irreverent book about the Habsburgs.

Transfer to the infantry was a standard punishment for refractory archdukes, a punishment not exactly flattering to that branch of the service. It was regarded as punishment because the infantry was non-aristocratic. This same degrading punishment was meted out by Franz Joseph to Archduke Johann Salvator, whose transgression consisted of having published a pamphlet criticizing the organization of the Austrian artillery. The Archduke compounded his trespass by permitting himself to be made an honorary citizen of Linz, the capital of Upper Austria, where he was punitively stationed. Like Leopold Wölfling, Johann Salvator later, in 1889, renounced membership in the Imperial family, took the name Johann Orth, and declared that he wanted to take up some profession which "would enable him to give up the shameful existence of a princely idler."[1] Archduke Albrecht was shocked by Johann Salvator's behavior and considered it an "outrageous disgrace" attributable to the loss of his religion which, within a few years, lowered him to the level of an adventurer in foreign lands.[2] Johann Orth did in fact have an adventurous life—or death. Being a licensed ship's captain, he bought a freighter which he allegedly intended to take around Cape Horn to Chile. The ship vanished mysteriously. But there have been persistent rumors that things were not what they seemed to be—that Johann Orth wanted to make it appear that he was shipwrecked in order to escape the supervision and persecution of the Austrian police; or that he had perhaps been murdered.

Another instance of archducal misconduct was furnished by Franz Joseph's brother, Archduke Ludwig Viktor, who had a mania for visiting public baths—a grave infraction of court etiquette. Once, dressed only in bathing trunks, the arrogant, physically and intellectually weak Archduke permitted himself to get into an argument with a man who, ignorant of his opponent's identity, proceeded to settle it by giving the Archduke a resounding slap in the face. The story spread through Vienna like wildfire. The Archduke was banished to his castle near Salzburg.

Low Marriages. Such blots on the family escutcheon caused much grief to the Emperor, who was forever concerned about the prestige and honor of his house. But what probably hurt him most was the increasing tendency among members of the Imperial family to marry beneath their station. In such cases he showed no mercy. The trend toward unequal marriages by members of the Habsburg family—a veritable "flight from the purple"—was started by Archduke Johann, who married the village postmaster's daughter Anna Plochl in 1829. This was before the reign of Franz Joseph. The Emperor Franz, Johann's brother, apparently did not have the same revulsion against such degradation of the Habsburg family as did Franz Joseph. He permitted his brother to marry Miss Plochl morganatically, which meant that the Archduke kept all his titles and privileges, but that his wife did not share them. Under Franz Joseph, on the other hand, there were no morganatic marriages (with one exception). An Archduke who insisted on marrying beneath his station was stripped of all his titles, privileges, income, and banished from the court if not from the country. There were several Archdukes who made such marriages in the reign of Franz Joseph, among them the previously mentioned Johann Salvator who married a ballet dancer of the Vienna Opera. (She presumably perished with her husband on the voyage in the South Atlantic.) Another was Archduke Ferdinand Karl, a brother of Franz Ferdinand, the heir to the throne who was murdered at Sarajevo in 1914. Ferdinand Karl married the daughter of a university professor and assumed the name Ferdinand Burg. When the professor urged his prospective son-in-law to consider well before stepping down to their own humble level of society, the Archduke replied: "Stepping down? No sir. I am not stepping down when I ask to be accepted in the circle which has been the creator and preserver of the arts and sciences. This circle has produced the greatest minds, who have ennobled humanity more than could any ancestral lineage."[3] The Emperor expelled him from the Habsburg family and stripped him of titles and income.

The only instance in which Franz Joseph allowed a morganatic marriage was that of the heir apparent, Franz Ferdinand, who married Countess Sophie Chotek in 1900. At first the Emperor seemed determined to forbid the marriage; and to expel the Archduke from the Imperial family, and bar him from the succession to the throne, if he should marry the Countess in defiance of Imperial prohibition. The intercession of leading ministers eventually persuaded the Emperor to consent to a morganatic marriage, but only after the Archduke solemnly renounced the rights of his descendants from the union to the throne. Since Hungarian law would have permitted Franz Ferdinand's wife to become Queen of Hungary, Franz Joseph insisted also on a law barring her from that honor, and her descendants from the succession to the Hungarian Crown. Only after these conditions had been met did the Emperor allow the marriage. Excepting the bridegroom, no member of the Imperial family was present at the wedding. The Emperor elevated the Countess to the rank of Duchess of Hohenberg, but missed no opportunity to humiliate her by emphasizing her inferior position—even beyond her death, as she and her husband were not given an archducal funeral.

Franz Ferdinand pained his uncle Franz Joseph not only by his low marriage, but by his incessant opposition to the Emperor's policies, his obvious impatience to become Emperor, resentment of Franz Joseph's longevity, and the establishment of a *de facto* "second government" which was continually at loggerheads with the Emperor's government. Franz Joseph never liked Franz Ferdinand and was not grieved, but rather relieved, by his death.

MAXIMILIAN, EMPEROR OF MEXICO (1832-67). A terrible blow was struck at the prestige of the house of Habsburg by the execution in Mexico of Franz Joseph's brother Maximilian. Of the four sons of Archduchess Sophie, Max was the most gifted and appealing, and was actually his mother's favorite. Handsome, witty, intelligent, full of fun, imaginative, romantic, unmilitary, with an engaging personality, he was quite unlike his stodgy, soldierly, pedantic brother Franz Joseph. In his youth he was interested in painting and sculpture, later wrote poetry, published books, and developed into a passionate builder. He was a dilettante, superficial, a weak character, easily influenced. In 1857 he married Princess Charlotte, daughter of King Leopold I of the Belgians. His beautiful, ambitious wife nourished Maximilian's dreams of power. The life of an idle prince was distasteful to him. "There are people," he wrote, "who consider the kind of life led by my younger brothers philosophical. To me, such an existence would mean a living death, and what is worse—I consider it ridiculous. There is nothing more miserable than the life of an endowed prince who leads a so-called care-free existence." (Letter to Baron Du Pont, September 19, 1865.)[4] Max considered himself born to be a ruler. Franz Joseph gave him no outlet for his ambitions. Though he made him Governor General of Lombardy-Venetia, he gave him no real power. But Max's opportunity came when a group of Mexican emigrés urged him, at the request of Napoleon III, to accept the Imperial Crown of Mexico. From boyhood, Max's hero had been his ancestor Charles V, in whose realm the sun never set. He dreamed of restoring that realm. He accepted the Mexican offer.

After decades of political unrest in Mexico, the Indian leader Benito Juárez had become President of Mexico in 1857 and had at once introduced revolutionary reforms. Among other things he revoked economic privileges of foreigners and stopped payment on loans made to his predecessors by European lenders. This gave Napoleon an excuse to intervene. Under the pretext of protecting European interests, with the approval of England and Spain, and with the United States embroiled in civil war, Napoleon sent an army under Marshal Bazaine to seize Mexico (1861). Napoleon wanted to crown his glorious career by extending his Empire over Latin America. Maximilan, with the blessing of the Pope who was concerned about Church property in Mexico, was installed as Napoleon's puppet Emperor.

Franz Joseph did not approve Max's Mexican venture, but neither did he oppose it, perhaps because he was anxious to be rid of a potential rival. As children, Franz Joseph and Max loved each other, but their relations cooled off and even became "extremely strained" as they grew older.[5] The ambitions of Max and Charlotte must have been a thorn in Franz Joseph's side. At one point, Napoleon III, whom Max admired, had approached Max with a plan to make him King of a separate kingdom of Lombardy-Venetia;[6] in 1861, a plan originating in England would have made Maximilian King of an independent Hungary,[7] and there were voices urging Franz Joseph's abdication in favor of Rudolf under Maximilian as regent. Max's departure for Mexico would end these vexatious possibilities. Franz Joseph demanded that Max renounce all his rights as an Archduke of Austria, then supplied a frigate to take Maximilian and Charlotte to their new home, and even permitted the formation of a "volunteer corps" under Austrian officers to assist in the conquest of Mexico.

The Imperial couple entered the Mexican capital with great

ceremony on June 12, 1864—the first Habsburgs ever to set foot on the soil of the new world which their family had ruled from 1504 until 1700. They were received with jubilation, efficiently staged by the French occupation troops. Maximilian probably had good intentions and imagined that he could somehow benefit the Mexican people and maintain his position as ruler above all parties in a country torn by the embittered struggle of the Indian peasants against the Spanish landowners. Eventually, Maximilian had to identify himself with the landed interests against the people. His government was recognized only where, and as far as, the soldiers of his French and Austrian invasion armies could terrorize the Mexicans into submission. Their own Juárez, not the foreign Maximilian, was the choice of the Mexicans.

Despite its tragic aspects for the Mexican people, and its tragic end for Maximilian himself, his Mexican adventure had a comic-opera air about it. While Bazaine's soldiers were trying to pacify the country by shooting and hanging Mexican peasants, Bazaine himself arranged lavish entertainments in Mexico City. Max and Charlotte held great court in the castle of Chapultepec and busied themselves with the formulation of a code of etiquette for their court; Maximilian bought silver helmets for his palace guards; he awarded the Order of Guadalupe to a long list of persons who had done nothing for him, for Mexico, or for the Virgin of Guadalupe;* every so-called victory was an excuse for another fiesta. Meanwhile the Emperor's Austrian and Belgian hangers-on were hatching real-estate deals to get rich quick.[8]

All the terror and ruthlessness, the looting and the scorched-earth policy of the invasion armies could not prevail over Juárez's Indians. But instead of sending more troops, Napoleon ordered the French occupation army to return home. The United States, finished with its civil war, had threatened intervention in Mexico against the European invaders. Bazaine urged Maximilian to abdicate and to return with him to Europe. Juárez gave Maxi-

---

* The list of recipients points up a difference between Max and Franz Joseph. It included the poets Grillparzer and Rückert, the theater director Heinrich Laube, the historian Palacký, and the Egyptologist Lepsius. Persons of this sort were rarely decorated by Franz Joseph, who confined his honors list almost exclusively to military and government persons.

milian an opportunity to escape, but vowed he would have him executed if he stayed. After some vacillation, Maximilian decided to stay. Surrounded by traitors and turncoats, the Emperor was captured at Querétaro where he had made his last stand. He and his two faithful generals Mejía and Miramón were condemned to death "for crimes against the nation and international law."[9] They were shot at sunrise on June 19, 1867. Before the execution, Maximilian had given each member of the firing squad a gold piece with the request that they shoot well, as it would not be fitting for an Emperor to writhe in agony. He insisted on giving Miramón the place of honor in the center, thanked General Mejía, encouraged the commanding officer who had nearly lost his nerve, said "Hail, Mexico!" then, struck by five bullets, slowly collapsed.

The news of Max's execution hit the Vienna court like a bombshell. Archduchess Sophie was a broken woman for the five remaining years of her life, unable even to press her attacks against the Empress Elisabeth. The execution of Maximilian was a terrible blow to the prestige of the Habsburg family. Emperor Franz Joseph had troubles of his own at the time of Maximilian's last fight and death in Mexico, had not wanted to hear about his brother's difficulties, and had done nothing to help him. Probably he had not expected Juárez, a half-breed Indian, to have the nerve to execute a Habsburg, whereas Juárez made a point of showing his disdain of European royalty. Unlike Franz Joseph in 1849, Juárez was mild in dealing with his enemies: He amnestied all the European officers who had been found guilty by court-martials and sent them home. He also permitted the body of Maximilian to be returned to Austria.

Empress Charlotte had returned to Europe in July 1866 to get help for her husband's desperate adventure. Napoleon, who had solemnly promised aid, had by this time written off his Mexican scheme and regretfully turned her down. From Paris she went to the Pope, who could do nothing. Suddenly, Charlotte begged the Pope to protect her, claiming that attempts had been made to poison her. She seemed out of her mind. Doctors declared her insane. She was kept at a convent in Rome for a while, was then moved to her castle Miramar near Trieste, and later taken back to her native Belgium where she lived in isolation until her death in 1927.*

CROWN PRINCE RUDOLPH (1858-89). Of all the many figures and fates among Franz Joseph's relatives which would—and did —furnish material for mystery stories, Franz Joseph's only son Rudolf continues to rank in first place. And of all his troublesome relatives it was his son who probably caused the Emperor most grief.

As a child, Rudolf was Franz Joseph's pride and joy, the cherished only son and direct heir; as an adult, he became increasingly alienated from his father; and his death was perhaps the severest blow to the Emperor's pride.

In many ways, Rudolf was more like his uncle Max than like his father Franz Joseph. Like Max, Rudolf was intelligent, had many interests, also scientific and literary, was a gifted writer, a dreamer, a romantic, with great charm and ambition. He was a maverick among the Habsburgs, a circumstance which secured him the benevolent interest and affection of educated circles in Austria. He loved and admired his mother, as he also admired Ludwig II of Bavaria. All these inclinations and admirations implied that he had little in common with his father—except a passion for hunting. What probably grieved Franz Joseph most was that Rudolf was not a military man.

---

* To the moot question whether Charlotte was really insane, there has been added another note of mystery: the question of the identity of the French General Maxime Weygand, who died in January 1965 at the age of ninety-eight. Newspapers reported that he was born in Brussels in January 1867, but that his birth is wrapped in mystery. The most credible information found in historical archives shows him to have been a natural son of the Emperor Maximilian of Mexico and a Saarland girl. Another version is that he was the legitimate son of Maximilian and Charlotte; that this legitimacy was concealed for reasons related to the problem of the succession; and that the child was adopted by a Belgian lawyer who had him educated in a Jesuit school.

The supposition that Charlotte had given birth to a child in January 1867 fits in with the mystery about her condition and her isolated detention, first in Rome, then in Castle Miramar, and finally in Belgium. Had the child's legitimacy been acknowledged—supposing the story to be true—he could have become the last Emperor of Austria instead of the French General Weygand. It is an intriguing question—again on the supposition of the whole story being true—who ordered the identity of Maximilian's heir to be concealed?

It is astonishing what unorthodox ideas Rudolf had developed even as a boy, while he was under the tutelage of persons whose clericalism, conservatism, and veneration of monarchy must have been unimpeachable. In 1873, when he was fifteen, Rudolf wrote to his teacher Baron Latour: ". . . the priests did most damage by teaching the people superstition and exaggerated piety to keep them base and servile, so that they (the priests) and the aristocracy could do as they pleased. . . . Men are free. . . . The institution of monarchy is a shambles which will collapse in the next storm . . ."[10] To his friend Moritz Szeps, a Viennese journalist, he wrote in 1883, from Prague: "From newspapers and private letters I learn what goes on in Vienna: financial fraud, thievery, riffraff in high places, raw arbitrariness, favoritism, corruption, decay of the state. . . . I wonder how long it will take such an old and tough structure as this Austria to burst asunder and crash."[11]

Such ideas were unheard of in a member of the Imperial family. No wonder that Franz Joseph was shocked. He was unable to understand his son's liberalism, his emancipated views on religion, his hatred of clericalism and reaction, his disdain of overbearing aristocrats—feudal brats, Rudolf called them—his questioning of the very foundations of the institution of monarchy and of the Austrian Empire. Relations between father and son were strained, lacked warmth and sincerity, and were purely formal. Rudolf was kept from every meaningful activity and participation in government; he was detested by Franz Joseph's ministers and courtiers, who were scandalized by his views, his friends, and his private life.

Rudolf seems to have led a dissipated life, with much wine and many women. When he went to Brussels to sue for the hand of Stephanie, daughter of King Leopold II of the Belgians and niece of the (allegedly) insane Charlotte of Mexico, he took a mistress with him and put her up in a Brussels hotel. His marriage with Stephanie was unhappy and produced no heir to the throne; they had only one daughter.

With no satisfactory outlet for his energies and ambitions, rebuffed by his father, increasingly disillusioned in his marriage, Rudolf toyed with ever more fantastic treasonable plans of power and conquest, with a coup d'état, with having himself proclaimed King of Hungary—while his activities were watched and his letters opened by the secret police. He also increased his dissipations. Crown Princess Stephanie said that after October 1888 Rudolf had aged markedly, and drank a lot. Others testified that he had become so moody and unpredictable as to suggest insanity.

The story of Rudolf's death is a twice-told tale. He was found dead, allegedly by his valet, in the bedroom of his hunting lodge at Mayerling near Vienna on the morning of January 30, 1889. With him, also dead, was the young Baroness Mary Vetsera, one of his mistresses. The court and government authorities tried from the start to conceal the truth about what had happened. The official version eventually given out, after some threadbare initial lies, was that Rudolf had shot himself in a moment of insanity. This was the conclusion of the medical report, based on an examination of Rudolf's brain, which disclosed features indicative of insanity.* As there was no hiding the fact that Baroness Vetsera had also died at Mayerling, the story generally accepted, and virtually amounting to part of the official version, was that Rudolf and Mary were desperately and hopelessly in love, that Rudolf wanted to marry the Baroness but of course could not do so, as divorce from his wife was impossible, that he could not break off his relationship with Mary as he had promised his father, and that he and Mary chose to die together rather than face separation or dishonor.

How Rudolf really died, and what the motives for his death were, remains a mystery. Almost the only thing that is certain about it is that the official version did not tell the whole story. It is not credible that Rudolf killed himself because he could not give up Mary. Marquis Bacquehem, the Minister of Commerce to whom all telegrams sent by members of the Imperial family had to be submitted, reported that it was clear that Rudolf had already tired of Mary, and that she was an embarrass-

---

* The medical report's emphasis on insanity served to defeat Cardinal Rampolla's objection to a Church burial for the Archduke as a suicide. The Emperor returned Rampolla's courtesy by blocking his election as Pope in 1903.

ment to him.[12] He had spent the night of January 27 to 28 with another mistress, Mizzi Kaspar, whom he had previously invited to die with him. Mizzi had refused; Mary apparently consented. Nor could Mary's possible pregnancy have been a reason for the lovers to kill themselves. For an unmarried girl to have a child may be a disgrace—but not if its father is the Crown Prince! And for the Crown Prince to have killed himself for this reason is a supposition even more farfetched. Extramarital affairs and illegitimate children were not matters to cause an Archduke to kill himself; they were frequent occurrences in the Imperial family, as in other sovereign houses.

Dozens of hypotheses have been advanced regarding the how and why of Rudolf's death, some credible, others not. Mr. Robert Payne, in an article previously referred to (see p. 47), suggests that the Minister-President, Count Taaffe, had arranged to have the Crown Prince murdered, and that in any case it is more likely to have been murder than suicide.[13] The difficulty with the murder theory is that the victims left farewell letters, some of considerable length. It is of course conceivable that Rudolf's death was an execution, possibly resulting from the discovery of his treasonable activities, that he was given an opportunity to die by his own hand, had intended to do so, but was dispatched by an executioner when he hesitated. Circumstances supporting this conjecture are: (1) In his farewell letters Rudolf stressed that he chose death to save his honor; significantly, he left no message for his father. (2) On January 29, before going to Mayerling, Rudolf told his cousin, Countess Larisch,* that he was in mortal danger, that at any moment Franz Joseph might order his personal belongings searched. She asked him why he did not confess to Franz Joseph. Rudolf replied this would be like signing his own death warrant.[14] (3) Rudolf's skull was shattered so badly that, as pictures show, it was hidden by a large bandage when he lay in state. It is not likely that a pistol shot would have caused such damage. Indications are that he was killed by a blow with a heavy object, such as a rifle butt or a champagne bottle.[15]

---

* Daughter of Empress Elisabeth's brother, Duke Ludwig in Bavaria, and his morganatic wife, Baroness Henriette Wallersee, nee Mendel.

The possibility that Rudolf's death was ordered by high authority cannot be ruled out. It would be absurd to deny it on the mere ground that a man like Count Taaffe (or some other high personage) would not have stooped to such methods of ridding himself—or, as he perhaps saw it, the state—of a dangerous enemy. History is replete with murders ordered by kings and ministers. But although, as Mr. Payne says, "suspicion seems to point heavily to the Prime Minister" (Taaffe), there is no proof. Whatever proof there might have been of the involvement of Taaffe or of other persons in high places was carefully locked away by Taaffe himself. The Emperor entrusted all documents pertaining to the death of Rudolf to Count Taaffe with the injunction never under any circumstances to disclose the secret contained in them. This is proof that the truth, or at least the whole truth, about Rudolf's death was not made public. The Emperor must have sensed that the Court Archives, secret in his day, would some day be opened to the public gaze, and he wanted to make sure that the truth about Rudolf would never be known. Count Taaffe took the papers to his castle Ellischau in Bohemia. Later it was said they had been lost in a fire, which may or may not have been intentional. In all probability, this most mysterious of all Habsburg mysteries will remain forever unresolved.

In 1900, eleven years after Rudolf's death, Crown Princess Stephanie married a Hungarian Count, Elemer Lónyay, who later was raised to the rank of Prince by the Emperor Karl, Franz Joseph's successor. Stephanie's father, the fabulously rich King Leopold II of the Belgians, disinherited her. Her daughter Elisabeth, Franz Joseph's favorite granddaughter, married Prince Otto Windisch-Grätz in 1902. In 1924 she was divorced, and later married Mr. Leopold Petznek, a Socialist politician. Franz Joseph, fortunately for him, had died before these events. Had he lived, he must have felt them as the worst degradation of his family's prestige and honor.

CHAPTER 13

Franz Joseph and His Constitutions

When the Emperor Franz, the grandfather of Franz Joseph, suffered from a cough one day, his physician said to him: "I am not worried about your cough. There is nothing like a good constitution." "What are you talking about!" the Emperor remonstrated, "I have no constitution and shall never have one!"[1]

Like his grandfather, Franz Joseph had a good physical constitution and a strong aversion to political constitutions. Unlike his grandfather who never did have a constitution, Franz Joseph ascended the throne as a supposedly constitutional monarch and ruled as a constitutional monarch through most of his reign. His admirers even praise him as the very model of a modern constitutional monarch.

THE KROMĚŘÍŽ AND MARCH CONSTITUTIONS.   When Franz Joseph became Emperor on December 2, 1848, the Reichstag—the Empire Parliament which had been convened in July 1848—was at work in Kroměříž (Kremsier) drafting a constitution. A few days earlier, on November 27, 1848, the Schwarzenberg ministry had declared its commitment to a constitution "sincerely and without reservation." The Kroměříž Parliament, for its part, worked sincerely and without reservation on the draft of a constitution which, in the opinion of historian Joseph Redlich, was comparable to the French Constitution of 1791 and to the American Constitution, and the best that Austria was ever offered. The Kroměříž constitution declared that all sovereignty rests in the people, and it vested real power in the people's representatives; it deprived the Emperor of absolute veto power; it abolished

Catholicism as a state religion; and it abolished all titles of nobility.

It is easy to understand that a constitution embodying such advanced democratic ideas was not permitted to see the light of day. On March 7, 1849, as the delegates arrived at the meeting hall to vote for adoption of the constitution, they found the room occupied by troops. Orders had gone out for the arrest of members identified as revolutionists, but Count Franz Stadion, the Minister of the Interior, who had been sent to inform the deputies that their Reichstag was at an end, allowed them to make good their escape. At the same time that their own constitution was so forcibly made to vanish, the deputies discovered that Franz Joseph had autocratically promulgated a constitution of his own, prepared in secrecy during the preceding three months, and mainly the work of Stadion, who had a reputation for liberal ideas and was regarded at court as a revolutionary. This constitution, known as the March Constitution, differed from the aborted Kroměříž constitution in many respects. Among other things, it applied to the entire Empire and ignored the problem of nationalities, whereas the Kroměříž constitution applied only to the Austrian (i.e., non-Hungarian, Western) part of the Empire, in view of the fact that Hungary had already been granted a separate constitution, and based representation on the several national groups. The March Constitution provided for a legislative Reichstag and, in addition, for a purely consultative and advisory Reichsrat (Empire Council). Of these two bodies, the Reichsrat was the only one actually put into operation, whereas the Reichstag, the real Parliament, never did meet.

THE SYLVESTER PATENT. The March Constitution was to become fully operative as soon as certain temporary difficulties were overcome, the government meanwhile decreeing laws which would later be ratified by Parliament. But soon Franz Joseph dropped all pretense. The entire constitution was rescinded on December 31, 1851, by the Sylvester Patent, so called because December 31 is St. Sylvester's Day. This Patent proclaimed the Emperor as absolute ruler—no constitution, no parliament, no nonsense.

On the face of the facts, Franz Joseph broke his solemn promise when he strangled the Kroměříž constitution and later reneged even on the constitution promulgated by himself and never put into effect. Some historians and biographers of Franz Joseph have excused these acts on the ground that he never accepted the idea that "constitutional" meant "parliamentary"; and that in revoking his own constitution he merely obeyed the dictates of duty because he had come to the recognition that the Empire was not ready for constitutional government on the Western model. This may be true, but does not alter the fact of breach of promise. Even Heller, one of the most adulatory biographers of Franz Joseph, concedes that the Emperor broke his word when he abrogated the March Constitution. Moreover, there are indications that neither Franz Joseph nor his mentor, Minister-President Prince Schwarzenberg, ever had the intention of living up to their promises to accept and abide by a constitution. On August 26, 1851, the date on which he initiated the coup d'état culminating in the Sylvester Patent, Franz Joseph wrote to his mother: ". . . today another big step was taken. We have thrown the constitution overboard and Austria has only one master. But now we must work all the more diligently. Let us thank God that after three years we have almost arrived where we should be." Under his signature, the mother wrote: "God be praised!! S [Sophie]."[2] The tenor of the letter, and Sophie's comment, suggest that the event had been hoped for, perhaps planned, from the outset. In fact, as previously mentioned, Ferdinand's abdication and Franz Joseph's accession had been engineered as a device for getting out of the promises so readily made to the people by the kindhearted Ferdinand. The new Emperor had not been a party to these promises and could therefore refuse to honor them.

The object of the maneuver to have the new ruler free from obligation to honor his predecessor's promises was, however, vitiated by Franz Joseph's accession promise to rule constitutionally. This promise had been put into the accession proclamation at the last moment by Schwarzenberg, who, of course, had written the entire proclamation. This is not to say that Schwarzenberg had any intention of making Franz Joseph a constitutional ruler. On the contrary, his aim was to restore the absolute power of the throne. But in Schwarzenberg's view, which he also made Franz Joseph's, ends justified means. The breaking of promises could be explained or forgotten. Reaching the aim was what counted. He had already broken his promise to the Empress Maria Anna, Ferdinand's wife, who had consented to her husband's abdication only on condition that absolutism be restored; Schwarzenberg had assured her of this, yet at the last moment slipped the promise of constitutionalism into the accession proclamation. That he intended to break this promise —and thus keep his promise to the Empress—was revealed only by later developments.

The reason for deliberately including a false promise in Franz Joseph's first pronouncement as Emperor was that the revolutionary furor of the people was by no means allayed, and Schwarzenberg wanted to assuage this furor by having the new ruler openly embrace constitutionalism. Hungary was yet to be defeated; the war in Italy was not ended; and the defeated Viennese, though cowed by the executions of the preceding month, might rise again if the government showed its real intentions too early. But by the end of the year 1851, these intentions could be openly shown, and autocracy proclaimed as the permanent system of government.

Proclamation of the Sylvester Patent was not expected to pass without popular resentment, and General Kempen, the commander of the police, had been ordered to beat down any opposition. But the people accepted the change without a murmur —at least in public. They knew Franz Joseph's police regime, which was as good if not better than Metternich's had been. Martial law in Vienna, Prague, Galicia, Hungary, and the ever-present soldiers, gendarmes, and policemen, made political expression risky. The Cabinet, too, accepted the coup d'état with barely a protest. Baron Kübeck, the old reactionary who was Franz Joseph's guide to autocracy, and the real author of the Sylvester Patent, commented in his diary on the courage and honor of the ministers, all of whom had been opposed to the revocation of the constitution, but quickly changed their minds when they saw that Franz Joseph was determined to have his way. Only one minister (the Finance Minister, Baron Krauss) resigned rather than break his oath. The others found that "their scruples were conquered by their self-sacrificing love for their posts."[3]

For the entire decade of the 1850's, Franz Joseph ruled as an autocrat. Metternich was invited back to Vienna as an adviser to the Emperor. Discontent and resentment quickly mounted. Yet, even this regime, as any ill wind, blew somebody some good. The Empire, which had been a collection of unconnected provinces united only by the person of the sovereign, became a unified state, a unified customs and trade area with freedom of movement for entrepreneurs, a centrally governed economic entity. In view of these advantages, the rising bourgeoisie put up with Franz Joseph's absolutism. The many nations of the Empire, on the other hand, condemned to silence for the time being, viewed past struggles only as a prelude.[4]

THE OCTOBER DIPLOMA. Defeat at the hands of Napoleon III and Victor Emanuel I of Sardinia-Piedmont in 1859, forced Franz Joseph to make another gesture in the direction of constitutionalism. The immediate need was to repair the shattered finances of the Empire. The government needed to borrow, but was unable to do so unless a responsible, parliamentary check was put on public expenditures.

On March 5, 1860, Franz Joseph convened a Reichsrat composed of archdukes, bishops, generals, high bureaucrats, and thirty-eight members of the provincial diets to work out a new constitution. This body was dominated by the old conservative Hungarian nobles, led by Count Szécsen, who saw an opportunity to regain their old privilege of aristocratic government in Hungary by making Franz Joseph believe that only with their program could he pacify the rebellious Hungarian nation. Austrian and Bohemian nobles supported the cause of the Hungarian magnates with whom they had many family ties and whose interests were the same as their own. Szécsen and his supporters proposed the re-establishment of provincial diets, in which they always had been dominant, and an enlarged and strengthened Reichsrat to function as an Empire parliament, but with power centered in the diets, that is, in the hands of the landed nobility. Franz Joseph distrusted the Hungarian nobles, had his police spy on them, and was afraid of Hungarian emigrés in Paris and Turin, but he was obsessed with the idea of bringing Hungary to heel and for this reason listened to the siren song of Szécsen and his cohorts. Events were soon to show that their claims were without foundation, as the Szécsen party had little following in Hungary.

On October 20, 1860, Franz Joseph approved Szécsen's new constitution in the so-called October Diploma. Thus the effect of the defeat of 1859, owing largely to the incompetence and negligence of aristocratic generals, was to hand more power to the aristocracy—at least on paper. In a letter to his mother, Franz Joseph indicated how seriously he intended to accept constitutional goverment: "It is true that we are going to get a touch of constitutional life," he wrote. "The power, however, will remain in my hands."[5]

THE FEBRUARY PATENT. This new aristocratic, federalist order of things was at once challenged by the bourgeoisie and by the military and bureaucratic champions of centralism and of German leadership, or primacy, in the Monarchy. Within a few months this group succeeded in changing Franz Joseph's mind. Anton von Schmerling, their leader, a German liberal, became the leading Minister. On February 26, 1861, by the so-called February Patent, a new constitution was proclaimed which again made the Monarchy a centralized and essentially German-dominated state. Hungary, where the old conservatives had meanwhile been repudiated, was again put under martial law and ruled by Franz Joseph's army and police.

In addition to reflecting the needs of the bourgeoisie, the new conception of the Empire was also a necessary condition for regaining and retaining leadership in Germany for Habsburg. Schmerling aimed for a state uniting all Germans, including the Austrians, under Habsburg leadership. Austria still had the presidency of the German confederation and there was still hope for the House of Habsburg to recapture the German Imperial crown renounced by Franz II in 1806 (see Chapter 14). To be successful in this bid for the German Crown, Austria had to appear as a German state and as a progressive, modern, liberal state—like Prussia. The October Diploma would have made the Monarchy relapse into a prebourgeois, feudal, and multinational state, unfit to compete with Prussia for German hegemony. The February Patent gave Austria the "new look" Schmerling thought would impress Germany.

Parliamentary representation in the Monarchy in those days was not based on the universal franchise, as in the United States or in Austria today, where the adult men and women in the several districts elect a representative by majority vote. At that time the provincial diets were organs of the "estates"—the propertied and educated elite. Membership consisted of bishops, rectors of universities and other institutions of higher learning, high aristocrats, large landowners, and leaders of the bourgeoisie. Schmerling's February Patent introduced a modicum of popular representation into these diets by changing hereditary into elective memberships. But election was by electoral interest groups called *curias*. One of these groups was composed of the owners of entailed estates,* another of ordinary landowners, one of cities and market towns, another of Chambers of Commerce and Industry, and one of rural communities. In the last-named it was of course again only men of property who could vote. Women had no vote at that time anywhere.

German preponderance was assured by the representatives of the bourgeois, urban, industrial and commercial groups, which were largely German even in the non-German provinces. Thus, in Budapest for instance, the city representatives conducted their discussions in German until 1872! Yet Budapest was, as it is today, the capital of Hungary. Nationalities as such got no recognition in the February Patent.

The Reichsrat in Vienna was composed of two co-equal houses: an Upper House with hereditary and appointed members, chosen with a view to their loyalty to Imperial and property interests; and a Lower House composed of members delegated by the several provincial diets. Representation of the various interest and national groups in this parliament was subject to all sorts of manipulations and at times grotesquely unequal.[6]

---

* Entailed estates were landed estates that legally could not be sold and that had to be handed down in accordance with a prescribed order (usually to the oldest son), so as to preclude the possibility of any member of the family dissipating the family wealth.

This, however, did not really matter, because the whole system was a pretense. The constitution was a mirage: There was no bill of rights and no guarantee for independence of the judiciary. The parliament was without essential legislative power: it had no real power to vote taxes and recruits; and the government could at any time suspend the Parliament and rule by decree under the notorious § 13 (in later years, § 14). This paragraph "allowed every ruling statesman to declare his own incompetence as a state emergency and to suspend the constitution. This law was used throughout the reign of Franz Joseph, from the time of Schmerling to the death of Austria, as the most convenient and repeatedly invoked instrument of Austrian statecraft."[7]

THE SCHMERLING THEATER. Despite the meaninglessness of this constitution which left all real power to the Emperor as before, Franz Joseph regarded it as the utmost concession he could make to constitutionalism. Two days after the proclamation of the February Patent he called in his ministers and exacted from them the solemn promise "to defend the throne with their full energy and united effort of all their powers against the extortion of further concessions by the Parliament, by the diets, or by the revolutionary masses." Any further limitation of sovereign power, the Emperor declared, would be unthinkable and inadmissible.[8]

Hungary, unwilling to accept the position of a province, and insisting on its historic privilege of being a self-governing, independent kingdom, refused to send delegates to Schmerling's Parliament. The Poles appeared at the first session of the central Parliament, but only to protest against the constitution, and thereafter absented themselves. The Italians stayed away altogether. The Czechs, too, condemned the centralist, pro-German constitution, and in 1862 withdrew permanently from Schmerling's sham Parliament. Istria and Venetia also had sent no deputies to the joint Reichsrat. There were protests throughout the Empire—in Prague, Galicia, Venetia, South Tirol, Dalmatia. Even among the Germans only the liberals supported the constitution, while the Catholic-Conservative elements rejected what they referred to as the "Schmerling theater."

ANOTHER RETURN TO AUTOCRACY. Franz Joseph virtually

ignored this entire parliamentary flim-flam. He was concerned only that Schmerling maintain the existing administrative and police apparatus and that the *Reichsrat* not only go through the formalities of approving additional taxes, but also, by the mere fact of its existence, facilitate the floatation of loans abroad.[9] After carrying on for a while with this fake constitution and sham Parliament, Franz Joseph suddenly shifted his course, dropped Schmerling, and repealed the constitution autocratically by a manifesto of September 20, 1865. This renewed return to absolutism delighted Archduchess Sophie and her coterie, who declared it *le triomphe complet et définitif*, while it left the peoples of the Austrian part of the Empire grimly disappointed, and the Hungarian part unreconciled as before.[10]

Franz Joseph had been persuaded to drop the constitution and its creator Schmerling, whom he had never liked, by a new adviser who was to have a dominant influence for a few years: Count Moritz Esterházy. Esterházy and his Czech protégé, Count Belcredi, who was named Minister-President, stood for rule by nobility and Church, against the German liberals; they wanted to undo the February Patent and return to the principles of the October Diploma. Belcredi intended to create a feudal federative state of five states: Czechia, Hungary, Poland, South Slavia, and Inner Austria. The landed nobility was to have preponderance of power. The Emperor was to be absolute ruler over these five states and of course keep the army and foreign affairs as his personal prerogative. The plan was never put into effect; it foundered on the rock of opposition by the German liberals and, especially, by the Hungarians, who never gave up their claims to an independent Hungary dominating its large Slav minorities.

Franz Joseph's second period of autocracy did not last long. He was soon forced into his final acceptance of constitutionalism by the Settlement with Hungary in 1867 (see Chapter 15). Hungary's open hostility during the war with Prussia in 1866 had convinced Franz Joseph that, if he hoped to get back at Prussia and to regain leadership of Germany, he must first win the support of his resentful Hungarian subjects. This was the object of the Settlement which granted Hungary independence, a constitution, and a separate parliament and government. Having granted them to Hungary, the Emperor necessarily also had to grant a constitution and a parliament to the Austrian part of his Empire.

THE DUAL MONARCHY. The Settlement of 1867 created the so-called Dual Monarchy of Austria-Hungary. The Empire was no longer one unit centrally governed from Vienna. There were now two separate parts, Austria and Hungary, with their separate governments in Vienna and Budapest.

The Settlement recognized Croatia, Slovenia, the Military Frontier, and Transylvania as belonging to Hungary. Although these countries were inhabited by non-Magyar peoples having not the slightest desire to live under Magyar rule, there was no question that the Hungarians were the ruling nation in this part of the Empire, which was officially called the Kingdom of Hungary. It was also known as the Eastern Half of the Empire, or Transleithania—the Leitha being the river separating Hungary from Austria.

The non-Hungarian part of the Empire had no similar, clearly dominant, national group which could give the country its name. It was therefore officially called the Kingdoms and Provinces represented in the Reichsrat (Empire Council—the Parliament). (See p. 17.) Generally, however, and even in some official contexts, this half of the Empire was referred to as Austria. It was also known as the Western Half of the Empire, or as Cisleithania. It included all the original Austrian provinces (Austria, Styria, Tirol, etc.) as well as the provinces of the Bohemian Crown (Bohemia, Moravia, Silesia), Dalmatia, the littoral province (including Trieste), and the Polish-Ruthenian provinces (Galicia and Bucovina). Although Bucovina is to the east of the "Eastern Half," yet it belonged to the "Western Half."

Although the two parts of the Empire were separate and independent, there were some respects in which they continued to form one entity: They had Joint Ministries of Foreign Affairs, of War, and of Finance. It may be more correct to say that these ministries were the monarch's own. Foreign affairs were the prerogative of the Emperor—not of the Austrian government and of the Hungarian government. It was the Emperor who made foreign policy, through his Foreign Minister. Similarly, the army was the Emperor's—not Austria's or Hungary's. There were, in addition to the Emperor's Imperial and Royal Army, also an Imperial Austrian Army and a Royal Hungarian Army, and these separate Austrian and Hungarian Armies were administered by corresponding ministries in Vienna and Budapest. But the Emperor's "Imperial and Royal" Army was neither Austrian nor Hungarian; it was "Austro-Hungarian." To finance these joint Austro-Hungarian enterprises, a joint Finance Ministry was needed, which again was separate and distinct from the Austrian Finance Ministry in Vienna and the Hungarian Finance Ministry in Budapest. The Joint Ministry of Finance was also charged with the administration of Bosnia and Hercegovina after these Turkish provinces were formally annexed in 1908; they belonged neither to Austria nor to Hungary, but to "Austria-Hungary"—or, more correctly, to the Emperor. Finally, to deal with matters affecting both "halves" of the Empire jointly, a sort of joint Parliament was created, composed of delegations from the two Empire Parliaments in Vienna and Budapest, and called "The Delegations." This complicated structure of government continued until the end of the Monarchy.

THE DECEMBER CONSTITUTION. When Hungary at long last regained its 1848 Constitution, Austria, as previously mentioned, also had to get a constitution. The "narrower" Reichsrat—representing only the Western Half—met in the summer of 1867 to draft a constitution for that part of the Empire. This constitution was adopted on December 21, 1867, and is known as the December Constitution. Again, as following the war of 1859, the struggle between centralism and federalism, and between the several nationalities, flared up, only that now it was in the context of the "Kingdoms and provinces represented in the Reichsrat," and not, as earlier, of the Habsburg Empire as a whole.[11]

The December Constitution was the work of the liberal German bourgeoisie. Like its predecessors, it again provided for provincial diets elected, not geographically, but by *curias* (electoral bodies) representing the several interest groups in each province. The central Parliament consisted of an Upper

House with hereditary and appointed members, and a Lower House with delegates sent by the diets. There was no direct representation, no direct election of deputies by the people. Not until 1873, after the Bohemian Diet had refused to send delegates to the Vienna Parliament, were deputies elected directly by the voters to the Lower House of the Vienna Parliament, though the franchise was not universal and was heavily weighted in favor of the Germans. The Slavs opposed the new constitution because, like its predecessors, it failed to recognize nationalities. The right of each nation to have schools, public offices, and courts conducted in its own language was recognized, but there was no recognition of the nation as such. The Czechs, especially, resented the Hungarian Settlement which recognized the independence of the Hungarian nation, while condemning the Czechs to continued subjection to Vienna. While Franz Joseph and Elisabeth were crowned in Budapest, Prague was under martial law. Czech nationalist demonstrations continued to flare up until the collapse of the Monarchy and were suppressed by army and police.

Despite its weaknesses, the December Constitution of 1867 was a great advance in the direction of modern government. The power and enormous apparatus of the police—meddling in everything, as much or more than in Metternich's time—was reduced; civil rights were secured; judges were protected from interference. Freedom of religion was introduced, marriage made civil, education freed from Church domination. In short, "Austria became part of Europe."[12] This liberalization of life was reflected in the physical renewal of Vienna and the economic expansion following the events of 1867.

ANTILIBERAL TENDENCIES. Franz Joseph and the ultra-conservative circles around his mother were far from reconciled to the new trends. The constitution had been forced on the Emperor, who continued to believe in his divine duty to rule autocratically. The first liberal ministry—the so-called Bourgeois Ministry—installed on December 30, 1867, and composed mostly of German bourgeois liberals (though the head of this bourgeois government was a Prince Auersperg), was not Franz Joseph's choice. He accepted it only because he was too beaten at the time to insist on his own way. But there was jubilation in court circles when this bourgeois ministry fell in April 1870.[13]

Franz Joseph next appointed a ministry of his own choice, under the presidency of the Polish Count Potocki, and composed chiefly of bureaucrats. Such bureaucratic ministries were used frequently by Franz Joseph from that time onward. They suited his taste better than parliamentary cabinets, which were often unable to function because of the many conflicting party interests.

On February 7, 1871, Franz Joseph unexpectedly appointed a new Cabinet under the presidency of Count Hohenwart, and including politically unknown men. The appointments came as a surprise even to Count Beust, who was then Chancellor of the Empire. The Emperor had followed the advice of Bohemian aristocrats, whose objective was twofold: to turn away from liberalism, and to form an independent Czech state on the Hungarian model and under the control of the big landowners. Though these aims were clearly to restore aristocratic power, the Hohenwart ministry, paradoxically, also foreshadowed a decidely progressive development.

One member of this new Cabinet was, though antiliberal, far from reactionary: Albert Schäffle. This previously liberal economist had come to recognize that the liberal-individualistic, that is, capitalist, society was untenable. He had been shaken by the misery of the workers in the industrial suburbs, and the mass graves into which their dead were thrown. He opposed parliamentary minority rule from which entire nations and classes were excluded, and he urged Franz Joseph to introduce the universal franchise to enable the masses of the people to improve their condition. Franz Joseph was inclined to lend ear to this advice, though for somewhat different purposes. He saw in the universal franchise a way to rid himself of the liberals whom he detested and to combat the nationalist movement. The masses were opposed to the German nationalist bourgeoisie as much as to the Czech nationalist aristocracy. This opposition could be profitably harnessed through the universal franchise. But as it turned out, universal suffrage was still a long way off.

On the urging of Count Andrássy, the Hungarian Minister-President, Franz Joseph dismissed the Hohenwart-Schäffle ministry on October 30, 1871, after only nine months in office. Universal suffrage and Czech nationalism were red rags to the Hungarian ruling class; and ever since the Settlement, Franz Joseph always accommodated himself to Hungarian wishes, for fear of losing Hungary altogether. So Hohenwart was dropped in another about-face, so characteristic of Franz Joseph's reign. Universal suffrage was put aside for the time being. The Czechs, who had been promised independence, were again disappointed, their resentment flared up anew. In Bohemia, the Emperor's promises were publicly offered for sale—printed on toilet paper, as the only paper they were worth being printed on. Czech opposition and restiveness never died down again until the collapse of the Monarchy. At one point, in 1880, Franz Joseph sent General Kraus, renowned for his brutalities in Venetia, as Governor to Bohemia, with orders to suppress by force all demonstrations against his regime. It was a return to the pre-March methods of Metternich.

PARLIAMENTARY REFORM. In 1893, Emil Steinbach, then Minister of Finance, proposed a change in the electoral law. The House of Representatives still was composed of representatives of the four *curias*: large landowners, Chambers of Commerce, cities, and rural communities. Steinbach's reform, announced on October 10, 1893, left the first two bodies unchanged, but provided that the representatives of the latter two *curias* should be elected by direct vote of the people. The people's parties rejoiced, while conservatives and liberals united to defeat the proposal. Growing restiveness and political awakening of the working people kept the question of electoral reform seething. Socialists and Young Czechs—a rapidly rising new radical party —demanded full popular representation. In February 1896, Minister-President Count Casimir Badeni proposed the addition of a fifth *curia*: universal, equal franchise. Parliament accepted this, and in March 1897 elections were held on the basis of this reform, with the result that fourteen Social Democrats (Marxian Socialists) entered the Lower House.

After this epochal innovation, the struggle for further parliamentary reform centered around the issue of universal suffrage. One Minister-President after another failed to accomplish this reform, as the parties representing the propertied classes naturally were opposed to giving the vote to the propertyless. Franz Joseph, who had become convinced of the desirability of universal suffrage by Steinbach's arguments, eventually forced its introduction in Austria. The opposing aristocrats, large landowners and bourgeois leaders gave in to the expressed desire of the Emperor and enabled Minister-President Baron Beck to push a great electoral reform bill through Parliament. From 1907 on, Austria had universal suffrage; it had, on the surface at least, become a modern democracy.

In Hungary, too, universal suffrage had been proposed by the government, in 1905, and it was this that had precipitated the issue in Austria. But in Hungary it did not come to the actual introduction of universal suffrage; the possibility of its introduction, however, served as a threat to keep aristocrats and nationalist extremists from tampering with Franz Joseph's control of the army, as they tried to do—and this was the one point on which Franz Joseph would not give in to the Hungarians. As elsewhere, so in Hungary the privileged classes were opposed to universal suffrage because they justly expected the underprivileged to use their votes against privilege and property. But also the nationalists, who elsewhere favored universal suffrage as strengthening the voting power of their nation, were opposed to it in Hungary, precisely because it would have strengthened the subject nations and endangered Magyar domination of them.

PARLIAMENTARY RULE AND NATIONALIST CONFLICT. With extension of parliamentary rule, the conflict of nationalities did not subside, as Franz Joseph expected, but on the contrary, increased in intensity. This was not necessarily because of extended parliamentary representation, but because nationalist sentiment rose *pari passu* with demands for representative government. Czech nationalism was especially troublesome, the Czechs continuing to want national independence on the Hungarian model and resenting the favored position of Hungary in the Monarchy. Franz Joseph's policy was a see-saw of now promising concessions to the Czechs and actually favoring them, now again giving in to the Germans and suppressing Czech aspirations by force.

One especially fateful event in this nationalist tug of war was Minister-President Count Badeni's language order of 1897. A dispute had been smoldering for decades regarding the language in which government business was to be conducted. The language of the central government of the Austrian (Western Half of the) Empire was German. Similarly, the language of the provincial governments had been German. All officials, therefore, had to know German, and many of them were Germans. But the non-German populations had the right to have government business conducted in their own languages. In Bohemia, for instance, Czechs could have their dealings with government conducted in Czech, Germans in German. In the Czech districts, therefore, officials had to know both Czech and German.

Badeni's order required all officials in Bohemia and Moravia, even in purely German regions, to know both languages. This was a blow to the German officials, since many of them did not know Czech, whereas all Czech officials knew German. Badeni's order in effect disqualified Germans from holding official positions in Bohemia and Moravia. The order unloosed a storm of protest in Parliament and in the streets of Vienna. As customary in such cases, the military intervened. The Hofburg was closed off, though Franz Joseph had left the city to visit his daughter in the country. Count Badeni was forced to resign, and his successor, Baron Gautsch, revoked Badeni's language order. This in turn led to riots in Prague, again giving the military an opportunity to teach obedience to recalcitrant subjects.

There was no escape from the dilemma that any concession to one national group provoked the ire of the rest. The struggle went on until final dissolution of the Monarchy in 1918, with frequent street disorders, fisticuffs in Parliament, military interventions, and proclamations of martial law. Disorders in Parliament, brought about by the conflict of nationalities, frequently paralyzed the legislative process, led to suspension of Parliament, and to government by § 14—the notorious escape clause which allowed the government to rule autocratically and thus to circumvent the supposed spirit of the constitution providing for representative government.

COMRADE FRANZ JOSEPH. Franz Joseph's espousal of the universal franchise put him on the side of the Socialists, whose party was clamoring most loudly for this reform. The Viennese joked about the ludicrous alliance of "k.u.k." (*kaiserlich und königlich*, i.e., imperial and royal) Socialists and "comrade" Franz Joseph. Had the Emperor become a Socialist? A democrat? A believer in the parliamentary system? None of these things. He was far from embracing the aims of the Socialists: he probably did not even understand them, beyond knowing that they were revolutionary, and hence bad. As for democracy, in the sense of the people knowing what they want and what is best for them, and deciding by majority vote what should be done, Franz Joseph would have none of it. To the end of his life he continued to believe in autocracy. He rejected the idea of people's sovereignty; he did not think the people were competent to govern themselves. The parliamentary system, too, he abhorred. He often said that the Monarchy could not be governed with a Parliament; there were too many conflicting class and national interests.

Why, then, did Franz Joseph accept the parliamentary system, and why did he favor the universal franchise?

(1) He had to accept the parliamentary system because he was forced to do so. Modern ideas of government had taken root too firmly even in Austria to make a return to open and admitted absolutism and autocracy feasible.

(2) The Austrian Parliament was not so much a governing body as it was advisory. Essential powers were reserved to the sovereign. When it came to a showdown, § 14 of the constitution could be—and repeatedly was—invoked to suspend Parliament and to give the Emperor absolute power.

(3) Franz Joseph saw in his acceptance of constitutionalism and of the parliamentary system a way of maintaining his power, which was his first and foremost objective throughout his reign. A remark he once made illuminates this point. "The parliamentary system is not the best, and could not be," the Emperor said, "but it is a saftey valve in the sense that the people feel they are represented."[14] In other words, it was a red herring: It gave the people a feeling that they were governing themselves through

their elected representatives, while actually they were ruled by the Emperor.

(4) This also explains why he favored the universal franchise. He did not do so because he approved of the principles of representative government, but because he believed it would further his goals. It would quiet the demands of the people's parties which clamored and demonstrated with increasing insistence for the universal franchise. They would feel that they got the power, while actually he, the Emperor, would keep it.

(5) There was another important reason for Franz Joseph's support of the universal franchise. He had been persuaded by Steinbach that national radicalism had its roots in the *curia* Parliament, and that if this type of parliament were replaced by one based on universal suffrage, nationalism would be destroyed. In Hungary, so the argument went, it was evident that Hungarian nationalism could be strong only because minorities (Croats, Serbians, etc.) were excluded from participation in government. In other words, the universal franchise was expected to marshal as yet unrepresented nationalist aspirations against the already established nationalist forces. This was a new application of the old established Habsburg principle of playing one nationality against the other. Andrássy had appealed to this principle when he pointed out to Franz Joseph the advantages to be derived from a separate Hungarian parliament: Two parliaments, he argued, are better for the Emperor than merely one, because what he could not get from one parliament, he would get from the other.[15] Count Taaffe maintained himself in office as Minister-President for fourteen years, from 1879 to 1893, by his skill in the game of keeping the nationalities in "a balanced state of mild dissatisfaction."[16]

Franz Joseph's admirers have claimed that his acceptance of the parliamentary system and of universal suffrage was due to his democratic spirit and to his sense of honor, which made him live up to his obligations once he had committed himself. Are these interpretations acceptable?

Spitzmüller, for instance, praises Franz Joseph for his democratic attitude in having favored the universal franchise.[17] But he continues by reporting that the Emperor was opposed to any further electoral reforms because he feared a weakening of the central power. This is as much as to admit that the Emperor was for reform only in so far as it would strengthen his power, or at least keep it from being weakened, but that he was opposed to reform if that reform was at the expense of his power. It was his desire for power, not his democratic spirit, which made him support universal suffrage.

As for the often-repeated assertion that Franz Joseph meticulously observed the letter and spirit of the constitution because his honor demanded it, this is hardly supported by the facts. Franz Joseph's honor did not keep him from overthrowing earlier constitutions granted by himself. In the Hungarian crisis of 1905 to 1906 over the question of the language of command in the army, the Emperor was again ready to abrogate the Hungarian constitution. In 1906 he had the Hungarian Parliament dispersed by a detachment of Honvéd (Hungarian infantry). It was not his honor, but his power, that Franz Joseph wanted to keep. Or, to put it differently, his honor always commanded him to preserve and expand his power. His acceptance of constitutionalism after 1867 can hardly be attributed to a change in his views about constitutionalism or about the dictates of honor. His honor would have compelled him to overthrow constitutionalism at any time if he had thought this would serve to increase or maintain his power. This was what he did in 1849, 1851, and 1865. If he did not do it after 1867 it was because he was unable to buck the trend of history any longer and because he found it to his advantage to make use of constitutionalism and of the parliamentary system to preserve his power.

CHAPTER 14

The Struggle
for German Hegemony

HABSBURG AND THE GERMAN CROWN. Not content with the many crowns he had inherited, Franz Joseph wanted to reach out for still another, the most glittering of all—the crown of the German Empire. Fifteen heads of the House of Habsburg had worn that crown, and four more, who had been German Kings, including Rudolf I who founded the dynasty, missed being emperors only because they failed to go to Rome for their coronation as Holy Roman Emperors (the official title of the German Emperors until the end of the Empire in 1806) by the Pope* (see Appendix C). To this impressive list should be added the Emperor Franz I (1745-65), who, though not a Habsburg but a Duke of Lorraine, was a member of the Habsburg family through his marriage with Maria Theresa, and was elected German Emperor by virtue of being the husband of the Habsburg heiress (see p. 86). Counting Franz I as a Habsburg, the German Crown had been in the Habsburg family from 1452 to the end of the Empire in 1806, with only one interruption, from 1740 to 1745, when a Wittelsbach was German Emperor as Karl VII. No wonder that Franz Joseph should have considered it his legitimate right to recover this crown, which his grandfather Franz II had renounced, perhaps too readily, in 1806 (see Appendix A), and which since that time had been in

---

* The last German Emperor to be crowned in Rome was Friedrich III, in 1452. He was also the first Habsburg Emperor.

storage, with no one to claim it. Surely, if anyone was to be German Emperor again, it should be a Habsburg. This seemed so not only to Franz Joseph, but to the other German princes, including the only one among them who could have challenged Habsburg's prerogative: the King of Prussia, Friedrich Wilhelm IV, who himself proposed that the German Empire be restored by Franz Joseph.

AUSTRIA VERSUS PRUSSIA. Franz Joseph's aspirations were justified not only by centuries of precedent, recognized by all German princes, but also by popular demands for a unified German state. After the demise of the Holy Roman Empire, the German states had been bound together in a loose confederation presided over by the Emperor of Austria as the mightiest and most illustrious of the German princes. By 1848 this confederation was a mere shadow without substance. A real union of the thirty-eight independent sovereign German states into one single national state like France or Great Britain, already foreshadowed by the German Customs Union of 1833, seemed a necessity. To create this German national state and draft a constitution for it was the task of the Parliament meeting at Frankfort in 1848. Though liberal and opposed to the absolutism of pre-March, this Parliament was not anti-monarchistic. It proposed restoration of the German Empire as a constitutional monarchy. Pending the choice of an Emperor, the Frankfort Parliament had created the office of Reichsverweser (Administrator of the Empire) and had entrusted this office to the Archduke Johann, brother of the Emperor Franz I of Austria and great-uncle of Franz Joseph. Archduke Johann was a man of the people and was known for his liberal ideas.

The choice of a Habsburg Archduke as Reichsverweser indicated the inclination of the Parliament, or at least of an important part of its membership, to restore the German crown to the Habsburgs, the historic claimants to it. There were, however, two factions on the question of whether Austria was to be included in the new German Empire at all: One party favored a "Greater Germany"; the other favored a "Smaller Germany." The Greater Germans favored the inclusion of Austria in the new all-German state. This was justified on the ground that

Austria had always been a part of the German Empire, that it was at the time a member of the German confederation, and that it would be absurd to exclude eight million Germans from an all-German national state. The champions of Smaller Germany argued for exclusion of Austria from the proposed German national state on the ground that Austria was a multinational state, not a German state, and that its inclusion would bring millions of non-Germans into the German national state.

If the Greater German idea were to prevail, the crown would necessarily have to go to the Emperor of Austria, who could not possibly cede first place to anyone else. On the other hand, if the idea of a Smaller Germany won out, the German crown could of course not possibly go to the Emperor of excluded Austria, but must be offered to the head of the largest and most powerful of the German states outside of Austria—that is, to the King of Prussia. The contest between the ideas of Greater Germany and Smaller Germany was, therefore, in effect a contest between Austria and Prussia for German hegemony and for the German Imperial crown.

Austria's action in beating down the revolution in 1848 and 1849 in fact eliminated it from the race for German hegemony. The execution of the emissary of the Frankfort Parliament, Robert Blum, by Windisch-Grätz, the enlistment of Russian aid against Hungary, the establishment of an autocratic, centrally administered, multinational and multilingual state stamped Austria as anti-liberal, more so at any rate than anti-liberal Prussia, and as emphatically non-German. Inclusion of the Habsburg Monarchy in a German national state was impossible. This was the fundamental reason for Prussia's eventual victory over Austria in the struggle over German hegemony. This was also the reason why the Frankfort Parliament offered the German crown not to Franz Joseph, but to Friedrich Wilhelm IV of Prussia.

SCHWARZENBERG'S "EMPIRE OF SEVENTY MILLIONS." Friedrich Wilhelm IV spurned the Parliament's offer of the German crown. He would not accept it from plebeian revolutionists. "No one," he wrote, "awards the crown but Emperor Franz Joseph, myself, and those who are our equals. And woe unto him who tries to do it without us . . ."![1] Had the King of Prussia been less fastid-

ious about who offered him the Imperial crown, the struggle
for it might have been over then and there. Of course Franz
Joseph would also have refused the crown if it had been offered
to him by the Frankfort Parliament. It is unimaginable that he
would have recognized any act of that detested, presumptuous
body, even an act of homage to himself. Franz Joseph saw the
German "problem," that is, the question of how to recapture
the German Imperial crown—as a purely dynastic one, even
as did the King of Prussia. To both these monarchs by the
Grace of God, the people's desire for unity, the people's desire
for anything other than to be obedient to the ruler, was mere
revolution. Who was to wear the Imperial crown was a matter
to be settled between crowned heads; it was impudence on the
part of the people to claim to have a say in it.

Friedrich Wilhelm IV did not, in fact, aspire to the crown.
He offered it to Franz Joseph on condition that he, the King of
Prussia, should be hereditary "arch warlord" of the Empire.
This was in effect a plan for Austria and Prussia to share German
leadership. Here Franz Joseph seems to have missed an opportunity. Had the two great powers in Germany—Austria and
Prussia—agreed on the re-establishment of the German Empire
on Friedrich Wilhelm's plan, their will would have prevailed;
Franz Joseph would have received the German crown not from
the German people but from the German princes. But Franz
Joseph and his Minister-President Prince Schwarzenberg were
not willing to share German leadership with Prussia. They
wanted full hegemony in Germany. They wanted an "Empire
of seventy millions" under the exclusive rule of Habsburg.
Prussia's rivalry had to be eliminated, preferably by armed
force.

An opportunity soon offered itself for a showdown. In 1850
the Elector of Hesse, also named Friedrich Wilhelm, and his
minister, Hassenpflug, tried to overthrow their country's constitution. They met with resistance, were forced to flee, and
appealed to the German confederation for help. Austria sent
troops to help the Elector; Prussia stood for defense of the constitution. War between Austria and Prussia was averted at the
eleventh hour by Czar Nicholas I who again, as in the year

before, came to Franz Joseph's aid and forced Prussia to give in. At a conference at Olomouc, Prussia agreed to withdraw her troops from Hesse. This was a diplomatic victory for Austria—the first, but also the last which Austria won over Prussia. Schwarzenberg never ceased to regret that it had not come to war, which he thought would have been won by Austria and her South German allies. This would have settled the question of German hegemony and enabled him to establish his Empire of seventy millions. He had missed his chance.

THE WAR OF 1859 AND THE GERMAN PROBLEM. In 1859 Franz Joseph decided on war with France and Sardinia-Piedmont to stop the aspirations of the King of Sardinia, abetted and incited by Napoleon III, to unify Italy under the house of Savoy (the name of the royal house of Sardinia). At that time more than five million Italians lived under Austrian rule, and Austria was the greatest Italian power, even as it was the greatest German power. Franz Joseph was jealous of his leading position in Italy and unwilling to make any concessions to Sardinia by releasing even a few of his resentful and rebellious Italian subjects to the Italian King. He expected to win the war—with Prussian help, as Prussia was obligated to come to Austria's aid when Reich territory was attacked. Franz Joseph had visions of the war being decided, not in Italy, but on the Rhine.

Here was an opportunity for Prussia. Prussia indicated its willingness to support Austria against France and Piedmont on condition that Franz Joseph concede German hegemony to Prussia. But the Emperor was not prepared to give up any of his claims in Germany any more than in Italy. Under the circumstances, Prussia merely tried to restrain Franz Joseph from starting the war, disclaimed responsibility to aid Austria on the ground that the war was about Lombardy and Venetia, which were not Reich territory, and even joined Russia and England in denouncing Franz Joseph's aggression. As a result of his unwillingness to make concessions either in Italy or in Germany, Franz Joseph eventually lost his position in both. Isolated and without allies, he was defeated by the French and had to give up part of his Italian possessions.

The war could have been won by Austria without Prussian

help, had its military leadership been moderately competent. The commanding general, Count Gyulay, a protégé of the almighty Adjutant General Count Grünne, was apparently a total failure. So were several aristocratic sub-commanders. Only General Louis von Benedek, destined to play a crucial role seven years later, covered himself with glory. But his victories could not turn the tide. Gyulay was relieved of his command "for reasons of health," and Franz Joseph himself assumed supreme command, knowing nothing of strategy or tactics, his military knowledge being mostly about drill, medals, and uniforms. The Austrian troops fought bravely, but they were "lions led by asses," as disrespectful observers put it.

On June 16, 1859, Franz Joseph wrote to his mother from Verona: "Dear Mama . . . our position is difficult . . . we have a numerically superior, very brave enemy . . . to whom even the most despicable means are welcome, who has revolution as his ally . . . we are everywhere betrayed in our own country. . . . I hope that perhaps after all Germany and that ignominious scum of Prussia will come to our aid in the last moment . . ."[2] A week later came the decisive Battle of Solferino, in which the numerically inferior (not superior) French and Italians defeated Franz Joseph.

Despite incompetent and corrupt military leadership, and despite Solferino, the Emperor still could have won the war, for "that ignominious scum of Prussia" was in fact willing to come to his aid after all. Napoleon, aware and afraid of this, proposed an armistice, which Franz Joseph accepted, giving up Lombardy. Austria being out of the war, Prussia of course did not pursue its intended intervention.

As was his custom, Franz Joseph shifted the blame for his defeat from himself to others: incompetent generals, corrupt administration, the defection of his oldest and most natural ally, Prussia. It was characteristic of the Emperor to regard himself as a knight in shining armor, surrounded by ignominious, unchivalrous enemies, and by false friends who betrayed him.

SCHMERLING'S REVIVAL OF SCHWARZENBERG'S DREAM. Much worse was soon to come to Austria from that "ignominious scum of Prussia." Otto von Bismarck was determined to throw Austria out of the German confederation and to put the German crown on the head of his King. Bismarck's star was rising. In September 1862 he became the head of the Prussian government, and from then on he dominated the political scene in Prussia, in Germany, and in all Europe, until 1890.

While Bismarck was preparing to capture the German crown for his King, Anton von Schmerling, who had become Austrian Minister of State in 1861, revived Schwarzenberg's dream of an empire of seventy millions—that is, an empire including the Austrian Monarchy and all of Germany under the Habsburgs. Schmerling's domestic policies—his attempts to make the Monarchy appear as a German state and as a constitutional state—were designed to demonstrate Austria's qualifications for German hegemony. On Schmerling's initiative, Franz Joseph called a meeting of the German princes at Frankfort in August 1863 to propose a new constitution for Germany. This, as Franz Joseph wrote to his mother, was "the last effort to unite Germany . . . in order to save the many sovereigns of Germany from destruction through the growing revolution."[3] Almost all the German princes responded to Franz Joseph's call, but the King of Prussia conspicuously stayed away. The Emperor was hailed and applauded in the anti-Prussian capital of the German confederation; his proposed constitution was adopted; and he basked in what he considered his victory. But it was an empty triumph, because the constitution was not to be effective until approved by Prussia, and Prussia would never approve a document which would force her into subservience to the interests of Austria.

THE DANISH WAR OF 1864. An armed showdown between the two great powers in Germany was rapidly approaching. But first they were to make common cause against Denmark—and it was a squabble over the spoils of that war that led to war between the victors two years later.

The bone of contention between Prussia and Austria on one side and Denmark on the other was the Duchies of Schleswig and Holstein. These had been awarded to Denmark by the Vienna Congress in 1815, but as they were inhabited mostly by Germans —and Holstein continued to be a member of the German confederation—there was strong sentiment in Germany that these two duchies should again be separated from Denmark. The issue was brought to a head by the accession of a new king, Christian IX, to the Danish throne. In violation of agreements with Prussia and Austria, Christian proceeded fully to incorporate Schleswig-Holstein into the Kingdom of Denmark. This set off a storm of protest in Germany. Prussia was determined to intervene. Franz Joseph could not stand aside and permit Prussia to assume the role of Germany's champion if he wanted to maintain and strengthen his position of leadership in Germany. He regarded it as a duty of honor to join Prussia in making war on Denmark.[4] Besides, he did not want Prussia to make territorial or diplomatic gains. Bismarck wished to secure the two duchies for Prussia. In view of this, the Emperor made an alliance with Prussia, which provided that no solution of the Schleswig-Holstein question was to be arrived at without the consent of both alliance partners.

Mistakenly relying on British help, Denmark rejected an ultimatum by Austria and Prussia, whereupon troops of these two powers entered Holstein on January 20, 1864. Reports of military successes elated Franz Joseph—though one would imagine them a matter of course when two great powers pounce upon one little one. Archduchess Sophie shared the joy of her son over the performance of the "dear soldiers, the only true support of their sovereign."[5] In the Peace of Vienna, Denmark ceded Schleswig and Holstein to Prussia and Austria. In bargaining about the division of the spoils, Franz Joseph tried to get a Prussian promise of help in case of an Italian attack for the purpose of seizing Venetia. But Bismarck refused, already planning to make common cause with Italy against Austria. Nor was he willing to cede any part of Prussian territory (in Silesia) to Austria in exchange for one of the duchies, confident that Prussia would eventually get them both without cost. The two victors agreed (at Gastein, August 14, 1865) to rule Schleswig-Holstein jointly, Austria occupying Holstein; Prussia, Schleswig. It was an arrangement comparable to the 1945 division of Berlin between the victors, and certain to lead to friction between them. Joint rule of the duchies prevented Prussia from annexing them outright, as Prussian public opinion, whipped up by Bismarck, demanded. But Bismarck foresaw his opportunity, created by the Gastein treaty, not only eventually to seize both Schleswig and Holstein, but also to have a military showdown with Austria, defeat her, expel her from the German confederation, and thus to make Prussia the uncontested leader in Germany.

EVENTS LEADING TO THE WAR OF 1866. These expectations were soon justified. In January 1866, Bismarck sent a sharp note to Austria, complaining that Austria was turning Holstein into a focus of revolutionary activity. Accusations were met by counter-accusations, notes followed upon notes. Austria decided to put the decision on Schleswig-Holstein into the hands of the German confederation, contrary to the agreement with Prussia. These exchanges of diplomatic volleys were accompanied by military preparations on both sides. War broke out on June 15, 1866. A few days later, Italy, too, declared war on Austria.

Historians have generally regarded Bismarck as the instigator of the war of 1866. It is certainly true that this statesman labored conscientiously to bring the war about, against the opposition of the Prussian royal family, especially of the Crown Prince, and also of the King, who only reluctantly gave in to Bismarck's demands for war against a German brother monarch. Bismarck kept up an intensive anti-Austrian propaganda, secretly allied himself with Italy against Austria, made sure of Napoleon's neutrality by hinting that he would permit that greedy Emperor to seize the left bank of the Rhine, and saw to it that the Prussian Army was prepared for war. But part of the credit must go to Franz Joseph. Though he ostensibly wanted peace and delayed mobilizing his army, he rejected opportunities for avoiding war by his inflexible insistence on maintaining his position of leadership in Germany. On May 16, 1866, King Wilhelm I of Prussia wrote to the Grand Duke of Weimar: "You ask . . . if there is no way left to avert [the imminent war]? Yes, there is a way, and this is to urge upon the Emperor of Austria . . . to accept the reform project which I proposed at Frankfort."[8] To be sure, such acceptance would have meant surrender of German hegemony by Franz Joseph—and Franz Joseph considered it a dictate of honor and duty not to surrender this hegemony, but rather to sacrifice thousands of lives in a futile attempt to hang on to it.

Similarly, Franz Joseph could have avoided war with Italy by selling Venetia to Italy. He rejected, as dishonorable, an offer to sell that province for 400 million florins, although the inhabitants were eager to be sold away from the Habsburg Empire. The war with Italy was especially senseless, since the Emperor, finding himself hard pressed and friendless, and suddenly threatened by Napoleon, who saw an opportunity to profit from Austria's distress, promised to cede Venetia to Napoleon—not to sell it, but to give it way, and not to Italy, but to France—regardless of the outcome of the war! This was the price Franz Joseph had to pay to buy Napoleon's neutrality. No matter which way victory went—and as it happened, Austria was victorious over Italy on land as well as on the sea—Venetia was lost to the Habsburgs and would be handed to Italy as a gift from Napoleon. The war could have been avoided by ceding —or selling—Venetia to Italy in the first place.

It was not only Franz Joseph's refusal to make timely concessions which marks him as a partial co-author of the war of 1866. The minutes of the April 25, 1866 meeting of his Council of Ministers indicate that the Emperor had decided to have war. His closing remarks at that meeting were that it was "urgently necessary to end the present tense and daily more intolerable situation through determined actions possibly leading to war."[7] After this, negotiations still went on with Prussia about simultaneous disarmament by both countries, but the decision had already been made: Franz Joseph's decision was for war. Also in a letter to his mother on May 11, 1866, Franz Joseph showed his warlike intention. ". . . It looks very much like war," he wrote, ". . . after spending so much money and sacrificing so much, we must show our teeth all the more . . ."[8] This indicates that it was not Prussia's provocation, but his "spending so much money"—on military preparations—that decided Franz Joseph to show his teeth, or to reach for his saber. It is the old story of armament, allegedly to ensure peace, itself becoming the driving force for war. The proverb *si vis pacem para bellum*, inscribed on the Vienna War Ministry building, is a fallacy. Preparing for war is a necessary condition for war. Only those who are armed can have wars. And often the preparations are precisely what unleashes war—as in the case of Austria in 1866. Incidentally, one wonders who the "we" are who spent so much money and sacrificed so much—Franz Joseph and his mother? Or was it their subjects, who had no stake in Imperial intrigues?

THE COURSE OF THE WAR OF 1866. Franz Joseph faced war on two fronts—against Prussia and Italy. Several of the German states were on Austria's side, but, except for Saxony, gave no substantial military assistance, though most of them would have been eager to have a go at Prussia, had Austria won initial victories. Napoleon, a potential ally against Prussia, was not prepared to seize this favorable opportunity, but in fact threatened war against Austria, as already mentioned, and had to be bought off with Venetia. The German population of Austria was lukewarm in its support of a fratricidal war. In Hungary, hatred of Franz Joseph was still deep-seated and caused many people openly to sympathize with his enemies. Franz Joseph's cautious Foreign Minister, Count Mensdorff, afraid that war would bring defeat for Austria, had warned that mobilization might give the enemies the excuse for war and make Austria appear guilty in the eyes of the world. The Austrian Chief of Staff complained that this policy was inviting the defeat the Foreign Minister feared; that not a moment was to be lost in mobilizing the army. The Emperor, as usual, was without a clear policy, vacillating and procrastinating, then coming to a sudden, rash decision which, again as usual, turned out badly for him: the decision for war.

Of the two theaters of war, the northern—Bohemia, Moravia, Silesia, where the Prussians would have to be met—was more important by far than the southern, where victory over a militarily inferior enemy was a virtual certainty. A chief problem for Franz Joseph was to whom to entrust the high commands in these respective theaters of war. After the debacle of 1859, he refrained from taking command himself and risking a second humiliation. A logical choice for the crucial northern army would have been the Archduke Albrecht (son of Archduke Karl, the first general to defeat Napoleon I, and the only Habsburg since Rudolf I who could be regarded as a real military leader), who was reputed to be a great strategist. But Franz Joseph chose General Louis von Benedek, who had gained most of his military experience in Italy where he had distinguished himself in 1859. In a list of Austrian generals prepared by the Prussian Army, Benedek was described as "no military leader, no strategist . . . very lucky, very brave, bold and daring soldier. Tremendously popular with the entire army, especially the enlisted men."[9] Benedek agreed with the Prussian estimate of his generalship and informed the Emperor that he did not feel himself capable of leading a great army and therefore could not accept command. Franz Joseph sent Archduke Albrecht to change Benedek's mind. Benedek accepted, declaring: "For the German theater of war I am an ass, whereas in Italy I could perhaps be useful. We are gambling, I am sacrificing my civic and military honor to the Emperor and only wish that he may not regret having given me this command."[10]

Archduke Albrecht was put in charge of the army in Italy, where, as expected, he promptly covered himself with glory, overwhelming the Italians at Custoza on June 24, while Admiral Tegetthoff with his tiny Austrian navy decisively defeated the Italian fleet near Lissa in the Adriatic Sea on July 20, 1866.

Benedek might not have proved to be so incompetent a general as he himself and the Prussians believed him to be, had he been allowed to manage things in his own way. But Franz Joseph, anxious to forestall defeat of the Saxon army under the command of his cousin and dearest friend, the Crown Prince Albert of Saxony, urged Benedek to march to the aid of Albert, against Benedek's better judgment. The result of this maneuver was that the Saxons were defeated anyhow and that Benedek's army had to join battle with the Prussians in an unfavorable position, with its back to the river Elbe. This was the Battle of Königgrätz, often also referred to as the Battle of Sadowa (in Bohemia), on July 3, 1866, the battle which decided the war. Despite all advantages of the Prussians in generalship and location, and especially in the superiority of the breech-loading rifle recently introduced by them and outshooting the Austrians three to one, the battle did not go badly for the Austrians at first. Bismarck, on the spot to watch the battle, doubted Prussian victory. The arrival at a critical moment of a delayed Prussian Army which now broke through a weakly defended spot in the Austrian position, decided the issue.

Benedek managed to save most of his army and to retreat in fairly good order. Militarily all was not lost for Austria. Victory in Italy had released the southern army, now rapidly being shifted to the north. Franz Joseph ordered his Ambassador in Paris, Prince Richard Metternich (son of the famous Chancellor), to egg Napoleon on to attack Prussia. Napoleon did not respond to Franz Joseph's plea. With the Prussians steadily advancing on Vienna, Baron Beust, the Saxon Premier, was sent to Napoleon to repeat the request for help. Beust prophetically warned Napoleon that unless he interceded now against Prussia, he would later have to face all Germany in arms. But Napoleon was not ready and in no mood to challenge the formidable victors of Königgrätz.

Franz Joseph tried to save what he could in a peace treaty with Prussia, trusting to the future to bring revenge and retribution. Bismarck, for his part, was eager for peace before possible French and Russian intervention. He had no desire to destroy the Monarchy now that he had won German hegemony for Prussia, but on the contrary intended to make an alliance with Austria. The peace, concluded at Nikolsburg on July 26, and made definitive at Prague on August 23, 1866, was remarkable for the generosity of the victors. The Emperor had to consent to (1) the dissolution of the German confederation; (2) the annexation by Prussia of Hannover, Hessen-Kassel, and Schleswig-Holstein; and (3) the reorganization of Germany without Austria. Austria also had to pay an indemnity of 20 million thaler (about 15 million U.S. dollars), but had to cede no territory. The only territory Franz Joseph lost was Venetia (which he had promised to Napoleon anyway) after a plebiscite showed its inhabitants almost unanimously for union with Italy. But Bismarck prevented Italy from getting also South Tirol as a reward for its defeats.

THE DISGRACE OF BENEDEK. Benedek assumed full responsibility for the defeat of the Austrian Army at Königgrätz. He had warned Franz Joseph, he had known and said that his command would cost him his civic and military honor, and now he, who had long sought retirement, got his wish—only instead of retiring as a hero, he was a disgraced failure. An article in the official *Wiener Zeitung* (December 8, 1866), published with the approval if not at the command of the Emperor, denigrated the unfortunate general outrageously. The loyal Benedek never said a word in his own defense. He took all the blame. He did not point out that the Emperor himself had interfered with his, Benedek's, decisions; he did not try to shift the blame onto others, though he could have pleaded that his chief of operations, foisted on him by Archduke Albrecht, was lazy and incompetent, and that two sub-commanders, both aristocrats, had disobeyed Benedek's orders and thus left a crucial sector of the front exposed.

Franz Joseph's treatment of Benedek is one of the darkest pages in the history of his reign. It is possible, however, that here, as in so many cases, Franz Joseph was merely carrying out the wishes of the Empress-Mother. Archduchess Sophie and her coterie of bigoted aristocrats, led by the sinister Count Grünne, had no use for the non-aristocratic, Protestant, Hungarian-born Benedek. If they smarted under the defeat of the army, the downfall of Benedek was not unwelcome to them. It is not impossible that his appointment to a command which many members of the court coterie believed to be hopeless was motivated by the desire to saddle him, rather than an Archduke or an aristocrat with the stigma of defeat. If victory over the Prussians had really been expected, command of the northern army would have been entrusted to Archduke Albrecht. As it was, the Archduke was sent to pick easy laurels in Italy. In addition, Albrecht was given the most competent chief of staff available, General Baron John, who was the real author of Albrecht's victories, while Benedek was surrounded by incompetents. In his last will and testament, Benedek, though keeping his promise not to reveal any facts that might have exonerated him, did allow himself to protest the shabby treatment accorded him by the government. On the strength of his promise to remain silent, he wrote, the government (he meant Franz Joseph) published the *Wiener Zeitung* article which not only fastened on him full responsibility for Königgrätz, which he was willing to assume, but even denied all his past merits. "This," he wrote, "is beyond my conception of right, fairness, and common decency."[11]

Franz Joseph knew that he had been unjust to Benedek, but made the injustice appear to have been dictated by considerations of state, by "duty." He reminded his generals that Görgei, the Hungarian general in 1849, wanted Deák to make clear that his surrender had been necessitated by the superior power of the enemy. Deák answered: "This is true, but as a Magyar I am compelled to see to it that the Magyars be kept in the belief that they were defeated only by betrayal. In your patriotism you must seek satisfaction for sacrificing your personal rehabilitation to your country."

"And Görgei said nothing"—the Emperor concluded—"but silently suffered the unmerited burden of accusation and reproaches. A nation possessing men who think this way is undoubtedly a great one."[12]

The application of this to the case of Benedek is clear. Benedek had to be the sacrificial lamb who took on himself all the blame so as to let the peoples of the Empire believe that all was well except for one erring general; that especially the self-respect and self-confidence of the army should be preserved by Benedek's profession of sole guilt and responsibility. It is reminiscent of the Moscow trials.

PUBLIC REACTION TO THE DEFEAT OF 1866. The defeat at Königgrätz was one of the few events in the reign of Franz Joseph that deeply stirred this unemotional, cold, matter-of-fact ruler. But while he grieved, blamed others for his misfortunes, vented his wrath, and complained to his mother about "the infamy and crafty swindle of which we were the victims, and all of it agreed upon long ago between Paris, Berlin, and Florence" (letter of August 22, 1866)[13]—apparently forgetting, or considering honorable, his own attempts to sick the "arch-scoundrel" Napoleon on Prussia—and while he plotted revenge, the peoples of his Empire went about their business unconcerned. It wasn't their war; they little cared what the Emperor and his Archdukes and princes and counts did. On the day of Königgrätz—July 3—the Viennese disported themselves at a fancy-dress affair in the Prater and at a Strauss concert in the Volksgarten; they were out for a good time and enjoying the summer day. As the Prussians approached the city, some inhabitants fled, but others went to the Vienna woods for a vantage point from which to watch the enemy troops, apparently regarding it more as a show than as a danger. Franz Joseph had broken the political backbone of the Viennese after 1848, and as absolute ruler had educated them to the political indifference which became typical of them. Having been denied their political freedom, they sought compensation in their freedom to amuse themselves. They amused themselves in the Prater and in their beer gardens and coffee houses, and by joking, often maliciously, about the incompetence of the high and mighty.

In his misfortune, "his" people did not rally around Franz Joseph; they railed at him. As he rode by, voices from the crowd shouted "Hail to the Emperor Max!"—broadly hinting that Franz Joseph abdicate in favor of his more popular brother (who was at that time in Mexico as Napoleon's puppet emperor). There was also much talk—too much for Franz Joseph's comfort— about a possible regency of Maximilian for the nine-year-old Rudolf.

Dissatisfaction with the government was widespread. All sorts of groups took advantage of Franz Joseph's momentary weakness to press their demands. The Hungarians, of course, led the procession—and actually got what they wanted. They even admired their restraint which kept them from raising the ante after Königgrätz! The Vienna City Council demanded a more liberal government. From all sides petitions and complaints came to the Emperor. The opinion was widespread that the Empire was on its last legs, that collapse was imminent. As one representative of the people put it, it looked as though the dynasty which started with Rudolf of Habsburg would end with Rudolf the Child. (Rudolf was the Crown Prince, Franz Joseph's son.)

FRANZ JOSEPH'S PLANS FOR REVENGE. Far from thinking of abdication, Franz Joseph thought of "revenge and retribution" for Prussia's "deceitful" attack, despite the magnanimous peace terms. He did not accept the terms of the Prague treaty as final, but still hoped to regain his now lost position of hegemony in Germany. Franz Joseph clearly advertised his plans for revenge by the startling appointment of Baron Ferdinand von Beust, a foreigner and a Protestant, as his new Foreign Minister on October 30, 1866. Beust had been Prime Minister of Saxony, but had to be dismissed at the insistence of the King of Prussia who regarded him as an arch villain and instigator of the "unnatural," fratricidal war. He was known for his anti-Prussian sentiments and his dislike of Bismarck who, in turn, had a low opinion of Beust as a conniver and schemer. Beust's appointment as Austrian Foreign Minister only one week after his dismissal by the King of Saxony naturally caused resentment in Prussia where it was interpreted as an insult and as a renewed challenge to Prussia. The insult was compounded when soon Beust was appointed Austrian Minister-President in addition to Foreign Minister, was made a Count, and was elevated to the rank of Chancellor of the Empire—the only man so honored in Franz Joseph's entire, sixty-eight-year-long reign.

Beust's scheme was to make an alliance with Napoleon and the South German States for a new war against Prussia. To achieve this design it was necessary first of all to come to terms with the Hungarians, that most obstreperous of all Empire peoples. In the war of 1866 the Hungarians had openly shown their hostility to the Emperor and their sympathy with the Prussians.[14] This had to be changed, and Hungary's support of Habsburg secured for the next war. On Beust's (and Empress Elisabeth's) urging, Franz Joseph accepted the proposals of Deák and Count Andrássy, granting virtual independence to Hungary. On June 8, 1867, the jubilant, suddenly pro-Habsburg people of Budapest witnessed the splendid, fairy-tale coronation of their King and beloved Queen. From now on, Hungary was no longer a threat to the Empire. As it turned out—and as many perceptive persons had foreseen—Hungary was now the focus of the Empire; during the rest of Franz Joseph's reign, the Hungarians ran the Monarchy.

With the Hungarian problem solved to their and his (though to no one else's) satisfaction, Beust lost no time in pressing his plans for revenge against Prussia. A meeting with Napoleon was arranged for August 18, 1867. This notwithstanding the execution in Mexico, on June 19, 1867, of Maximilian, for whose death

Napoleon was in some measure responsible. Archduchess Sophie, at any rate, considered Napoleon the murderer of her son. Under the circumstances it would have been too raw to have Napoleon come to Vienna, or Franz Joseph go to Paris. The meeting was therefore held at Salzburg. Napoleon arrived with Empress Eugénie and a general, but without any of his ministers; Franz Joseph with Elisabeth and all his ministers. No agreement was arrived at, but the way was prepared for one. The true intentions of the two monarchs was clearly proclaimed by their public statements that their meeting had none but purely social purposes! Eyewitnesses commented on the striking contrast between the unmajestic, pompous, paunchy appearance of Napoleon and the tall, slender, elegant Franz Joseph; and especially on the contest between the two famed Imperial beauties: Eugénie's beauty verging on the meretricious, while Elisabeth's was pure, angelic, and Imperial.

There were further discussions between Austria and France. Relations between these countries became steadily more friendly, and an alliance, though not formally concluded, seemed morally implied. In 1869, Franz Joseph assured Napoleon that "we consider France's cause our own and shall contribute in every way possible to the success of French arms."[15] Meanwhile, relations between France and Prussia were deteriorating, and tension between Berlin and Vienna was near the breaking point by 1869. The opportunity for Franz Joseph's revenge seemed to have arrived. Archduke Albrecht was sent to Paris to discuss a joint military campaign. In June 1870, the French General Lebrun came to Vienna to continue military talks. The Archduke seemed to be dreaming of defeating Moltke (the Prussian general who defeated the Austrians at Königgrätz), but the Austrian War Mininster feared another Königgrätz if Albrecht was to be in command. On June 14, 1870, Lebrun was received by Franz Joseph, who approved all military arrangements but declared that above all he wanted peace; that if he was to go to war, he would have to be forced into it. In other words, before the world, Austria must appear as the innocent party, pounced upon by the brutal Prussians![16]

END OF THE STRUGGLE FOR GERMAN HEGEMONY. The war

between France and Prussia broke out earlier than expected; Franz Joseph's military preparations were not complete. A complication was the alliance of all German states with Prussia; this meant that in case Franz Joseph lived up to his obligation to Napoleon he would have to go to war not only against Prussia but also against Bavaria and Saxony, his old allies and friends. Worst of all, the French soon suffered reverses. These circumstances persuaded Franz Joseph to stay on the sidelines. From Paris came anguished cries for help. Where was Austria? The agreement called for Austria to have 150,000 men in Bohemia ready to attack Prussia. Urgent telegrams were sent from Paris to Vienna. It was an embarrassing situation for the chivalrous Franz Joseph, always so meticulous about keeping his word and now in a position of having to break it. But the embarrassment did not last long. The French were defeated; Napoleon was captured by the Prussians; France became a Republic; and on January 18, 1871, in the Hall of Mirrors at Versailles, Wilhelm I of Prussia was proclaimed German Emperor. Not only the Franco-Prussian War, but the struggle for German hegemony was over. Prussia had won, Habsburg had lost. More correctly, all this had already taken place in 1866 and even earlier, but Franz Joseph did not understand and accept the verdict of 1866 until 1871.

Recognizing that his chances for revenge against Prussia and for regaining the German Imperial crown had vanished, Franz Joseph fired Beust and made Andrássy Foreign Minister. This presaged a drastic change in foreign policy. Andrássy had been opposed to a policy of revenge from the first. He—and Hungary —could have no advantage from strengthening Franz Joseph's position in Germany. Hungary's power had grown out of Franz Joseph's weakness and his ejection from the German confederation. Andrássy's policy aimed at shifting the focus of Habsburg interests to the east, to the Balkans, against Russia, whose hostile intervention against Hungary in 1849 he had not forgotten, and at an alliance with Germany. He succeeded in both. Toward the end of his term as Foreign Minister he arranged for the occupation of Bosnia and Hercegovina by Austria-Hungary, and he concluded an alliance with Germany. These two achievements of Andrássy were to prove important steps in the undoing of the Habsburg Monarchy. The occupation of Bosnia foreshadowed the eventual collision with Russia; the alliance with Germany —cornerstone of Franz Joseph's foreign policy through the rest of his reign—doomed Austria to defeat with her northern ally. The alliance with Germany also weakened the Habsburg Empire by sharpening the conflicts between the nationalities in Austria: On the one hand, it encouraged German nationalism in Austria, while on the other hand, the Slavs saw in it nothing but a means for strengthening the positions of the Germans and Hungarians in the Monarchy at the expense of the Slavs.

Thus ended the chapter of Franz Joseph's bid for the German Imperial crown. It was not the Habsburgs, but the Hohenzollerns who restored the German Empire—the Second Empire. The crown of Charlemagne, instead of being put on the head of Franz Joseph, was placed on exhibit in the Imperial treasure vaults in Vienna, where it can still be seen today.

CHAPTER 15

The Hungarian Settlement

After the defeat of his army by the Prussians at Königgrätz, Franz Joseph was obsessed by a desire for revenge. This made him do things he would under different circumstances have rejected as "dishonorable": He curried favor with Napoleon, the "arch scoundrel" and arch enemy; he also gave in to Hungarian demands for independence, which until then he had rejected as utterly impossible, because incompatible with the idea of a centralized state. Also, to give independence to Hungary meant to reward traitors and to punish the loyal. But this had now apparently become necessary in Franz Joseph's view, because Hungary's support had to be won if he was to succeed with his plans for revenge against Prussia and for regaining German hegemony.

HUNGARY RULED FROM VIENNA, 1849-67. Hungary had been ruled by the Vienna government as a conquered and occupied country after the defeat of the Hungarian Revolutionary Army and the liquidation of the Kossuth government by the Russians in 1849. In 1861, Schmerling's short-lived constitution provided for representation of Hungary in an all-Empire Parliament in Vienna. But the Hungarians, led by the revered Ferencz Deák, refused to play Schmerling's game and insisted on restoration of the 1848 constitution, which had been approved by Emperor Ferdinand and which made Hungary an independent kingdom within the Monarchy rather than an Austrian province.

Under these circumstances it is not suprising that there was little pro-Habsburg sentiment in Hungary. Franz Joseph was still remembered for the executions at Arad where the revolutionary generals had been hanged to the strains of Haydn's Emperor hymn (which the Hungarians renamed the Hangman's hymn). Kossuth was still the national hero of the Hungarians, continuing in exile to agitate for Hungary's liberation. Once, when Franz Joseph rode through a Hungarian village, he was hailed by the people with shouts of *"Vivat!"* Why didn't the people use the customary *"Eljen!"*, the Emperor wanted to know. The mayor explained that he had carefully coached them to shout *"Vivat!"* because they were so accustomed to shout *"Eljen Kossuth!"* that he was afraid their "Eljens" might again be for Kossuth.

Hatred of Franz Joseph had been softened by the genuine affection and admiration of Hungarians for Empress Elisabeth, their Queen. Her beauty, her charm, and the love for the land and people of Hungary which she felt and expressed from the first day of her first visit to that country had won her the love of the people. Their *"Eljens!"* for her were loud and came from the heart; those for Franz Joseph came from reluctant lips.

Hungarian opposition continued, occasionally punctuated by open rebellion. Hungarian political leaders refused to budge from their demands for autonomy, for their own parliament and government, while the Emperor was equally determined not to budge from his insistence that Hungary accept its position as a province like any other in the Monarchy, with representation in a central Parliament in Vienna, to which the Hungarians refused to send delegates. In this impasse, Franz Joseph's Minister of State, Anton von Schmerling, continued absolutist rule in Hungary, declaring: "we can wait"—implying that Hungary would eventually come to terms.[1]

HUNGARY IN THE WAR OF 1866. As it turned out, it was the Hungarians who could wait and Franz Joseph who had to come to terms. During his war with Prussia, as mentioned earlier, the Hungarians had been openly "disloyal"—that is, in the Emperor's eyes; in their own, they were then, as always, loyal to what they regarded as Hungary's interests. They celebrated Prussian victories and cheered Italian prisoners of war; in many places youths hid in the forests to escape being made cannon fodder for Franz Joseph; in Budapest students stuck red feathers on their hats to show their revolutionary spirit. More than 2,000 enlisted in the legion formed by General Klapka, one of the leaders in the Revolution of 1848-49, to fight on the side of Prussia. In the last days of the war, Franz Joseph had sent Elisabeth to Hungary to drum up support for the dynasty. She reported to him on the people's ugly mood and warned him that unless he came to terms with the Hungarian leaders—Deák and Andrássy—there would be another revolution.

After the defeat of Königgrätz, Franz Joseph was ready to follow her advice. Within a week of the disastrous battle he called Deák to Vienna for secret talks. Deák stuck to his original demands—the same he had made in 1848 and ever since—not less, not more, though in view of the Emperor's desperate situation he could have raised his demands. As it was, Deák demanded *de facto* dissolution of the Empire into two separate parts, thus ending Schwarzenberg's centralized state. Count Belcredi, who had become Minister-President in 1865, was opposed to the Hungarian proposal. But the new Foreign Minister, Beust, urged concessions to Hungary as essential to a foreign policy of revenge.

ALTERNATIVES OPEN TO FRANZ JOSEPH. Franz Joseph vacillated between two alternatives. On the one side were Deák's demands, supported by a large majority of the Hungarian people. These demands were for reinstatement of the Hungarian constitution of 1848; a separate parliament and government for Hungary, which would mean a privileged position for Hungary among the nations of the Empire and the end of the "unitary state" idea of Schwarzenberg and Schmerling; only military and foreign affairs were to remain the joint responsibility of Hungary and the non-Hungarian parts of the Empire, or more correctly, were to remain the personal preserve of the Emperor. A minority in Hungary wanted to deprive the Emperor even of this vestige of his power and to make Hungary an entirely independent country, with only the person of the King identical with the Emperor of Austria. This minority proposed a mere "personal union," whereas Deák was for a "real union" of Hungary with the rest of the Empire; for "dualism"—the "Austro-Hungarian" Empire.

On the other side was the plan of the Minister-President, Count Belcredi. This plan conceded most of Deák's demands, but insisted on a joint parliament; like Deák, Belcredi was for liquidating the unitary, centrally governed state of Schwarzenberg and Schmerling, but instead of granting independence only to Hungary, he would have created a federation of national states, which he expected to be dominated by Catholic conservatives. Somewhat incongruously, he imagined that such a federation could be consistent with a strong, central Imperial power.

Beust and Deák—and Elisabeth who all along had supported Hungarian demands for independence—won out over Belcredi. Franz Joseph fired Belcredi, made Beust Minister-President, and accepted Deák's demands. He also offered Deák the post of Minister-President in the first Hungarian government. But Deák declined, urging instead the appointment of Count Gyula Andrássy, whom Franz Joseph accordingly did appoint to head the Hungarian government.

COUNT GYULA (JULIUS) ANDRASSY. Count Andrássy was a man who had had a colorful career in Hungarian politics and was destined to be one of the dominant figures in the reign of Franz Joseph. Andrássy had been one of the leaders of the Hungarian Revolution of 1848-49; he had been sentenced to death, but escaped to France. His wealth was confiscated, and he was hanged in effigy. Paris society knew the handsome fugitive as *le beau pendu*. In 1857 an amnesty, proclaimed by Franz Joseph largely on the urging of Elisabeth, allowed Andrássy to return to Hungary, where he promptly resumed his political activities. Abandoning the extreme line of the still exiled Kossuth, Andrássy joined the more moderate Deák and became his confidant and close collaborator. Andrássy adored the Empress Elisabeth whom he called "Hungary's beautiful Providence," and she in turn admired the handsome, dashing, lordly Andrássy, with his somewhat Gypsy-like air, looking so magnificent in the oriental splendor of his Hungarian Magnate's attire. She was fond of him, believed in him, and supported his political ambitions. Elisabeth's daughter, Archduchess Valerie, recorded that her mother was attached to Andrássy in true, staunch friendship, as perhaps to no other person.[2]

THE SETTLEMENT. Appointment of a separate Hungarian Ministry was announced on February 18, 1867; the Settlement was approved by the Hungarian Lower House on March 30, by the House of Magnates on April 3, 1867. The Vienna Parliament, too, was required to approve the Settlement. For this purpose, the suspended Vienna Parliament had to be reconvened and asked to change the constitution to allow for Hungarian autonomy. Beust successfully railroaded the measure through Parliament, though he was unable to get Czechs and Croats to approve what they considered an outrage.

The Settlement (see pp. 139-140) provided: (1) A separate Parliament and government for Hungary (including all the provinces of the Hungarian Crown, such as Croatia, Slovakia, Transylvania). (2) Restoration of the Constitution of 1848, which gave most power to the Hungarians, and especially to the Hungarian landowners, little power to the other nationalities in the Hungarian provinces. (3) Military and foreign affairs to be jointly administered by a deliberative body consisting of "delegations" from the two Parliaments, and by three Joint Ministers—for Foreign Affairs, War, and Finances. (4) The renewal of the terms of Settlement every ten years.

As a reward for agreeing to the settlement, and in order to solemnize this historic compact with fitting ceremony, a magnificent, fairy-tale coronation of Franz Joseph and Elisabeth as King and Queen of Hungary was arranged for June 8, 1867. Though Franz Joseph had drawers full of crowns, this was his only coronation; the other crowns were never formally put on his head. Popular enthusiasm, ancient symbolic rites, solemn ceremonies, dreamlike splendor, and a glorious June day combined to whip up emotions to a fever pitch of exultation. The frenzied *"Eljens"* to the beautiful young Queen *Erszébet* brought tears of pride and joy to the eyes of her who had no small part in bringing about all this joyousness. The climax came when Count Andrássy, acting for the Palatine (viceroy), together with

the Prince Primate of Hungary, the Archbishop of Esztergom
(Gran), put the Crown of Saint Stephen on Franz Joseph's head.
It was a great triumph—Franz Joseph receiving the Hungarian
crown from the man whom eighteen years before he had
sentenced to be hanged! Count Crenneville, the Emperor's
Adjutant General, shuddered at the thought of former traitors
now bestowing crowns.[3]

TREASON REWARDED. Hungary's joy was not shared by the
other peoples of the Empire. There was general resentment
against the preference accorded to the Hungarians. The Emperor had given in to the people who had been his enemies
from the day he ascended the throne and had slighted those who
had fought for him. This preference for his enemies was epitomized by his gift of 100,000 gold ducats, which he had received
as a coronation gift from the Hungarian people, to the widows
and orphans of the men who had fallen in 1848 and 1849, fighting for the Hungarian revolutionists. This act, inspired by
Elisabeth, was probably motivated by noble sentiments; but it
enraged those who had fought for the Emperor and who now
received nothing for their pains, while the Emperor rewarded
his enemies, whom he had previously condemned as traitors!

NATIONALITIES PROBLEM SHARPENED BY SETTLEMENT. An immediate and continuing response to the Hungarian Settlement
was that other nationalities in the Empire demanded similar
"settlements." The Czechs, who incidentally had been the only
people to suffer from the war of 1866 which took place on their
territory, reasserted their claim to an independent Kingdom of
Bohemia, including all the lands of the Crown of Saint Wenceslaus; but they were unsuccessful. The day that saw Budapest
festively celebrating Franz Joseph's coronation as King of Hungary, saw Prague under martial law. Croatia was worst offended,
as it had loyally supported the Emperor in the Revolution and
in his war against the Hungarians in 1848-49, yet now was
delivered to these same Hungarians, its arch enemies, Croatia
being counted as one of the provinces of the Crown of Saint
Stephen. (The Croatians, however, did make their own Settlement with Hungary in 1868, which assured them a small measure
of autonomy within the Kingdom of Hungary.) Franz Joseph

turned a deaf ear to the petitions and complaints of the Germans and Romanians in Transylvania. In fact, throughout the remaining half-century of his reign, Franz Joseph never showed any interest in the problems and demands of national minorities in the Kingdom of Hungary.

That the national aspirations of all Empire peoples other than the Hungarians had to be frustrated was a direct consequence of the Hungarian Settlement; for the chief, if unexpressed, condition of the Hungarian Settlement was precisely that no other nation was to receive similar concessions. Hungary demanded absolute sway over its national minorities. Had Franz Joseph granted independence to the Czechs or to the Poles, this Hungarian hegemony would have been threatened: The Slav minorities, the Germans, and the Romanians in Hungary would have demanded the same. For this reason Hungarian policy absolutely opposed demands for autonomy of any other national group in the Empire. Its aim was to create in Cisleithania—the Austrian part of the Dual Monarchy—a situation similar to that which existed in Transleithania. There the Hungarians were the master race dominating the non-Magyar minorities; in Cisleithania the Germans were similarly to be the master race dominating non-German minorities in their part of the Empire. This, in the view of Hungarian leaders, would have settled the nationalities problem. In fact, however, the nationalities problem could not be settled in this way, but became a source of progressive disruption of the Empire.

It was ironical that the Hungarian Settlement, designed to prepare the way for revenge against Prussia, strengthened precisely those national groups in the Empire that would not support such plans: the Hungarians and the Germans. Even as Franz Joseph was plotting with Napoleon against Prussia in 1867, Andrássy let the French ruler know that Hungary would never allow Franz Joseph to carry out his anti-Prussian plans. This showed not only how Hungarian policy conflicted with the aims of the Austrian Emperor, but incidentally gave proof of the actual power wielded by the Hungarian government in Empire affairs. Andrássy was the head of the Hungarian government at that time, but he was not Franz Joseph's Foreign Minister; yet he presumed to make foreign policy on his own, in contradiction to that of the Foreign Minister, Beust.

HUNGARY'S PRISONER. It was an open secret that the Emperor was dominated by the Hungarian Cabinet and that his own Foreign Minister had little influence, as the Italian envoy to Vienna reported to his government.[4] With the Hungarian Settlement, Franz Joseph had in fact made himself the prisoner of "a group of intractable, ruthless large landowners, who so firmly seized the reins of the joint enterprise that Austria was actually ruled—via the [Austro-Hungarian] Monarchy—by Hungary."[5] From the time of the Settlement to the end of his reign almost fifty years later, Franz Joseph made the Settlement the cornerstone of his domestic and foreign policy, was always anxious to accede to Hungarian demands, in fact kowtowed to the Hungarians. Foreign diplomats recognized and reported this shift of power from Vienna to Budapest. In Austria, people joked bitterly about having to learn Hungarian, as in our day the Hungarians might joke about having to learn Russian—the language of their new "master race."

Hungary in effect ruled and exploited the entire Monarchy. Though having only two-fifths of the population (including of course its non-Magyar population) of the Empire, it had an equal voice in decisions affecting the Monarchy—and often the decisive voice. Yet Hungary paid only one-third of the taxes.[6] With every ten-year renewal of the Settlement, Hungarian demands became bolder. They claimed one-half of the Austro-Hungarian Bank, four-fifths of which was owned by Austrians while the Hungarians were its principal debtors, and they managed to get an Hungarian appointed as Governor. If it had not been for the First World War, it is likely that Hungary would have become entirely independent by the time of the next renewal of the Settlement, in 1917. How much Hungary was an independent country by that time, and not a part of the Empire, was proved by the way Hungary, with plenty of food, was permitted to withhold that food from the starving rest of the Empire. The independent Hungary established in 1919 was, of course, not part of the plans of Hungarian leaders: It was a truncated Hungary, with no national minorities to rule and exploit, and with no Austro-Hungarian Empire to run.

No abasement was too degrading for Franz Joseph in his efforts to appease the Hungarians, who rewarded his subservience by heaping indignities upon him. Examples of Franz Joseph's obsequiousness abound. In 1906, he arranged for the solemn return of the remains of Imre Tököly to Hungary. This Tököly had helped the Turks besiege Vienna in 1683, fought the Habsburgs, and ended his days as a Turkish pensioner. (At that time the Turks were the arch enemies of the Habsburgs.) Ferencz Rákóczy was another Magyar traitor (from the Habsburg point of view) whose memory Franz Joseph honored. Rákóczy had constantly fought on the side of the Turks and of Louis XIV of France against the Habsburgs. Franz Joseph had a representative put a wreath on the monument to General Bem, a Pole who had fought the Habsburg regime in Vienna in 1848, escaped from there to continue his fight as one of the most successful leaders of the Hungarian Army in 1849, escaped again and became a Turkish general as "Murad Pasha."

This honoring of valiant foes could have been motivated by magnanimity; but while Franz Joseph genuflected before his and his ancestors' Hungarian enemies, he acted quite differently when it came to honoring the memory of a brave Hungarian soldier who gave his life fighting *for* the Emperor. Colonel Hentzi, a Hungarian-born Swiss, defended Buda for the Emperor against the Hungarian Revolutionary Army under Görgei. His brave defense delayed Görgei and prevented his marching on Vienna. Thus Hentzi really saved Franz Joseph. Hentzi died in this battle on May 21, 1849. Fifty years after Hentzi's death, Franz Joseph, instead of sending flowers, gave in to Hungarian pressure and ordered the removal of the monument which had been erected on the spot of the hero's fall! Franz Joseph was indeed living up to the reputation for ingratitude enjoyed by the house of Habsburg ever since Wallenstein was murdered in 1634, and was thus rewarded for his services to the Emperor Ferdinand II!

As a reward for these abasements, the Hungarians made Franz

Joseph accept the son of the Hungarian arch traitor (from the Habsburg point of view) Lajos Kossuth as a minister, filled their textbooks with praise of such Habsburg enemies as Zápolya, Bocskay, Béthlen, Tököly, the two Rákóczys, and Kossuth, and erected a monument to George Washington, who "had freed his country from the King and made it independent."[7]

The remarkable part was that Franz Joseph came so completely under Hungarian domination not because he liked the Hungarians or their aspirations and policies, but simply because he was afraid of them. He was afraid that unless he made concessions to them, they would break away from him completely. He was willing to make concessions to them as long as they permitted him to keep his army and control over foreign policy. The army was the one thing Franz Joseph was always willing to fight for. Even here, however, the Hungarians challenged the Emperor's power. There was a Hungarian Army, the Honvéd, which was Hungarian from A to Z, even as there was an Austrian Army, the Landwehr. But the main army was Austro-Hungarian, and it was this army the Emperor had to defend against Hungarian encroachments. The language of command of the joint army was German. The Hungarians wanted to make it Hungarian for all regiments recruited in Hungarian territory, even though the recruits were non-Magyars. To grant this request would have meant the end of a joint army. To prevent this, to save his army, Franz Joseph was willing to violate the Hungarian constitution even as an old man, in 1905, when he appointed as Hungarian Minister-President a General who stopped parliamentary nonsense by sending a detachment of the Honvéd into Parliament to close its proceedings. To the end of his reign, Franz Joseph succeeded in restraining the Hungarians from taking the army away from him. As for foreign policy, the Emperor maintained his hold on it by conducting it entirely in accordance with Hungarian wishes, much of the time under the management of a Hungarian as Foreign Minister.

In his fear that unless he gave in to the Hungarians, they would break up his Empire, Franz Joseph permitted them actually to break it up. This was what the Settlement amounted to in effect. When the agencies of the joint Austro-Hungarian government

—the Delegations and the three Joint Ministers—were installed on December 21, 1867, the official rhetoric emphasized the unity of the Empire; but the fact was that this unity had been ended. The two parts of the "Dual Monarchy" were separate and independent of each other and generally pursued contradictory aims. The Empire had broken apart; its final dismemberment was foreshadowed by the Settlement of 1867. After that the Empire was unified in appearance only, if in that. Perhaps this was all Franz Joseph cared for, appearances always being of prime concern to him. It was his achievement that he held on for another half-century to this appearance and to whatever reality was left of his Empire.

CHAPTER 16

The "Mission" of the Habsburg Empire

"IF AUSTRIA DID NOT EXIST, WE SHOULD HAVE TO CREATE IT." The dissolution of Franz Joseph's Empire, begun in 1867 with the Hungarian Settlement and reaching its final consummation in 1918, has raised a still continuing debate over what the use of this remarkable conglomerate may have been. The hodgepodge character of the Habsburg Empire provided ready arguments for its enemies to condemn it as an anachronism, a political monstrosity inevitably tottering toward collapse. Devotees of the defunct Empire claim, on the contrary, that it served useful and necessary functions. They like to quote, and to accept like a Papal *ex cathedra* pronouncement, the famous statement of the Czech historian František Palacký that "if the Austrian state did not exist we should have to create it in the interests of Europe and humanity." The same thought was expressed by Talleyrand in a letter to Napoleon after the Battle of Austerlitz, when Napoleon seemed to be toying with the idea of liquidating the Habsburg Empire. Talleyrand warned that the continued existence of that entity was indispensable to the welfare of civilized mankind. These and similar assertions by other statesmen, including Bismarck and Andrássy, and by a host of historians, are cited in support of the contention that the polyglot, multinational Habsburg Empire fulfilled some necessary mission; that it was therefore a "desirable" institution and that its demise is regrettable or even tragic.[1]

The question, however, is not whether the Habsburg Empire was good or bad—which may be left for partisans to fight about; but whether there existed some inner logic, some geographic, economic, historical, ethnic, or other "necessity" for this empire.

THE GEOGRAPHIC ARGUMENT. The geographic argument, most generally advanced, is that the lands of the Danube basin, no matter by whom inhabited, form a natural geographical unit. The Habsburg Empire—the "Danube Monarchy," as it was often called—was the response to this geographic demand for unity.

Even if this mythical necessity were conceded, the Habsburg Empire cannot be regarded as having been a response to it.

(a) The Habsburg Empire did not develop out of the need for political or administrative unity of the peoples inhabiting the Danube basin; it grew out of the land grabbing and power pursuit which was the avowed and sole purpose of dynastic rulers. Furthermore, it was only in the century preceding the accession of Franz Joseph that attempts had been made to unify these diverse territories and to bring them under one centralized administration. Until the reign of Maria Theresa (1740-80) the several parts of the Empire had been treated as separate possessions, separately administered. The administrative unity of the Empire was lost again in 1867 with the division of the Empire into an Austrian and a Hungarian component, each virtually independent of the other.

(b) According to the "Danube thesis," the Habsburgs should have ruled also Bavaria and Romania—the source and the mouth of the Danube—as they indeed desired and attempted at times; but they would have had no business in most of Bohemia and Galicia, in Silesia, Istria, Italy, South Tirol, Dalmatia—all lands not belonging to the Danube basin, but none of which the Habsburgs showed the slightest intention of relinquishing.

The Habsburg Empire was the "Danube Monarchy" only in the sense that the Danube is the greatest river flowing through its territories; not in the sense that it was an empire built around that river and unifying all the Danube basin lands. If there exists a need for such unification, it has not manifested itself strongly. Never—before or under the Habsburgs—had the lands of the Danube basin formed a political or administrative unit; and there have been no attempts to create such a unit since the dismemberment of the Empire.

THE ECONOMIC ARGUMENT.   The economic argument for the "necessity" of the Habsburg Empire is closely related to the geographic and equally invalid. The formation of the Empire through successive acquisitions of territories had nothing to do with economic considerations, except that each new acquisition meant added wealth for the ruler. For the people it could mean an economic setback, rather than a benefit, to come under Habsburg rule. This was so in the case of Bohemia when it was reconquered, and Roman Catholicism reimposed on the people, by the Habsburg Emperor Ferdinand II in 1620. The consequence was that some 150,000 Protestants—many of them craftsmen and generally the most productive element of the population —emigrated, throwing the country into a severe economic decline.

In the period of mercantilism, when rulers in most European countries consciously encouraged industry and trade, built roads, abolished internal tolls, and erected external protective tariffs, the Habsburgs did the same in the territories under their rule. This happened mostly in the eighteenth century. Whether at that time or later the several provinces benefited from their common rule by the Habsburgs is questionable. They might conceivably have done bettter singly, as did the many small German states. Advocates of independence for the several parts of the Empire argued that their respective countries suffered because their inability to follow an independent economic policy retarded their economic development. In any case, most of the Empire provinces were economically backward as compared with western European countries.

Assertions that the misery of the succession states in the years after World War I is attributable to the dismemberment of the Empire, and that this misery would have been avoided had the Empire been preserved, confuse cause with effect: The Empire collapsed because of the extreme misery suffered by its people. The assertion that the succession states would have been better off if they had maintained their union is pure speculation. Facts indicate that economic conditions, that is, production and income, in the succession states improved after 1919, the year in which the misery inherited from World War I was at its worst. The world-wide depression of the 1930's of course also hit the succession states; but this was a general breakdown in the capitalistic world, which had nothing to do with the presence or absence of an Austrian Empire. Today those of the succession states that are communistic report sensational economic progress. The two succession states still in the capitalist camp—Austria and Italy—are enjoying unprecedented prosperity, without benefit of a Habsburg Empire.

THE HISTORICAL ARGUMENT. The historical "mission" supposedly performed by the Habsburg Empire was to defend the peoples comprised in it—as well as Europe as a whole—first from the Turks, later from the Russians. Ironically, it was directly in response to Habsburg territorial ambitions that the Turks first invaded Austria and besieged Vienna in 1529. Ferdinand I (brother of Emperor Charles V) claimed the Hungarian crown in 1526 on the strength of an agreement made by his grandfather Maximilian I with King Ladislaus II of Hungary in 1515. A majority of Hungarians, however, elected a king of their own, John Zápolya, and there was war. King John Zápolya, far from feeling the need for union with Habsburg against the Turks, called upon the Turkish Sultan Soliman for aid against the Habsburg invader. Soliman accepted the invitation, attacked Austria, but also occupied most of Hungary. For a century and a half the greater part of Hungary remained under Turkish rule, an arrangement acceptable to the Hungarian nobles and of no interest to the peasants who suffered misery and servitude regardless of who ruled their country. When the Turks besieged Vienna a second time, in 1683, they were defeated, not by Austrians and Hungarians, but by armies led by the Duke of Lorraine and by King John Sobieski of Poland.

As for the Austrian "mission" to be a bulwark against Russia, the Habsburg ruler, far from defending his subjects against the Russians, actually called for, and got, Russian help in putting down the rebellious Hungarians in 1849, thus repaying the earlier Hungarian appeal to the Turks for help against the Habsburgs.

It goes without saying that the Habsburgs tried to defend their territories against the land-grabbing designs of their neighbors, among whom the Turks were for a long time the most dangerous. All rulers try to defend their possessions. But to say that it is the "mission" of rulers to defend their lands is again to confuse cart with horse. The Habsburg Empire defended itself in order to exist; it did not exist in order to defend itself, much less to defend Europe, or Western civilization.

THE ETHNIC ARGUMENT. The ethnic "mission" of the Empire may be conceived of as that of uniting ethnically and linguistically unlike peoples for common purposes, instead of letting them waste their energies fighting each other. A peaceful, harmonious union of peoples speaking different languages is quite conceivable: It actually exists in the Swiss Confederation, a voluntary union of German-, French-, Italian-, and Romansh*-speaking groups who have lived together for centuries without faction and friction. But in the polyglot Habsburg Empire, the involuntarily associated national groups were in a continuous war of each against all, occasionally united in their opposition to the Imperial power. Far from existing for the purpose of uniting divergent national interests, the Empire nurtured national antagonisms in order to secure its existence. The Habsburg rulers had traditionally played one nation against the other in the ancient game of "divide and rule." This system was taken over and continued by Franz Joseph, in whose reign conflict between nationalities became increasingly vehement. Franz Joseph's favorite Minister, Count Taaffe, coined the oftquoted phrase that one "must keep all the nationalities in a state of mild dissatisfaction." And Franz Grillparzer, whom Habsburg-loyal Austrians revered as their greatest poet, wrote about "the shameful Machiavellian schemes of the leaders who, to make sure that the Imperial family would be the sole unifying link among the states, nurture the mutual antagonisms of the several provinces."[2]

DESIRABILITY OF MULTINATIONAL UNIONS. All this is not to say that union of many diverse peoples was not, and is not still, desirable on many counts. All participating peoples could benefit from it. But the fact is that the Habsburg Monarchy was not

---

* Romansh is a Raeto-Romanic dialect, spoken in the Canton of Grisons (Graubünden).

animated by any mission to achieve such benefits, and did not achieve them. Moreover, the argument in favor of union on various levels—political, economic, cultural, scientific—does not apply merely to those countries which happened to be ruled by the Habsburgs, but to all countries; it is the argument for a United States of Europe, or for a United States of the World, or for a World Health Organization, or a World Postal Union. There is no particular virtue in a union, on any of these levels, of only or specifically those countries which formerly constituted the Habsburg Monarchy.

WHY DID STATESMEN ARGUE THE "NECESSITY" OF THE HABSBURG EMPIRE? The brief examination in this chapter suggests that there was no real "mission" to be fulfilled by the Habsburg Empire. Why, then, did statesmen argue the "necessity" of this empire? There are undoubtedly many answers to this question —different ones in the case of each of the men who made such claims—and it would be straying too far from the subject of this book to go into them. But a common denominator to which they can all be reduced is: national interest. When Palacký, Bismarck, Andrássy, and others discovered that the Austrian Monarchy was a "necessity," it was because the existence of the Monarchy seemed to them an advantage, and its possible demise a danger, to their national interests at the time.

Palacký's statement, contained in a letter to the Frankfort Pre-Parliament in 1848, reflected his fear of a union of Austria with Germany, in which the Czechs would have been a hopeless minority. Czech nationalism had a better chance when confronted by fewer Germans. At the same time Palacký saw in the preservation of the Monarchy a bulwark against Pan-Slavism, which would have engulfed the Western Slavs as appendages to Russia.[3] Had he believed in the possibility of complete independence for the Czechs, he would perhaps have been less fervent about the necessity of an Austrian Monarchy, even as his disciple Masaryk, the first President of the Czecho-Slovakian Republic, under different conditions, not only failed to see the necessity of the Austrian Monarchy, but on the contrary considered it an enemy of the "interests of Europe and of humanity."

Bismarck's reason for insisting on the preservation of the

Monarchy was clearly that it was advantageous to Germany. As long as the Monarchy existed, it provided a convenient buffer for Germany, too weak to be a danger, but a possibly useful ally; while if the Monarchy were dismembered, the pieces might be gobbled up by Russia, increasing the danger threatening from that neighbor.

Andrássy's reasons for considering the Monarchy a necessity were the most obvious of all: Hungary ran the Monarchy, and Andrássy ran Hungary.

The argument for the "necessity" of the Monarchy reduces itself to the argument that a weak neighbor is a good neighbor to have: He is not dangerous; he serves as a buffer against more dangerous neighbors; and he may be a useful ally. This was why the Western powers—and the Monarchy—discovered, in the last century, that Turkey was "necessary" and had to be defended against the Czar's appetite for Turkey. The classic case of the "necessary" country, of course, is Switzerland—a danger to none of its neighbors, a protection for all.

If the argument for the "necessity" of the Monarchy is interpreted in this sense, as consisting in the weakness of the Monarchy, there may be some validity to it. Even then, however, it is questionable, as the Monarchy, though weak in many respects, was a constant threat to its southern and eastern neighbors.

CHAPTER 17

The Economy of Franz Joseph's Empire

One of the arguments in support of the idea that the Habsburg Empire had a mission to fulfill, as mentioned in the preceding chapter, was the economic argument: that the union of many small nations into one great empire made possible a greater economic development, a higher level of economic performance, than could have been achieved by the several countries separately. "Looking back," as one economic historian put it, "we must conclude that the countries of the Danube Monarchy never knew a better, a happier time than that of the Old Emperor."[1] Such arguments and assertions are hard to prove or disprove, as they reflect nostalgia and personal preference rather than objective facts. It may be useful to turn to the facts and briefly review the nature of the economy of the Monarchy and its development in the reign of Franz Joseph.

FRANZ JOSEPH'S REIGN A PERIOD OF EXPANSION. The period of Franz Joseph's reign—from the middle of the nineteenth century to World War I—was one of economic expansion throughout the Western world. In emulation of England, which had already gone through the Industrial Revolution in the preceding three quarters of a century, Germany, the United States, France, and other nations turned to machine industry and grew rich. The Monarchy followed the general trend. Production and wealth grew, though not as much as in some other countries, notably in neighboring Germany.

THE EMPIRE'S ECONOMY AT THE TIME OF FRANZ JOSEPH'S
ACCESSION. When Franz Joseph became Emperor, the provinces
of his Empire were predominantly agricultural. Nearly 70 per
cent of the total working population worked on farms and in
forests. Agriculture was backward; productivity was low. The
medieval system of serfdom had not been abolished until 1848.
As serfs, forced to cultivate their lords' lands, the peasants worked
reluctantly and resentfully. They were mostly illiterate and
ignorant and stuck to antiquated methods of cultivation. The
great landlords were content to leave well enough alone; they
had no interest in interfering with a system which assured them
wealth and leisure, even though it condemned the working people
to poverty and misery. It was the same familiar situation found
wherever large estates of absentee landlords are worked by an
enslaved, ignorant peasantry, as for instance today in most Latin
American countries.

Manufacturing industry was limited to areas inhabited by Germans, mostly in Bohemia, Silesia, Lower Austria, Styria, and to
the few larger non-German cities of the Empire, such as Budapest, Trieste, Zagreb. In these, too, industry, as also trade and
finance, were concentrated in the hands of Germans and Jews.
There were few large factories. Manufacturing was carried on
in small shops, largely by handicraft methods. Industry and trade
also flourished in the Italian provinces soon to be lost to Franz
Joseph. The provinces Franz Joseph seized in 1878—Bosnia and
Hercegovina—were poor compensation for the lost Italian territories; they were the most underdeveloped part of the Empire.

THE EMPIRE ECONOMY BEFORE 1848. The Empire economy
had seen better days. In the eighteenth century it had flourished
under the mercantilistic policies of Karl VI, Maria Theresa, and
especially under the Emperor Joseph II. In Joseph's reign the
Empire became for the first time a unified economic area; internal
tolls were eliminated; and a central administration was established.
Many manufacturing enterprises were started under protection
of external tariffs and with government encouragement. Serfdom was abolished. All these reforms, however, were promptly
undone by Joseph's successors Leopold II and Franz II (Franz
I of Austria). Emancipation of the peasants was rescinded, and

internal tariffs were reintroduced. In 1793, duties were restored on goods moving between Austria and Hungary. Encouragement of industry gave way to positive discouragement. Emperor Franz was afraid of factories and machines as potentially nurturing an industrial proletariat and revolutionary ideas.

After the Napoleonic wars, English free-trade ideas were spreading all over Europe. The Monarchy, too, moved in the direction of liberalization, at least in again abolishing internal tolls. But liberalism in economics was yoked to reaction in politics. Metternich was not willing to join the German Customs Union formed in 1833, fearing the liberal ideas which had fathered this union.

TREND TOWARD LIBERALISM AFTER 1848.   After the Revolution of 1848, the Empire economy took a definite turn toward liberalism. Feudal obligations of peasants were finally abolished. This was the one important, enduring success of the Revolution. The peasants no longer worked for a landlord, but for themselves, and were thus encouraged to improve their production. The landlords were compensated for the loss of their ancient rights. Many of them invested the compensation money in new enterprises, thereby stimulating economic development. The entire Empire was made into a free-trade area, as the last tolls on goods moving between Austria and Hungary were again removed in 1850. In foreign trade the Empire always relied on protective tariffs and never embraced outright free trade, but came near to it in the thirty-year period after 1848. A determined effort was now made to join the German Customs Union, though chiefly for political, not economic, reasons: It had become clear that Austria could not maintain, or regain, its pre-eminence in the German confederation except as a member of the Customs Union. For the same reason Prussia blocked Austrian membership on every occasion.

PROPERTY INTERESTS DOMINANT.   Though Franz Joseph regarded the Empire as his private domain, which he ruled as an absolute monarch, the more real if less visible ruler was the class of property owners—as indeed it was in the entire Western world. Large landed proprietors, financiers, and factory owners called the tune. Not the welfare of the people, but the interests of property owners inspired, or determined, government policy in every respect, be it in taxation, foreign trade, railroads, or anything else. To cite one example: The state had paid 377 million guilders for the construction of state railways in the early years of railroad building, then sold them, in 1854 and 1858, to private interests for 165 million guilders—a loss to the government, and correspondingly a virtual gift to the buyers, of 212 million guilders. This transaction was hailed as "wise" by the representatives of capitalist interests. Thereafter, railroad development was in private hands—domestic and foreign—the government confining its participation to the granting of subsidies and the guaranteeing (and paying) of interest on private railroad obligations. Beginning in 1881 (in Hungary, 1876), the state nationalized the railroads, buying them from the private owners who could no longer squeeze a profit out of operating them, at prices considered by Minister-President von Koerber to be "ruinous" to the state.[2]

Of course, these transactions were always defended as being in the interest of the state, but their effect was to put money into the pockets of capitalists. As in other countries, the capitalists in the Monarchy regarded the state as an agency for the protection of private property, and the taxes which they were willing to pay, as a fee for this service. "The night watchman state, not the welfare state, was their ideal."[3] They preached the doctrine of laissez faire and wanted the government to keep out of their affairs, but turned to that same government when they needed tariff protection, subsidies, or other forms of aid. Under this system the economy grew: The working people—the proletariat, the feared "mob"—grew in numbers; the property owners grew in wealth.

RAILROADS. Economic growth in the Franz Joseph era was sustained by investment in railroads, buildings, and factories. In 1848, the railroads were still in their infancy: The entire Monarchy had only 666 miles of railroads; by 1870, it had 6,214 miles; by 1914, 28,460 miles. This was a sizable railroad network, putting the Monarchy in fourth place in continental Europe, after Germany (38,962 miles), France (38,527 miles), and Russia (31,070 miles).[4] In the 1850's, Austria was the first country to build a railroad over steep mountains—the Semmering railroad, opened in 1854, a triumph of engineering—connecting Vienna with points to the south. Railroads were expensive undertakings, especially when built in difficult terrain. The total invested in the construction of railroads in the Monarchy was over one billion dollars, a huge sum for that time. But not only this large direct investment in railroads stimulated economic activity and growth; equally if not more important were the indirect effects on the building and manufacturing industries. Railroads needed rails, rolling stock, stations, and numerous other buildings. It was largely around the railroads that the iron and steel and machine industries grew up. These in turn stimulated other industries in a chain of mutual cause and effect. The entire Franz Joseph era was one of railroad building. The economy, therefore, had continuous, although uneven, stimulation from this source.

EXPANSION OF VIENNA. The second great stimulus to economic growth was building activity, occasioned especially by the expansion of the city of Vienna and, to a lesser extent, by similar expansions of some of the smaller cities of the Empire.

The old city of Vienna, what is now called the "Inner City," had been a fortress surrounded by walls and moats. Between these fortifications and the suburbs lay a strip of land about a third of a mile wide. This was the so-called Glacis—bare land, with no buildings and only a few trees. The function of the Glacis was to deprive attackers of cover and to enable the defenders to mow them down more easily. Already in Napoleonic days the fortifications were no longer useful in defense against an enemy army; the city was in fact surrendered to Napoleon without defense. But a government obsessed with fear of revolution was loath to part with walls which continued to provide protection against possible attacks by the "mob" from the suburbs. Because of this danger, the walls were not only left standing, but even strengthened in 1818, and proved useful in 1848, when the dreaded event occurred.

In 1857, Franz Joseph ordered the razing of the walls and the expansion of the city, to connect and unite it with its suburbs. In the place of the walls, a beautiful wide avenue was to ring the Inner City—the Ringstrasse, officially opened in 1865, and ever since then Vienna's parade street, lined with magnificent public buildings, parks, theaters, and the palaces of Vienna's nineteenth-century plutocracy. Blocks upon blocks of apartment houses also went up along and beyond the Ringstrasse, on what had been the Glacis. To this day, the Ringstrasse with its grand buildings stands as a monument to the reign of Franz Joseph. Vienna became one of the most splendid capitals of the world. But pomp did not interfere with protection. To cope with the dreaded attacks by the "mob," that is, the working people in the suburbs, the Ringstrasse was planned "with special consideration for the requirements of military strategy." Military barracks were built as strong points at strategic spots, and the Ringstrasse laid out so as to enable the military to shoot at demonstrators with rifles or grapeshot.[5] The Hofburg (Imperial residence) was protected by a strong, high iron fence with gates that normally remained open but could be closed in an emergency.

The economic effects of the great rebuilding scheme continued to be felt for a long time: A large stretch of previously unused land near the center of the metropolis was opened to development; new speculative possibilities were created; profits and profit prospects were raised by the boost given to the building industry; for twenty-five years the former Glacis region was the scene of building activity unequaled even by the great rebuilding after the bombings in World War II. The Ringstrasse structures, incidentally, were sturdily built and stood up well under allied bombing.

FACTORIES. The development of industry was the third great factor sustaining the economic expansion in the Franz Joseph era. At first, factories were started mainly by entrepreneurs from Germany, France, England, and other foreign countries, even as Austrian railways were in the hands of mostly foreign capitalists. The Monarchy was in effect a colonial territory of the West. Soon, however, the foreigners became Austrians and were joined by native Austrian capitalists.* By 1914, machine production in the Empire had become established in a number of industries. An important industry was the beet-sugar industry, with many fac-

---

* Heimito von Doderer's latest novel[6] revolves around the theme of an English manufacturer settling in Austria in the last century.

tories in Bohemia, Moravia, Silesia, and Galicia. The growth of this industry can be gauged by the quantities of sugar beets processed: in 1843, 300,000 tons; in 1890, 7,600,000 tons; by 1914, 14,000,000 tons. Sugar became the leading export item in the early 1900's. Other important mechanized industries were grain mills, especially the large steam flour mills in Budapest; breweries in many parts of the Monarchy, producing 700 million gallons of beer in 1913, much of it for export; iron and steel, machines, scythes, sickles, enamel ware, paper. The most important single industry in the Monarchy in value of output and number of persons employed (except for the construction industry, if all ancillary and dependent trades are counted as part of the building industry), was the textile industry. This industry had been started in the reign of the Emperor Leopold I (1658-1705) and was to a large extent still carried on under the inefficient and outmoded "domestic system," that is, by workers, especially weavers, working in their homes and not in a factory. In the reign of Franz Joseph, however, factories increasingly took the place of domestic production in the textile industry.

FINANCIAL INSTITUTIONS. Accompanying the economic expansion, the banking and credit system of the Monarchy also grew. There were savings banks, mortgage banks and mortgage associations, and a few large commercial banks. In 1882, the Postal Savings Bank was created, a notable institution which introduced an efficient, simple payment and clearing system still used in Austria today and preferred to the check system used in the United States. The volume of payments made through this institution increased from about $250 million in 1887 to about $3,000 million in 1913, reflecting the growing popularity of the payments system as well as the expansion of the economy.

The large commercial banks not only financed, but also launched and controlled industrial ventures in the last twenty-five years of the Franz Joseph era. In 1914, the largest of these banks, the Creditanstalt, had interests in fifty-seven enterprises, forty-three of them industrial.[7] The Creditanstalt was to play a key role in the financial troubles of the early 1930's. It was the collapse of this institution in 1931 that set off a world-wide financial crisis, leading first to a moratorium on German external debts, then to suspension of repayments by Great Britain and France of their war debts to the United States, and eventually to the abandonment of the gold standard by the United States.

THE CRASH OF 1873. The financial collapse of 1931 was the second great international crisis that had started in Vienna. The first was in 1873. Years of prosperity had spurred speculation in corporation shares and real estate. Banks extended credit to the speculators at high interest rates. These high rates in turn attracted foreign lenders, especially from Germany, which had just collected a one-billion-dollar indemnity from France after the Franco-Prussian War of 1870-71. It was an ideal time for promoters of corporations, reminiscent of the Mississippi Bubble in France and the South Sea Bubble in England—the two famous orgies of speculation in shares of companies founded ostensibly to exploit the riches of the South Sea and of the Mississippi territory, which ended with catastrophic crashes in 1720. In Austria, in 1872 and 1873, 530 corporations were chartered with a share capital of three billion guilders—the equivalent of $1.2 billion, an enormous sum for those days in Austria.

Indications of impending collapse of fantastically inflated stock-exchange values caused large banks and cagey speculators to get out of the market in the first four months of 1873; others hopefully waited for the May 1 opening of the Vienna World Exposition, which they expected to start another upward surge in the stock market. The Exposition was to show the world the prosperity and progressiveness of newly industrialized Austria. With much fanfare, Emperor and Empress opened the Exposition in the presence of an illustrious gathering of royal personages, including the Prince of Wales and the German Crown Prince. It rained, and the opening-day crowd was disappointingly small. A few days later cholera broke out. Share prices did not rise; instead, the bottom dropped out of the stock market on May 9, 1873—"Black Friday." Paper millionaires became paupers overnight. A frantic crowd of thousands pushed and shouted outside the stock-exchange building, trying to find buyers for securities. Stocks selling for a hundred guilders the day before were traded for pennies. Many securities found no buyer at any price. As stock prices dropped, the suicide rate rose, and people joked grimly about the dangers of walking on the Ringstrasse where so many ruined speculators were throwing themselves out of windows. It was the crash of the century. Inevitably it spread to other financial centers and also reached New York, where similar overoptimistic speculation in railroad and industrial securities had led to an equally precarious situation, awaiting only some appropriate event to precipitate collapse. The "founders' period"—the years of reckless promotion of corporations for the purpose of profiting from such promotions—was over, at least for a while.

HALF A CENTURY OF PEACE. Despite the financial bloodletting of 1873, the Empire economy, after a few years of stagnation, recovered and embarked on renewed expansion, lasting, with occasional reverses, until the outbreak of war in 1914. Supporting this new expansion were the same factors responsible for the earlier growth: railroad building, mechanization of industry, building activity occasioned by urbanization and growth of population. These developments had not run their full course by 1873 and were only temporarily interrupted by the stock-market disaster. Their resumption was aided by a prolonged period of peace and by the long overdue stabilization of a chronically afflicted currency.

The long period of peace enjoyed by the Monarchy lasted from 1866, the year of the war against Prussia, until 1914—almost half a century. It was interrupted only by the occupation of Bosnia and Hercegovina in 1878. This military action had been authorized by the Great Powers at the Berlin Congress in the same year, and was expected by the Empire authorities to involve nothing more than the marching in of some military units to take possession. Nevertheless, it assumed the proportions of a war in the face of determined resistance by the Bosnian people, whose consent had of course not been asked. After initial defeats of the Imperial Army, several army corps had to be committed to the "pacification" of Bosnia. Even so, however, the enterprise was not a full-scale war and at any rate had little impact on the economy of the Monarchy. Not counting the Bosnian affair as a war, then, the Habsburg Empire was at peace for forty-eight years. Emperor Franz Joseph came to be known as a "peace-loving" monarch. He, himself, apparently considered himself as such; and he was reproached for his addiction to peace by his war-lusty Chief of the General Staff in the last years of his reign, General Baron (later Field Marshal Count) Franz Conrad von Hoetzendorf.

Although it is mostly Franz Joseph who is singled out as an especially peaceful monarch, the fact is that all the major European powers were at peace during the half-century before World War I. The wars they did wage, such as Great Britain's Afghanistan War in 1878-80, were mostly minor actions, more or less on the scale of the occupation of Bosnia. Only Russia had a real war with Turkey in 1877-78 and another with Japan in 1904-05, and England had the Boer War in 1899-1902. Even these wars were of course incomparably smaller than the subsequent world wars. Germany had no war under the Emperor Wilhelm II before 1914, in fact none from 1871 to 1914. France, too, had no major war, nor had Italy. The Spanish-American War of 1898 was merely an excuse for American seizure of Spanish colonies, with casualties caused not so much by fighting as by disease.

The explanation of this phenomenon of a prolonged peace, so strange in a world of nation-states eternally at each others' throats, is not to be found in a sudden desire for peace on the part of monarchs and ministers, but rather in the desire for profits on the part of bankers and businessmen. Ample profits could be made from investing in railroads, factories, and building. Wars would only interfere with these profits by creating uncertainties, hindering the flow of funds and goods across national boundaries, and by necessitating higher taxes. The capitalists of that era wanted peace, and the international *haute finance*—Rothschild or Hirsch, for instance—did what it could to restrain the warlike propensities of monarchs and of their ministers and generals. How much nineteenth-century capitalists wanted peace is illustrated by the reaction of Vienna speculators to the news of the Austrian Army's rout at Königgratz in 1866. Instead of panicking, they followed the lead of Baron Eduard Todesco, one of the big financiers of the time, who calmly bought securities on the ground that the defeat was a blessing because it assured peace and, consequently, profits. Events proved him right. It was not until after the turn of the century, when investment opportunities seemed to dwindle, that war appeared as an attractive alternative source of profits.

CURRENCY. The currency of the Empire had been unstable throughout most of the nineteenth century. The Napoleonic wars had left the Monarchy with an inconvertible paper currency, which fluctuated greatly in terms of the standard silver coin. Attempts to restore a stable currency had not been successful by the time Franz Joseph became Emperor and in fact not until 1896. In the period from 1848 to 1878, the silver guilder could at times buy as many as 1.53 guilders in paper. In the 1870's the avalanche of silver from newly discovered American mines and from demonetization of silver in the United States, Germany, France, and British India made silver cheap, reduced the premium of silver over paper guilders, and even raised the value of paper guilders above that of silver guilders in 1878. The Austrian mint still permitted the coinage of silver for private account in unlimited quantities. There was, consequently, danger that silver would come pouring into the Austrian mint from other parts of the world which had gone over to the gold standard and where silver was no longer freely coined. This would have lowered the external value (i.e., value in terms of pound, dollar, mark, etc.) of the Austrian guilder. To prevent such depreciation, coinage of silver for private account was stopped in 1879. Following the world trend, the Monarchy adopted a single gold standard in 1892. A new currency, based on the *crown* as the monetary unit, was introduced. One dollar equalled approximately five crowns. The transition to the new gold currency was completed by 1896, and from then on until 1914, the Monarchy had a stable currency, for the first time in a century.[8]

THE EMPIRE ECONOMY ON THE EVE OF WORLD WAR I. By 1914, the economy of the Monarchy was prosperous. The usual picture presented of it shows it as nearly self-sufficient, well balanced, almost a paradise on earth. But the mere fact that the Empire economy collapsed comparatively early in World War I suggests that prewar conditions were not as wonderful as they seemed from a later vantage point. Geographically, the development of the Monarchy had been quite uneven. Wealth and culture were concentrated in a few industrial centers, while most regions remained backward in all respects. In the prosperous industrial sections, as well as in agriculture, wealth was concentrated in a few hands, while the masses lived in poverty. There was a fairly large number of prosperous professional people, shop-keepers, and tradesmen in the German parts of the Monarchy, but the non-German sections lacked a substantial middle class.

EMIGRATION. One indication that conditions were not entirely satisfactory was the large emigration. By 1907 the Monarchy led all countries in number of emigrants. Three hundred and eighty-six thousand persons, mostly Poles, Ruthenians, and Galician Jews, emigrated in that year, 338,000 of them to the United States. In one way this was an advantage to the Empire economy, because it kept unemployment down and improved the balance of payments by the amounts of money the emigrants sent from abroad to their families at home. But on the other hand it drained Galicia of the more intelligent, enterprising workers, "leaving behind the typical lazy and drunken Polish or Ruthenian peasant who, in return for inferior wages, did still more inferior work."[9]

AGRICULTURE. By 1914, Empire population had risen to nearly 53 million (from about 38 million in 1848). This population was

Number of persons employed in various types of activity, as per cent of all persons employed, in selected countries.[10]

Country	Year	Agri-culture	Industry & Handi-craft	Trade & Trans-port	Number of per-sons in labor force as per cent of total population
Austria	1910	53.08	22.64	9.85	56.1
Hungary	1900	68.6	13.4	4.1	45.9
Germany	1907	35.2	37.5	12.4	45.5
Italy	1901	59.4	24.5	7.4	50.1
Switzerland	1901	30.9	44.9	13.0	46.9
France	1901	41.8	35.5	9.5	51.3
Great Britain	1900	13.0	45.8	21.3	44.0
United States	1900	35.9	24.1	16.3	38.4

mostly rural. Whereas Germany had forty-eight cities with more than 100,000 inhabitants, Austria-Hungary had only nine. Despite considerable industrial development, the Monarchy was still predominantly agricultural. About 60 per cent of the working population worked on farms; correspondingly smaller proportions of the working population were employed in industry and trade. The table on page 198 shows how the Monarchy compared with other countries in this respect.

Because a high proportion of the population was in the labor force even before World War I (see table above), no substantial labor reserves could be drawn upon during the war to replace the men called into the army. The consequence was a decline in output, which even in the first two years of the war was severe, but which became catastrophic by 1918. An added difficulty was the continuing low farm productivity, indicated by the comparative figures in the following table.

Output of selected crops, in cwt. per 10,000 square meters.
Average 1908-1912[11]

Country	Wheat	Rye	Barley & Oats
Austria	13.7	13.8	14.6
Hungary	12.6	11.5	12.6
Germany	20.7	17.8	20.1
Norway	16.6	15.9	18.1

Considering that climate and soil in the Monarchy were on the whole more favorable than in Germany and, especially, in Norway, the backwardness of Empire agriculture was even greater than indicated by the figures. This backwardness was due in large measure to the low level of education of the agricultural population. On the eve of World War I, the illiteracy rate was still about 22 per cent for the population as a whole. In 1912, 60 per cent of the agricultural population of Hungary were illiterate.

INDUSTRY. Industry, despite great advances in mechanization, was not highly developed, compared with Western countries. The proportion of the working population employed in industry in the Monarchy was only about one half that of Germany. Of those employed in industry, most still worked in small shops with handicraft methods. This was in part the result of a deliberate policy of the conservative parties which favored small trades as against large factories because the latter bred the radical proletariat, whereas the small tradesmen formed the core of bourgeois conservatism. The products of these small industrial enterprises were famed for their high quality: the fine leather ware of Vienna, Bohemian glass, gloves, fashion goods, in fact all manufactures requiring skills. But wages were low and volume of output small. The same tendency to favor small enterprises showed itself in retail and wholesale trade. Small specialty shops were preferred. There were no large department stores comparable to those in countries to the west of the Monarchy. Wholesale trade, too, was discouraged by restriction and taxation.

CARTELS. In those branches of industry in which the business unit was larger, or in which the factory had superseded the small shop, cartels to control prices and divide markets and profits were widely used in Austria and Hungary. The leading cartels were the sugar cartel and the iron cartel, each embracing all works in their respective industries. There were cartels also in jute, machines, alcohol, petroleum (of which the Monarchy was an important producer), and in many other branches of industry—in all well over a hundred cartels.

EXTERNAL TRADE. The value of exports and imports of the Monarchy had increased from $220 million a year at the time of Franz Joseph's accession to $1,300 million in 1913. In the latter year, comparative figures (imports plus exports) for other countries were:[12]

Great Britain	$5,730 million
Germany	4,506 "
United States	3,594 "
Netherlands	2,462 "
Belgium	1,162 "

The relatively small volume of the Monarchy's external trade should not, however, be taken as an indication of backwardness. The economy of the Empire was more self-sufficient than those of the countries named, except the United States, and consequently less dependent on foreign trade. England and Germany had a foreign trade equal to about 40 per cent of their respective total production; the Monarchy's was perhaps not more than 20 per cent of its gross product. About 45 per cent of Austro-Hungarian foreign trade was with Germany.

TARIFF WARS. Foreign-trade policy was guided largely by the interests of the big landowners. Following the general trend, the free-trade policy of the first three decades of Franz Joseph's reign gave way to increasing protection. A customs war with Romania from 1882 to 1893 broke out after the Monarchy first restricted, then entirely embargoed, cattle imports from Romania, chiefly in the interest of Hungarian cattle raisers. Similar Hungarian pressures led to the so-called hog war with Serbia, lasting until 1911. Imports of cattle and hogs from Serbia were forbidden on veterinarian grounds. The Serbian economy, highly dependent on livestock exports, was able to find other buyers for cattle, but not for hogs, to compensate for the lost Empire market. In 1911, the embargo was modified to allow the annual importation of 50,000 hogs, but only as pork, that is, slaughtered. This belated concession was welcome to the Serbians, but could not erase the deep resentment against the Monarchy caused by the earlier total embargo and the resultant hardships inflicted on the Serbian peasants. The hog war was a major factor leading to the deterioration of Empire-Serbian relations before 1914 and to World War I itself.

ECONOMIC POLICY. The Monarchy's economic policy in general was confused and contradictory. In industry, Hungary subsidized large enterprises, while in the Austrian part of the Monarchy corporations were heavily taxed. Hungarian railroad freight rates were used as protection and subsidy to Hungarian producers, to the detriment of Austrian industry. While Austria generally preferred small business, large establishments were favored in agriculture. The landed aristocracy dominated foreign-trade policy, though industrial interests also influenced tariff legislation in favor of higher duties. The Austrian and Hungarian parts of the Empire supposedly formed one unit in external relations, but occasionally went their separate ways. Thus the Brussels sugar convention of 1902 specifically recognized that Austria and Hungary participated as separate contracting parties. In 1906 Hungary passed a separate tariff (which raised duties on agricultural products—not because of any danger of foreign competition, but merely to raise prices and hence profits of landowners). That Hungary followed independent policies harmful to the Austrian economy indicates that Austria had no advantage from union with Hungary and contradicts claims that such a union was in fact an economic boon to both halves of the Austro-Hungarian Monarchy. Economically, the union had ceased to exist long before the political separation in 1918.

The absence of a coherent and consistent economic policy was perhaps primarily due to the lack of interest and understanding of the top bureaucrats whose task it would have been to formulate policy. They reflected the mentality of the Emperor in this respect, as in everything else. Franz Joseph apparently did not consider it one of his duties to formulate economic policy or to see to it that his ministers formulated it. His ideas of government centered on administration, not on policy; on the police and the army, not on the economy. Economic questions seemed to be entirely outside of his perspective. In an age of explosive economic expansion, his Empire flourished despite his neglect, though, not surprisingly, at a rate below its potential, and below the actual performance of its northern and western neighbors.

CHAPTER 18

The Making of World War I

Of the many conflicts of interests which for years had made a general European war seem inevitable, the one that actually set it off in 1914 was the tension between the Habsburg Monarchy on the one side and Serbia backed by Russia on the other side. This tension had been fed by a series of incidents going back to the beginnings of Franz Joseph's reign.

THE CRIMEAN WAR. After Franz Joseph had ascended the throne amidst war and revolution in 1848, Czar Nicholas I, who then ruled Russia, was the faithful friend who reconquered rebellious Hungary for the Habsburg ruler. The Czar asked no reward for this service to a brother autocrat, but took it for granted that Franz Joseph would be on his side if Russia were to get into war. Opportunity for Franz Joseph to show his gratitude came soon, in the Crimean War between Russia and Turkey from 1853 to 1856. This war was motivated by the Czar's urge to expand his power and possessions in the Balkans at the expense of the crumbling Turkish Empire. Nicholas proclaimed himself the champion of Christians oppressed by infidels and sent his army into Turkey to liberate them. England and France, not sharing the Czar's Christian zeal, came to the aid of Turkey, sending expeditionary forces to the Crimea, where several battles, and finally the fall of Sevastopol, in favor of the Western powers and Turkey, decided the war.

Franz Joseph, instead of siding with his benefactor, came near to declaring war against him when Russian troops occupied the Danube principalities of Moldavia and Walachia, then under Turkish sovereignty, now parts of Romania. The massing of Austrian troops along the Austro-Russian border and an Austrian ultimatum in 1854 forced Russia to withdraw from the Balkans. Nicholas was shocked by Franz Joseph's perfidy. The world was indeed amazed by Austria's ingratitude, as Prince Felix Schwarzenberg had prophesied. Franz Joseph said he did not enjoy playing false to his friend in need. "It is hard to act against former friends," he wrote to his mother on October 8, 1854, "but in politics this is unavoidable. . . ."[1] Austria's interests clashed with those of Russia in the Balkans, and Franz Joseph saw in Russia the Monarchy's "natural enemy." If Russia was not the enemy until then, she became so after this incident. Never did Austria regain the trust of the Russian government. The seeds of the catastrophic war which eventually destroyed both empires were in the betrayal of 1854; subsequent incidents intensified Russian resentment.

Not only the long-run, but also the short-run harvest of Franz Joseph's Crimean War policy turned out to be bitter fruit for the Emperor. Having deeply offended Russia, he made an alliance with France and Great Britain and promised to enter the war on their side, but then reneged on his promise. This infuriated the Western powers, so that they nearly recalled their envoys from Vienna.[2] Napoleon got his revenge by fomenting Italian nationalism against Austria and eventually defeating Franz Joseph at Magenta and Solferino in 1859. By his "naive cunning"[3] in the Crimean War, Franz Joseph lost all potential allies and found himself isolated in the showdown with France and Italy.

OCCUPATION OF BOSNIA AND HERCEGOVINA, 1878. After losing first Lombardy in 1859, then Venetia in 1866, Franz Joseph longed to recover his prestige, as he saw it, by adding some territory to his Empire. The opportunity came in 1876. Russia, again forced to intervene in the Balkans, ostensibly in behalf of the oppressed Christian subjects of the Turkish Sultan, invited the Monarchy to divide the Balkans with her. Austria-Hungary was to liberate Bosnia and Hercegovina and make it an independent state, while Russia would do the same for Bulgaria. Count Andrássy, at that time Franz Joseph's Foreign Minister, rejected the idea of an independent Bosnia because this might give ideas of independence also to the South Slavs in the Monarchy—Dalmatians, Croats, Slovenes. But it was agreed that the Monarchy could occupy Bosnia and Hercegovina after Russia had finished with the Turks, as a reward for Austro-Hungarian neutrality. Russia won against Turkey, and in the Treaty of San Stefano (March 3, 1878) created a new order in the Balkans, declaring Serbia, Montenegro, and Romania entirely independent countries, greatly enlarging Bulgaria, and temporarily occupying that country. Now Andrássy, a Russian-hater ever since Russia's invasion of Hungary in 1849, thought the time propitious for attacking Russia while her armies were still tied down in the Balkans. He accused Russia of having violated her treaty obligations; Franz Joseph professed to be outraged by Czar Alexander II's "infidelity"; indignant letters were exchanged by the two Emperors. War between Austria-Hungary and Russia was averted by the convocation of the Berlin Congress (June 13-July 13, 1878), at which the European powers deprived Russia of most of the fruits of her victory over Turkey, but gave Austria-Hungary a mandate to occupy Bosnia and Hercegovina. Although the two Turkish provinces were only to be occupied by the Monarchy, and not annexed—the Turkish Sultan retaining sovereignty—it was a foregone conclusion that the newly won territories would never willingly be returned by the Monarchy.

The acquisition of Bosnia and Hercegovina has often been presented as an "achievement" for which credit is due to Franz Joseph. The seizure of the two provinces supposedly brought him to the pinnacle of his career. After defeats and territorial losses, the Monarchy had seemingly regained its prestige as a Great Power. But this new glory was bought at a high price.

In the first place, the Monarchy suffered a near-fiasco in occupying the provinces. Instead of receiving its liberators from Turkish oppression with open arms, the population rose against the invading army and defeated it in several engagements. It took a considerable military effort on the part of the Monarchy finally to subdue the Emperor's unwilling new subjects. This display of military weakness largely offset the prestige supposedly won by territorial expansion.

Secondly, Bosnia and Hercegovina were poor countries, inhabited by poor, illiterate people—who stayed poor and illiterate to the end of Habsburg rule. Social conditions in the two provinces remained scandalous. Nothing was done to free the peasants; promises to give towns and villages self-administration were not kept; in 1906 only 14 per cent of all children of school age were in school.[4] Economically and culturally it was no advantage for the Monarchy—this apartment house inhabited by so many quarreling tenants—to receive these two additional poor families, Bosnia and Hercegovina; it lowered the quality of the neighborhood and intensified the dissension among the tenants.

Thirdly, and most disastrously, the acquisition of Bosnia and Hercegovina, though perhaps at the moment a proof of its power, also doomed the Monarchy by arousing the undying enmity of Russia. Russia had again been betrayed by the Monarchy. Whereas the Czar had been largely deprived of his share in the Balkan loot, the Monarchy had got *its* share, and Austria-Hungary had become a Balkan power. A clash with Russia was bound to come. That the incident which eventually set it off occurred in Bosnia (Sarajevo) is symbolic of the role played by that Balkan province in the struggle between the Great Powers.

PANSLAVISM AND SERBIAN NATIONALISM. Though relations between Russia and the Monarchy were strained after 1878 and war threatened on several occasions, still an uneasy peace was managed. Especially during the building of the Trans-Siberian Railway, Russia needed peace with Austria-Hungary. In 1897 the two countries agreed to maintain the status quo in the Balkans and to consult with each other on any proposed territorial changes. For ten years this agreement was the basis of peace between the two countries, and of European peace.

While things remained quiet on the surface, Russia and Serbia nevertheless continued their anti-Habsburg activity. This activity took the form of Panslav and Serbian nationalist agitation. The Panslav movement aimed at uniting all Slav peoples, which in effect would have meant their incorporation into the Russian Empire and the concomitant liquidation of the Habsburg Empire. The Serbian nationalist movement, fomented and supported by Russia, aimed at unifying all South Slav nations into a "Great

Serbia"—the present Yugoslavia—again, of course, requiring the liquidation of the Habsburg Empire. Austro-Hungarian occupation of Bosnia and Hercegovina was a thorn in the side of Serbia, which naturally wanted these South Slav provinces for itself. In 1878, Serbia had consented to the occupation, in exchange for some territory awarded to it by the Berlin Congress on Andrássy's urging. Serbia's Prince (later King) Milan was, in fact, pro-Habsburg, and his son Alexander I, who succeeded him in 1889, was interested in himself rather than in Serbia. But the nationalist movement flowered again after nationalists had murdered Alexander I and installed Peter I Karageorgevich as King of Serbia in 1903. From then on relations between Serbia and the Monarchy steadily deteriorated. Fuel was added to the fire of discord by the Monarchy's trade policy, which hurt the vital Serbian hog industry in the interest of Hungary; and by the impetus given to Russia's Balkan schemes after her Asian expansion drive had been halted by Japan's victory in the Russo-Japanese War of 1904-1905.

ANNEXATION OF BOSNIA AND HERCEGOVINA, 1908. While Russia and Serbia plotted to destroy the Habsburg Monarchy, the Monarchy plotted to destroy Serbia and to fortify Habsburg power in the Balkans. As a first step, Baron Aehrenthal, Franz Joseph's Foreign Minister since 1906, thought the time had come for converting occupation of the two Turkish provinces into annexation—that is, for liquidating nominal Turkish sovereignty over them and incorporating them permanently into the Habsburg Empire. Even as in 1878, many voices in the Monarchy warned against this step. In fact, no national or other interest group supported it. But Franz Joseph, still intent on expunging the stigma of earlier defeats and losses of territory, insisted on "defending his good rights"[5] in Bosnia and Hercegovina; and Aehrenthal was eager for a diplomatic victory which, as it turned out, got him the title of Count in the following year.

On September 16, 1908, Aehrenthal met with the Russian Foreign Minister, Izvolski, who agreed to the annexation on condition that Russia get the Dardanelles with the help of the Monarchy. Russia did not get the Dardanelles, but Aehrenthal at once proclaimed annexation of Bosnia and Hercegovina, Franz

Joseph signing the annexation decree on October 5, 1908. Aehrenthal had acted quickly, precisely because he had expected that Russia would not get the Dardanelles, and he did not want to lose his prize just because Russia lost hers.

The annexation declaration was an affront to Serbia, to Turkey, and to all the signatories of the Berlin Treaty of 1878, since it was a violation of that treaty. Izvolski was furious, claimed Aehrenthal had "cheated" him by not telling him that the annexation had already been prepared when the two Foreign Ministers had made their agreement. The German Emperor Wilhelm II was deeply hurt that Franz Joseph had not consulted with him. King Edward VII of England thought Aehrenthal a "slippery fellow" for confronting the world with a *fait accompli* that could be undone only by war. It was another instance of *"l'Autriche triche."* The Monarchy was not averse to war. The Chief of Staff, General Conrad, fully intended the annexation to provide an opportunity for war against Italy and Serbia. Austria-Hungary mobilized its army. But Russia was not ready, and peace was saved by the willingness of Russia and the other powers to amend the Berlin Treaty so as to legalize the annexation, and by Serbia's acceptance of the decision of the powers.

Aehrenthal's maneuver had been successful. But hatred of the Habsburg Monarchy in Russia and Serbia had now become irreconcilable.

CREATION OF ALBANIA, 1912. Events in the Balkans rapidly moved toward a climax. The Turkish Empire was crumbling. Italy, encouraged by Austria-Hungary's success in annexing Bosnia and Hercegovina, seized Tripoli and Cyrenaica from the Turks in 1911. In 1912, Serbia, Bulgaria, Greece, and Montenegro, with Russia's blessing, pounced on the Turks and virtually drove them out of Europe. Serbia displayed unexpected military power in this war and expanded its territory considerably. In the following year the Balkan states fell out among themselves over the spoils of their joint victory, and again Serbia was victorious. Little Serbia was on the way to becoming a large country.

To block Serbia from reaching out to the Adriatic Sea, Austria-Hungary created the new state of Albania. This again nearly led to war between the Monarchy and Serbia. The Monarchy massed its troops near the Serbian border and presented an ultimatum to Serbia. Peace once more was preserved by Serbia's submission to Austro-Hungarian demands (on October 18, 1913) and also by Germany's reluctance to back her ally in a war about some "miserable Albanian goat pastures." Serbian hatred of the Monarchy reached a fever pitch.

MURDER AT SARAJEVO. Such was the tense situation when on Sunday, June 28, 1914, Archduke Franz Ferdinand, the heir apparent to the Habsburg throne, and his morganatic wife, Duchess Sophie von Hohenberg, were murdered at Sarajevo, the Bosnian capital, by the Bosnian nationalist fanatic Gavrilo Princip, one of several assassins sent to Sarajevo on that day by the "Black Hand," a secret South Slav terrorist organization. Franz Ferdinand had gone to Bosnia for army maneuvers directed against Serbia, despite warnings that an assassination would be attempted.*

The first reaction of the world to the Sarajevo double murder was shock and indignation rather than fear of war. There was no indication that Serbia had anything to do with the assassinations. Princip and his fellow assassins were subjects of the Monarchy, not of Serbia. Soon, however, the Vienna government did make Serbia responsible for the crime, in order to have an excuse for going to war against Serbia. In a meeting of the Austro-Hungarian Council of Ministers on July 7, 1914—a meeting famous in the annals of World War I, since it was then and there that the war was born—the ministers agreed to present Serbia with demands that the Serbian government would have

---

* It was ironical that the Serbian nationalists should have chosen Franz Ferdinand as their victim. He was sympathetic to South Slav aspirations and championed "trialism," i.e., an Austro-Hungarian-South Slav Empire in place of the "dualism" of the Austro-Hungarian Empire. It may be objected that "trialism" was merely a device to head off the South Slav movement for an independent Great Serbia, unconnected with the Habsburg Monarchy, and that this circumstance made Franz Ferdinand an object of special hatred by the South Slav nationalists. According to this reasoning, every partial concession must be regarded as a deliberate attempt to make the more radical solution less attractive. It borders on the absurd to regard Franz Ferdinand as deserving the hostility of the (Austrian) Serbians *because* he was willing to make concessions to them.

to reject, thus giving the Monarchy an excuse for military intervention. Only the Hungarian Minister-President, Count István (Stefan) Tisza, was opposed to this decision. In a letter to the Emperor he wrote: ". . . after painfully scrupulous reflection, I cannot share responsibility for the proposed military aggression against Serbia . . . I must declare that in spite of my devotion to . . . Your Majesty, or I should say more correctly precisely because of this devotion, I could not share the responsibility for the exclusively and aggressively warlike solution."[6]

AUSTRIA-HUNGARY'S ULTIMATUM TO SERBIA. Foreign Minister Count Leopold von Berchtold, after a visit to Ischl to inform the Emperor of the ministers' decision, reported to them that Franz Joseph consented.* Even earlier, on July 5, Franz Joseph had agreed that war against Serbia was necessary, provided that Germany would promise to come in on the Monarchy's side. In the days following the July 7 meeting, a report had come from an Austrian Foreign Ministry official who had been sent to investigate Belgrade's possible responsibility for the assassinations. The official informed his superiors that there was not a shred of evidence that the Serbian government had arranged, abetted, or even known about, the crime. Disregarding this information, the Imperial government, on July 19, drafted the intentionally unacceptable note to Serbia. This time, all the ministers, including Tisza, approved.† The note assumed Serbia's responsibility for the murders and demanded what amounted to surrender of Serbian sovereignty to the Monarchy. Unless unconditionally accepted within forty-eight hours, Austria-Hungary would break off relations with Serbia.

---

* The minutes of the July 7 meeting are signed by Franz Joseph with the comment: "I have taken note of these minutes. Vienna, August 16, 1914." The date is puzzling. Did Franz Joseph not see the minutes until August 16? And if so, did he not know what had been decided at this meeting until that date, almost three weeks after the war had started? Or was he confused about the month, meaning July 16, not August 16? Even if he saw the minutes on July 16, the question remains: why so late?

† Tisza's conversion to the war party has not been fully explained. Perhaps, as Tschuppik suggests, he had become convinced that he could not change his colleagues' decision for war and, instead of washing his hands of it by resigning, decided to stay on to protect Hungarian interests as well as he could. He was murdered on October 30, 1918, having left no oral or written explanation of the circumstances that made him switch sides.[7]

At 6:00 P.M., Thursday, July 23, the Emperor's envoy in Belgrade, Baron Wladimir Giesl, handed the note to the Serbian government. On Saturday, at five minutes to 6:00 P.M., Serbia's Minister-President Nikola Pašić handed his country's reply to Baron Giesl: Serbia accepted almost all conditions, but did not unconditionally accept the note in its entirety, trusting in the good will and chivalry of the Emperor.

In the Austrian view, Serbia had rejected the ultimatum. Half an hour later Baron Giesl and his entire staff, having foreseen Serbia's "rejection" of the note, departed from Belgrade. That same evening, Franz Joseph ordered mobilization against Serbia and Montenegro. Austria-Hungary's declaration of war against Serbia followed on July 28, 1914. Franz Joseph had signed the declaration on the strength of Berchtold's report to him that Serbian troops had already attacked Austro-Hungarian Army units near Temes-Kubin. On the following day Berchtold admitted that the report of Serbian aggression was "unconfirmed" and that he had struck the reference to it from the declaration of war.

In retrospect, Franz Joseph's rejection of Serbia's conciliatory reply to his ultimatum was to be expected as a necessary part of the plot to start a war. At the time, when it was not known outside of the innermost circles of the Vienna government that already on July 7 the Monarchy had decided on war, this rejection and the subsequent declaration of war was unexpected and seemed unreasonable. Emperor Wilhelm II said he would not have gone to war on the basis of Belgrade's reply. Sir Edward Grey, Britain's Foreign Secretary, tried to get the Monarchy to call off the war and offered mediation, promising that Franz Joseph's honor would be vindicated and his prestige enhanced. The German Chancellor, Theobald von Bethmann-Hollweg, pleaded with Berchtold to accept the British offer. But Franz Joseph decided that the war must go on.

CHAPTER 19

The Peace Emperor

In a manifesto issued to his peoples on July 29, 1914, Emperor Franz Joseph said: "It was My most fervent desire to dedicate the years which by the Grace of God are still left to Me to works of peace and to preserve My peoples from the heavy sacrifice of a war. Divine Providence has decreed otherwise. The machinations of a hate-filled enemy force Me, after long years of peace, to reach for the sword to preserve the honor of My Monarchy, to defend its prestige and power position, to secure its property. . . . I follow the path of duty . . ."

These words correspond to the image of the old Emperor as a man of peace—as well as a man of honor and duty—an image supported by his benevolent, grandfatherly appearance, and by his great age itself, a time of life rarely associated with bellicosity. A peaceful man, many of his contemporaries believed him to be, and many people still believe him to have been. It is the image of him spread by historians and biographers, and the image which Franz Joseph must have had of himself when he called himself a "peace emperor." Yet it was he who plunged Europe into World War I. How can the peaceful words be reconciled with the bellicose actions? Several explanations are possible.

WAS FRANZ JOSEPH FORCED INTO WAR? One possible explanation is that the manifesto truthfully stated the situation or, at least, Franz Joseph's view of the situation: He was forced into war by Serbia, by the demands of his honor, prestige, and duty. This interpretation, however, need not be taken seriously. The facts already recited are sufficient to show that Serbia surely did not force Franz Joseph into war. The machinations were the Monarchy's, not Serbia's. And as for honor and prestige and duty, these too did not "force" Franz Joseph into war, for if they had, why would the Emperor have made his going to war conditional on Germany's support? Had German support not been guaranteed, would "the machinations of a hate-filled enemy" and honor and prestige and duty still have "forced" Franz Joseph to declare war? The answer supplies itself: It was not a question of being forced at all, but of deliberately choosing war as seemingly advantageous to the Monarchy at the time.

Was Franz Joseph Mentally Competent? Was the Emperor perhaps "forced" in another sense, namely forced by his attendants to sign a document the meaning of which he did not understand? According to some reports, the Emperor no longer had a clear mind in 1914 and signed whatever was put before him without knowing what it was. One story has it that when the declaration of war against Serbia was submitted to him, he muttered: "What? Again these damned Prussians!" Evidence on the question of Franz Joseph's condition in his last years is contradictory. Some say he was completely senile; others that he was entirely lucid and mentally alert until his death. If he had really been incapacitated, it is unlikely that his heir apparent, the ambitious and impatient Franz Ferdinand, who resented the old man's tenacity, would have permitted him to stick to the throne.

Was Franz Joseph Misled by His Ministers? Perhaps the Emperor, though mentally alert, was isolated and a prey to the schemes of his ministers and other advisers? Foreign Minister Berchtold, for instance, misinformed him about Serbia's alleged attack on Imperial military units, and perhaps kept important information, such as Grey's mediation offer, from him. That ministers misinformed him is undoubtedly true, but it is also a truism. Rulers are always prisoners of their advisers, who may feed them false information or withhold information from them. From whom else could rulers receive information and advice?

Did Franz Joseph Think War Advantageous? Perhaps the Emperor was indeed a man of peace, but only in the sense in which most rulers are: He was for peace as long as his or his country's honor or safety did not "force him to reach for the sword"—which, translated into less highflown words, means that he was for war only when he thought it was to his advantage. He did not always see war as a desirable enterprise, but he had seen it so several times in his reign, and he probably saw it so in 1914.

WAR HAWKS AROUND FRANZ JOSEPH. There are rulers, and advisers of rulers, who are for war always and on principle, though of course even these professional war hawks tend to cloak their bellicosity with arguments of morality or expediency. The chief representatives of this category are generals, whose trade, after all, is war. It is as natural for them to urge, on every occasion, their country's need for war as it was for Molière's goldsmith, Monsieur Josse, to argue that only jewels would restore the health of the play's ailing heroine.*

Of the many professional war agitators in the Monarchy during the last few years of Franz Joseph's reign, none was more of a war hawk than the Chief of Staff, General Franz Conrad von Hoetzendorf. When measured by the standards of General Conrad, Franz Joseph may well appear as a man of peace. To Conrad, his own government as well as that of allied Germany, seemed in a veritable peace conspiracy. Germany, he complained, was responsible for permitting the crisis of 1913, which had almost led to war, to peter out without one; in the future, he insisted, the government of the Monarchy would have to see to it that Germany accommodate herself to the requirements of the Monarchy! Conrad berated Berchtold for not seeking war with Russia.[1] In his eagerness for war with Italy, he sent staff officers to spy in Italy, which naturally made the Italians, then nominal allies of the Monarchy, suspicious, and elicited anguished protests from the Austro-Hungarian Ambassador in Rome. Conrad's incessant prodding of Foreign Minister Aehrenthal to arrange a war with Italy and Serbia eventually led Franz Joseph to remonstrate with him: "These continued attacks" (on Aehrenthal), Franz Joseph said to Conrad, "especially reproaches because of Italy and the Balkans

---

* *L'Amour Médecin,* Act 1, scene 1.

... these are directed against me. I make [foreign] policy, this is *my* policy."[2] Franz Joseph dismissed Conrad as Chief of Staff on November 30, 1911, soon after this conversation, but reinstated him a year later, on December 12, 1912, on Franz Ferdinand's urging.

FRANZ JOSEPH'S FOREIGN POLICY BELLICOSE. Peace-loving as Franz Joseph may appear in comparison with Conrad, he was not quite so peace-loving a ruler as he himself and his panegyrists proclaimed. As his angry outburst against Conrad indicates, it was he, the Emperor, who made foreign policy. This, and the army, were the prerogatives which he had not surrendered to any parliament. As his censure and (temporary) firing of Conrad also shows, Franz Joseph did really personally control foreign policy—at least until the end of 1911, when he had the scene with Conrad. If Aehrenthal had not had Franz Joseph's approval, if he had not followed the Emperor's wishes in carrying out the Monarchy's foreign policy, Franz Joseph could have, and presumably would have, dismissed Aehrenthal. Austro-Hungarian foreign policy was Franz Joseph's policy.

Now, Austro-Hungarian foreign policy, that is, Franz Joseph's foreign policy, in the last few years of his reign, could not easily be stigmatized as "peaceful," any more than the foreign policy pursued in his earlier years. Figuratively, Franz Joseph always had his finger on the trigger; he was quick to send ultimatums and to threaten military action if his wishes were not respected. Rankling defeats in 1849, 1859, and 1866, and the initial fiasco in Bosnia in 1878, undoubtedly made Franz Joseph more cautious in later years. But the prolonged peace for which the latter part of Franz Joseph's reign is noted was not due to a policy of good will toward all neighbors or to an absence of bellicosity. This prolonged peace, it should be remembered (see pp. 196-197), was kept not only by Franz Joseph, but by all the European Great Powers. Germany, generally regarded as bellicose, stayed out of war even longer than Austria-Hungary—from 1871 to 1914. (World War I was Wilhelm II's first war, though he had been Emperor for twenty-six years; Franz Joseph, in the first twenty-six years of his reign, had four wars.) But far from being dedicated to peace in this period in which there happened to be no major war, the European powers stumbled from crisis to crisis in a game of "chicken," in which one or the other, fearing disaster, yielded in the last moment—until one time neither side yielded and there was a collision. The two decades preceding 1914 were especially tense; alliances were being formed; armies and navies were being prepared for the showdown by all the Great Powers—including the Monarchy.

For years the Monarchy had followed an "activist" policy, meaning essentially a policy leading to a victorious war, which would solve the Empire's increasingly troublesome internal difficulties. Internal corruption and decay were to be cured by an external bloodletting—a mirage much like that pursued by the Czarist regime in Russia. The specific aims were to conquer Serbia in order to "solve" the South Slav problem (consisting of the irrepressible desire of these peoples, fomented by the nationalist activities of their intellectual leaders, to be out of the Monarchy and to form their own independent state, as they eventually did in 1918); to have a dominant position in the Balkans; and to wage preventive war against Italy to forestall defection of the Italian population still under Habsburg rule, or even to win back (at least Archduke Franz Ferdinand seems to have had this wish-dream) the lost Italian provinces. How anxious the Vienna government was to foment war against Serbia was illustrated by an incident in 1909: the well-known historian Heinrich Friedjung had written articles in the leading Vienna newspaper, *Neue Freie Presse*, denouncing anti-Monarchy agitation emanating from Serbia. He named names and said he could prove his accusations with documents. Some Serbs and Croats who felt wronged by his accusations took him to court, where Friedjung presented documents furnished him by the Austro-Hungarian Legation in Belgrade. But these documents now turned out to have been forgeries! The effect of the trial was to increase Serb hatred and to degrade the Monarchy even further in the eyes of the world.[3]

Not only the extremist General Conrad, but all the members of the top cabinet (Foreign Minister, Austrian Minister-President, Hungarian Minister-President, Joint Ministers of War and Finance, Chief of Staff) were for war. Berchtold had said: "I do

not want to expose myself to the reproach, which Aehrenthal had to hear in 1908, of having prevented a reckoning with Serbia."[4]*
At the fateful meeting on July 7, 1914, the Joint Minister of War, General Baron Krobatin, regretted that the Monarchy had already missed two opportunities for solving the Serbian question by war; Count Stürgkh, the Austrian Minister-President, urged that a "psychological situation" had been created which absolutely called for war with Serbia; how such a war was to be started was a matter of detail, but in any case quick action was required. Bilinski, the Joint Minister of Finance, also favored war, for no better reason than that the military governor of Bosnia, General Potiorek, whom he must have regarded as an authority on the subject (though the General's competence was questioned by other participants of the conference), had for years urged an armed showdown with Serbia. The Hungarian Minister-President Tisza, as already mentioned, was the only dissenter. Tschuppik[6] ascribes this to Tisza's Calvinist rectitude and claims that Tisza was the only "man of character" in the group. The minutes of the historic meeting reveal that this "man of character" pleaded with his colleagues, not that they refrain from starting a war with Serbia by dispatching an unacceptable ultimatum to that country, but that they formulate the ultimatum in such a way as not to make its unacceptability clearly recognizable, since "otherwise we would have no possible legal justification for a declaration of war." What he wanted, apparently, was more hypocrisy, not less bellicosity.

The responsible leaders of the Monarchy who spoke and acted in this manner were the spokesmen of Franz Joseph's policy—for it was *his* policy, as he insisted; and though he *said* that he did

---

* Berchtold is customarily identified as the real instigator of World War I. For instance S. L. A. Marshall writes: "Berchtold . . . the deep-eyed villain of the 1914 summer's tragedy . . . betrayed the peace deliberately by lying, deceiving, double-dealing and committing folly unequaled."[5]
That he maneuvered Austria-Hungary into war "deliberately by lying," etc., is unquestionably true. Whether he "committed folly" is questionable; such a judgment must be based on an understanding of his aims. From his point of view, plunging the world into war may have seemed wise. But wise or foolish, Berchtold was certainly not alone in wanting the war and plotting to bring it about. The entire Council of Ministers of the Monarchy, and Franz Joseph himself, "betrayed the peace deliberately."

not want war he surrounded himself with war hawks and approved their decision to wage a war of aggression in full knowledge that there was no legal justification for it. Franz Joseph's part in the plotting of the war which was "forced on him by the machinations of a hate-filled enemy" is further attested by the revelation of Baron Spitzmüller, probably the most Byzantine of all of Franz Joseph's adulators, that it was the Emperor himself who persuaded Tisza, the lone dissenter at the July 7 meeting, to change his mind and vote for war.[7]

AUSTRIA NOT ALONE RESPONSIBLE FOR WORLD WAR I. The facts here recited show the part Franz Joseph and his government had in launching aggressive war against Serbia. It should be added at once, however, that Austria could not claim sole credit for having started World War I. Other rulers and statesmen were also plotting war. The Russian Foreign Minister Sasonov admittedly steered toward a general European war; France supported Russian aggression plans. That all belligerents had a share in bringing about the war of 1914-18 has been stressed by most historians who dealt with the question and has been thoroughly established.

DID FRANZ JOSEPH DECIDE TO MAKE PEACE IN 1917? Baron Stefan Kray, one of Franz Joseph's secretaries during the last years of his reign, wrote that "there can be no doubt that already in the fall of 1916, Franz Joseph in all seriousness considered making peace. I have subsequently heard from one of his confidants that exactly one month before his death, on October 21, 1916, when he was informed of the assassination of the Austrian Minister-President Count Stürgkh by the Social Democrat Friedrich Adler, he saw in this fact the first visible sign of beginning defeatism and, under the impact of this impression, declared he wanted to end the war in the coming spring. It can hardly be doubted that Emperor Franz Joseph with the help of his high authority recognized by all the world, and putting the full weight of his universally beloved and revered personality into the scales, would have succeeded . . ."[8] Approximately the same account is given by Franz Joseph's valet, who puts the Emperor's remark on the day of his death (not thirty days before his death), says it was made to Minister-President Koerber, and attributes it to information supplied to the Emperor by himself, the valet, about the sufferings and growing disaffection of the people.[9]

The report about Franz Joseph's determination to make peace is puzzling on several counts. (1) Was the Emperor's "honor," etc., which allegedly necessitated the war in the first place, satisfied by two years of bloodletting without victory? Were not the hate-filled enemies continuing even more than in 1914 to plot the destruction of his house and his Empire? (2) Why should the sufferings of the people move Franz Joseph to make peace in 1916, when in 1914 he knew, and stated in his manifesto, that war means suffering? (3) If the Emperor could have made peace in 1916 by reason of being popular and revered in the enemy countries, could he not have avoided war on the same grounds in 1914? (4) If the Emperor had it within his power to make peace, why only "in the spring" of 1917? Why not at once? What did he expect to gain from continuing the slaughter for a few months?

The assertion that Franz Joseph wanted to stop the war lacks conviction. The fact at any rate is that he did not stop it and made no attempts to stop it. There is no proof that he ordered his army command to arrange for a truce, or his Foreign Minister to arrange peace talks with his enemies. Moreover, it is highly doubtful that Franz Joseph did in fact have the power to make peace, that is, to surrender to his enemies. By the end of 1916 things had gone too far to be called off merely because of a change of heart of the old Emperor. In July 1914 he could have restrained the war hawks in his own government, if he had wanted to do so, and his German ally would have been grateful to him for it. But then he showed no desire to prevent war. By November 1916 the army ruled the Monarchy, and the German Army ruled the Austrian Army. One may easily imagine how the generals—in the Monarchy and in Germany—would have reacted to any action on the part of Franz Joseph to make peace. It is harder to imagine Franz Joseph wanting to take such action.

Course of the War Until Franz Joseph's Death. As in his previous wars, so also in World War I, Franz Joseph's armies at first suffered reverses. The army under General Potiorek that was to chastise the Serbians was badly mauled by them instead. On the Eastern front, the Russians occupied most of Galicia and threatened to invade Hungary. It was again a case of "lions led by asses." Chief of Staff General Conrad, billed as a great strategist, was defeated everywhere, and his fellow war conspirators—Berchtold, Stürgkh, and Tisza—wanted him fired for incompetence. Conrad blamed his defeats on the inadequacy of the army—a strange excuse to be pleaded by a general whose job it was to prepare the army adequately. However much the armies were beaten, the General's personal success was attested by his being made a Field Mashal and a Count. The man who was fired was not he, but Berchtold, who was replaced by one of Tisza's protégés, Baron (later Count) Burián—a more "energetic" man.

Burián's immediate problem was to keep Italy—the Monarchy's ally!—from joining the host of the Central Powers' enemies. Germany's suggestion that the Monarchy cede the part of South Tirol inhabited by Italians to Italy, in order to keep this ostensible ally at least neutral, was huffily rejected by Franz Joseph as inconsistent with his honor—just as he had rejected the opportunity to buy Italy off in 1866 by letting that country buy Venetia from him. Franz Joseph was not going to barter away his subjects! When it became clear that Italy was actually going to attack the Monarchy, and Burián belatedly, and in disregard of Franz Joseph's honor, did offer South Tirol to Italy after all, it was too late—again as in 1866. Italy had signed a treaty with England and France on April 25, 1915, and declared war against Austria on May 23, 1915. As the Monarchy was already reeling under Serbian and Russian blows, Italy could expect an easy military victory. In this expectation the Italians were disappointed; they were never able to break through the Austrian defenses, but eventually, though after Franz Joseph's death, were routed by the Central Powers and had to call for French and British military assistance.

Elsewhere, too, the initial reverses suffered by Franz Joseph's armies were followed by victories, though with the assistance of German troops and under the command of German generals. The Russians were driven out of Austro-Hungarian territory, and all of Serbia was occupied, as was also Romania, which had declared war against the Central Powers in August 1916. Romanian troops invaded Transylvania, but were driven out again and decisively defeated in November 1916 by German and Bulgarian armies.

PORTENTS OF REVOLUTION. By the end of November 1916, the military situation of the Monarchy appeared favorable. But military victories were deceptive. Economic conditions were even then verging on catastrophe. Production had declined, the food supply was dwindling, chiefly because of a labor shortage, as millions of men were in the army, and many had been killed or incapacitated. The Monarchy's grain harvest in 1916 was only one-half its prewar volume. Starvation was already sapping the strength and the will to win of the people. Hungary, still with plenty of food, shut herself off from the rest of the Empire, instead of relieving the shortages in Cisleithania. There were hunger riots and protest marches to Schönbrunn, where Franz Joseph was about to end his earthly days. The Slavs in the Monarchy had been opposed to the war from the beginning; most of them sympathized with the enemy, some openly. Treason was rampant among the Czechs. But now the German Austrians, too, became restive. Parliament had been closed ever since 1913. There was no legal way for popular resentments to express themselves. Government became increasingly authoritarian and repressive, surveillances and arrests mounted. On October 21, 1916, Friedrich Adler, the son of Austria's Socialist leader, Dr. Victor Adler, assassinated the Austrian Minister-President Count Stürgkh in a desperate attempt to shake up the government and to arouse the masses to effective protest against intolerable conditions.

These were portents of revolution—the revolution which the youthful Franz Joseph had beaten down in 1848 and 1849, but whose return he had feared throughout his reign. Now, at the end of his life, it was knocking at his door again. Now, as sixty-eight years before, Franz Joseph's Empire was in convulsions, in war and violence, run by generals and policemen. But this time there would be no Schwarzenberg, no Windisch-Grätz, no Czar Nicholas—and no youthful Franz Joseph—to save the Habsburg Empire. This time it was the end.

FRANZ JOSEPH'S DEATH. While his Empire was dying, Franz

Joseph, too, was approaching his end. He had been in good health most of his life, was rarely ill; it was only in his last years that he had repeatedly suffered from coughs. The cough came again in early November 1916. Franz Joseph knew he would succumb this time, but he kept up his routine of signing papers and receiving visitors to his last day. Weak and feverish, he was taken to bed. He reminded his valet to wake him at the usual time: "tomorrow morning at half past three!" But there was no tomorrow. Franz Joseph died at five minutes after nine o'clock on the evening of November 21, 1916, at Schönbrunn, the place of his birth.

A hearse drawn by eight black horses, preceded by a squadron of Hussars and flanked by members of the Imperial Guard, left Schönbrunn at ten o'clock at night on November 27. Along the way his fast horses had so often taken Franz Joseph, crowds were waiting to see him drive slowly past for the last time. In ghostly procession the dead Emperor was taken to the Hofburg. There he lay in state until November 30, when he was entombed in the Habsburg family crypt in the nearby monastery of the Capuchin order, in accordance with the rules of court etiquette.

Titles and Territories
of Franz Joseph on
His Accession to the Throne

The awesome list of titles claimed by Franz Joseph in his proclamation of December 2, 1848 (see p. 10) testifies to the exalted station of His Imperial and Royal Majesty and reflects
the feudal and dynastic origins, as well as the geographic
composition and the extent of the empire he inherited. Most of
the titles claimed by Franz Joseph corresponded to territories
over which he ruled, though some did not.

With the first and grandest of his titles—Emperor of Austria—
Franz Joseph proclaimed himself ruler over all the enumerated
kingdoms, duchies, and principalities. The reason why he called
himself Emperor of Austria rather than, for instance, Emperor
of Bohemia or Emperor of Hungary, is that the Archduchy of
Austria—a small part, but the center, of the Empire, with the
capital city of Vienna—was the nucleus around which the Habsburgs had built their empire over the centuries. They were the
"House of Austria." Franz Joseph continued to bear the title
"Archduke of Austria" as ruler of Austria proper; as ruler of
the whole galaxy of kingdoms belonging to him as the Head of
the House of Austria he was a king of kings—an emperor—the
Emperor of Austria.

The title "Emperor of Austria" was a recent one (see pp. 85-
86). For centuries the Habsburgs had claimed a virtual monop-
oly of the title and dignity of "Holy Roman Emperor," which

was what the German Kings or Emperors were called (see page 149). But in 1804, when Napoleon crowned himself "Emperor of the French" and regarded himself as the new Charlemagne, the Emperor Franz II, grandfather of Franz Joseph, saw that his days as Holy Roman Emperor were numbered. Not wishing to give up the Imperial title, he assumed the hereditary title "Emperor of Austria." This corresponded better to reality: He was in fact the ruler of the many realms which composed his newly designated empire, whereas he had no power over the German kings and princes; and the title "Holy Roman Emperor" had for a long time been a hollow, though hallowed honor. As expected, Napoleon did demand the liquidation of this historic curiosity. Franz abdicated as German Emperor on August 6, 1806. The nearly 900-year-old Holy Roman Empire of the German nation had ceased to exist.

Of the several kingdoms claimed by Franz Joseph, those of Illyria and Lodomeria were fictional. No such kingdoms existed as administrative units. Illyria was a vague, collective designation for Carinthia, Carniola, the Windish* March, Friuli, Trieste, Istria, Gradisca, Gorizia, Dalmatia, Dubrovnik (Ragusa), Zadar (Zara), and Kotor (Cattaro)—possessions claimed separately in Franz Joseph's list and approximately embracing the Empire provinces inhabited by South Slavs. Napoleon had briefly seized some of these in 1805 and 1809 and had given them their ancient name "Illyria." Lodomeria was a principality in Volhynia, which later became a division of Galicia.

The title "King of Jerusalem" was a pious pretense. The city and the Holy Land had been under Turkish rule for centuries; the "Latin Kingdom of Jerusalem" had ceased to exist in 1291. But ever since the Emperor Frederick II had entered the city and crowned himself King of Jerusalem in 1229, the German Emperors, and after them the Emperors of Austria, had held on to the title "King of Jerusalem," perhaps for the prestige it gave them among their devout Christian subjects.

The two Lusatias, of which Franz Joseph claimed to be Margrave, had been lost to Saxony by his ancestor Ferdinand II in 1635. Also lost were Kyburg and Habsburg—the possession from which the dynasty had derived its name. Lorraine, from which the dynasty of Habsburg-Lorraine derived its second name, had been surrendered in exchange for Tuscany in 1737. Tuscany,

---

* An ancient name for "Slovenian."

Modena, and Parma with Piacenza and Guastalla belonged to branches of the house and not to its head, and thus were not under the jurisdiction of the Emperor, though he claimed the titles. Hohenembs and Sonnenberg, not easily found on ordinary maps, and the cities of Trento (Trient), Bressanone (Brixen), Feldkirch and Bregenz are located in Tirol and Vorarlberg; Teschen is a city in Silesia; Friuli is a region in Venetia; Dubrovnik (Ragusa), Zadar (Zara), and Kotor (Cattaro) are cities in Dalmatia; the Windish March, no longer known by that name, is a part of Carniola.

One territory belonging to Franz Joseph's Empire, but not represented in his list of titles, was the Military Frontier. As the name indicates, this was a strip of land under military government, set up in the seventeenth and eighteenth centuries as a "living wall" to keep out the Turks. It was later merged with Hungary and today forms part of Yugoslavia and Romania.

Franz Joseph's Chief Ministers

From the beginning of his reign to the Settlement with Hungary in 1867, Emperor Franz Joseph's chief ministers were his Foreign Minister and his Minister-President (in some cases bearing the title Minister of State, Chancellor of the Empire, or Guiding Minister). Mostly, the Foreign Minister was also the Minister-President.

After the Settlement with Hungary divided the Empire into Austria (Cisleithania) and Hungary (Transleithania), there were three governments in the Monarchy: the Austrian government, the Hungarian government, and the Joint Austro-Hungarian government. The Joint Austro-Hungarian government had jurisdiction over foreign affairs, the Joint Austro-Hungarian Army, and joint finances, with a Joint Minister in charge of each of these three departments. The Minister of Foreign Affairs presided over the Council of Ministers called to discuss questions of concern to the Monarchy as a whole, and including the three Joint Ministers, and the Austrian and Hungarian Minister-Presidents.

Hungary had its own government in 1848-49, but it was revolutionary and not recognized by Franz Joseph. From 1849 to 1867, Hungary was administered by Austrian military governors.

Franz Joseph's Foreign Ministers:

1. Prince Felix Schwarzenberg	Nov. 21, 1848–Apr. 5, 1852
2. Count Karl Ferdinand von Buol-Schauenstein	Apr. 11, 1852–Mar. 17, 1859
3. Count Johann Bernhard von Rechberg	Mar. 17, 1859–Oct. 27, 1864
4. Count Alexander von Mensdorff-Pouilly	Oct. 27, 1864–Oct. 30, 1866

5. Baron (later Count) Friedrich
   Ferdinand von Beust
   (Chancellor of the Empire)   Oct. 30, 1866–Nov. 8, 1871
6. Count Julius Andrássy   Nov. 14, 1871–Oct. 8, 1879
7. Baron Heinrich von Haymerle   Oct. 8, 1879–Oct. 10, 1881
8. Count Gustav Kálnoky   Nov. 20, 1881–May 2, 1895
9. Count Agenor von Goluchowski   May 16, 1895–Oct. 24, 1906
10. Baron (later Count) Alois
    Lexa von Aehrenthal   Oct. 24, 1906–Feb. 17, 1912
11. Count Leopold Berchtold   Feb. 17, 1912–Jan. 13, 1915
12. Baron (later Count) Stefan Burián   Jan. 13, 1915–Dec. 22, 1916

Franz Joseph's Austrian Minister–Presidents:

1. Prince Felix Schwarzenberg   Nov. 21, 1848–April 5, 1852
2. Count Karl Ferdinand von Buol-
   Schauenstein (Guiding Minister) Apr. 11, 1852–Aug. 21, 1859
3. Count Johann Bernhard von
   Rechberg (Guiding Minister)   Aug. 21, 1859–Feb. 4, 1861
4. Anton von Schmerling
   (Minister of State)   Feb. 4, 1861–June 26, 1865
5. Count Alexander von
   Mensdorff-Pouilly*   June 26, 1865–July 27, 1865
6. Count Richard Belcredi   July 27, 1865–Feb. 7, 1867
7. Baron (later Count) Friedrich
   Ferdinand von Beust
   (Chancellor of the Empire)   Feb. 7, 1867–Dec. 30, 1867
8. Prince Karl Auersperg   Dec. 30, 1867–Apr. 12, 1870
9. Count Alfred Potocki   Apr. 12, 1870–Feb. 4, 1871
10. Count Karl von Hohenwart*   Feb. 6, 1871–Oct. 30, 1871
11. Baron Ludwig von Holzgethan*   Oct. 30, 1871–Nov. 25, 1871
12. Prince Adolf Auersperg   Nov. 25, 1871–Feb. 15, 1879
13. Karl von Stremayr*   Feb. 15, 1879–Aug. 12, 1879
14. Count Eduard Taaffe   Aug. 12, 1879–Nov. 11, 1893
15. Prince Alfred Windisch-Grätz   Nov. 11, 1893–June 19, 1895
16. Count Erich von Kielmansegg*   June 19, 1895–Sept. 30, 1895
17. Count Kasimir Felix Badeni   Sept. 30, 1895–Nov. 30, 1897
18. Baron Paul Gautsch   Nov. 30, 1897–Mar. 5, 1898
19. Count Franz von Thun   Mar. 5, 1898–Oct. 2, 1899
20. Count Manfred von Clary   Oct. 2, 1899–Dec. 21, 1899
21. Heinrich von Wittek*   Dec. 21, 1899–Jan. 18, 1900
22. Ernst von Koerber   Jan. 19, 1900–Dec. 27, 1904
23. Baron Paul Gautsch   Jan. 1, 1905–Apr. 30, 1906
24. Prince Konrad Hohenlohe-
    Waldenburg-Schillingsfürst   May 2, 1906–May 28, 1906
25. Baron Max Wladimir von Beck   June 2, 1906–Nov. 7, 1908
26. Baron Richard von Bienerth   Nov. 25, 1908–June 28, 1911
27. Baron Paul Gautsch   June 28, 1911–Oct. 28, 1911
28. Count Karl von Stürgkh   Nov. 3, 1911–Oct. 21, 1916
29. Ernst von Koerber   Oct. 31, 1916–Dec. 13, 1916

---

* Indicates Interim Ministry.

Franz Joseph's Hungarian Minister-Presidents:

1.	Count Julius Andrássy	Feb. 17, 1867–Nov. 14, 1871
2.	Count Melchior Lónyay	Nov. 14, 1871–Dec. 4, 1872
3.	Josef Szlávy von Okány	Dec. 4, 1872–Mar. 1, 1874
4.	Stefan Bittó von Sárosfalva	Mar. 21, 1874–Feb. 28, 1875
5.	Baron Adalbert von Wenckheim	Mar. 2, 1875–Oct. 20, 1875
6.	Koloman Tisza von Borosjenö	Oct. 20, 1875–Mar. 13, 1890
7.	Count Julius Szapáry	Mar. 13, 1890–Nov. 17, 1892
8.	Alexander Wekerle	Nov. 17, 1892–Jan. 14, 1895
9.	Baron Desider von Bánffy	Jan. 14, 1895–Feb. 26, 1899
10.	Koloman Széll	Feb. 26, 1899–June 27, 1903
11.	Count Karl Khuen-Héderváry	June 27, 1903–Nov. 3, 1903
12.	Count Stefan Tisza	Nov. 3, 1903–June 11, 1905
13.	Baron Geisa von Fejérváry	June 18, 1905–Apr. 8, 1906
14.	Alexander Wekerle	Apr. 8, 1906–Jan. 17, 1910
15.	Count Karl Khuen-Héderváry	Jan. 17, 1910–Apr. 16, 1912
16.	Ladislaus von Lukácz	Apr. 22, 1912–June 5, 1913
17.	Count Stefan Tisza	June 10, 1913–June 15, 1917

Source: Spuler, Bertold: *Sovereigns and Governments of the World*, Part II, 2nd edition. Würzburg, A. G. Ploetz, Verlag, 1962.

APPENDIX C

Habsburg Rulers

Appendix C
Habsburg Rulers
(Dates in parentheses refer to their reigns)

As German Kings

Rudolf I—1218-91 (1273-91)

(son) Albrecht I—1248-1308 (1298-1308)

(son) Friedrich III, The Handsome
1286?-1330 (1314-30)

Albrecht II—1397-1439 (1438-39)

As German (Holy Roman) Emperors

(cousin) Friedrich III—1415-93
(King 1440-86)
(Emperor 1452-93)

(son) Maximilian I—1459-1519
(King 1486-1519)
(Emperor 1508-19)

As Dukes of Austria

Albrecht I (1282-1308)

Friedrich I (1308-30)

(brother) Albrecht II, The Wise—1298-1358
(1330-58)

(brother) Albrecht III (in Lower and
Upper Austria—1365-95)

(son) Rudolf IV, The Founder—1339-65 (1358-65)

(brother) Leopold III (in Styria, Carinthia,
Tirol, etc., 1365-86)

(son of Albrecht III) Albrecht IV—(1395-1404)

(son) Albrecht V—1397-1439
(1404-39)

As Archdukes of Austria

Friedrich V (1439-93)

Maximilian I (1493-1519)

Charles I (1519-22)

Ferdinand I (1522-64)

Maximilian II (1564-76)

Rudolf V (1576-1612)

Matthias (1612-19)

Ferdinand II (1619-37)

Ferdinand III (1637-57)

Leopold I (1657-1705)

Joseph I (1705-11)

Karl II (1711-40)

(daughter) Maria Theresa—1717-80 (1740-80)

Joseph II (1780-90)

Leopold II (1790-92)

Franz I (1792-1835)

As Emperors of Austria

Franz I (1804-35)

(son) Ferdinand I—1793-1875 (1835-48)
(nephew) Franz Joseph I—1830-1916 (1848-1916)
(grandnephew) Karl I—1887-1922 (1916-18)

(grandson) Charles V—1500-1558 (1519-56)
(brother) Ferdinand I—1503-64 (1556-64)
(son) Maximilian II—1527-1576 (1564-76)
(son) Rudolf II—1552-1612 (1576-1612)
(brother) Matthias—1557-1619 (1612-19)
(cousin) Ferdinand II—1578-1637 (1619-37)
(son) Ferdinand III—1608-57 (1637-57)
(son) Leopold I—1640-1705 (1658-1705)
(son) Joseph I—1678-1711 · (1705-11)
(brother) Karl VI—1685-1740 (1711-40)

[Husband of Maria Theresa, Franz Stephan of Lorraine 1708-65
—German Emperor Franz I (1745-65)]

(son) Joseph II—1741-90 (1765-90)
(brother) Leopold II—1747-92 (1790-92)
(son) Franz II—1768-1835 (1792-1806)

Notes

Preface

1. Spitzmüller, Dr. Alexander Freiherr von, *Kaiser Franz Joseph als Staatsmann*, Wien, Manzsche Verlags- und Universitäts-Buchhandlung, 1935. p. 9.

2. Gopčevič, Spiridion, *Österreichs Untergang-Die Folge von Franz Josefs Missregierung*, Berlin, Verlag von Karl Sigismund, 1920, p. 240 *et passim*.

Chapter 1

1. Ernst, Dr. Otto, *Franz Joseph I. in seinen Briefen*, Wien, Rikola Verlag, 1924, p. 7.

Chapter 2

1. *Allgemeine Zeitung*, Augsburg, December 7, 1848.

2. Corti, Egon Caesar Conte, *Vom Kind zum Kaiser, Kindheit und erste Jugend Kaiser Franz Josephs I. und seiner Geschwister*, Graz-Salzburg Wien, Verlag Anton Pustet, 1950, p. 331.

3. *Ibid.*, p. 336.

Chapter 4

1. Charmatz, Richard, *Lebensbilder aus der Geschichte Österreichs*, Wien, Danubia Verlag, 1947.

2. Fischer, Ernst, *Österreich 1848. Probleme der demokratischen Revolution in Österreich*, Wien, Stern-Verlag, 1946, p. 93.

3. Corti, *Vom Kind zum Kaiser*, p. 287.

Chapter 5

1. Tschuppik, Karl, *Franz Joseph I. Der Untergang eines Reiches*, Hellerau bei Dresden, Avalon-Verlag, 1928, p. 75.

2. Pusztay, A. von, *Thronfolge und die pragmatische Sanction in Ungarn*, Preßburg, 1849, pp. 128-29.

3. Corti, Egon Caesar Conte, *Mensch und Herrscher. Wege und Schicksale Kaiser Franz Josephs I. zwischen Thronbesteigung und Berliner Kongreß*, Granz-Wien-Altötting, Verlag Styria, 1952, p. 4.

4. Redlich, Joseph, *Kaiser Franz Joseph I. Eine Biographie*, Berlin, Verlag für Kulturpolitik, 1928, p. 63.

5. Kiszling, Rudolf, *Fürst Felix zu Schwarzenberg: Der politische Lehrmeister Kaiser Franz Josephs*, Graz-Köln, Hermann Böhlaus Nachf. Ges. M.B.H., 1952, p. 106.

6. Redlich, J., p. 72.

7. Friedjung, Heinrich, *Der Kampf um die Vorherrschaft in Deutschland 1859 bis 1866*, 2 Bände 6. Auflage, Stuttgart und Berlin, J. G. Cotta'sche Buchhandlung Nachfolger, 1904, Band I., p. 60.

8. Tritsch, Walther, *Metternich und sein Monarch*, Darmstadt, Holle Verlag, 1952, p. 677.

9. Heller, Dr. Eduard, *Kaiser Franz Joseph I. Ein Charakterbild*, Wien, Militärwissenschaftlicher Verlag GM Franz Schubert, 1934, p. 41.

10. Spitzmüller, p. 13.

11. Charmatz, pp. 59 ff.
12. Tschuppik, p. 67.
13. Weckbecker, Wilhelm, editor, *Von Maria Theresia zu Franz Joseph*, Berlin, Verlag für Kulturpolitik, 1929, p. 193.
14. Spitzmüller, p. 13.
15. Helfert, Joseph Alexander Freiherr von, *Die Thronbesteigung des Kaisers Franz Joseph I.* (Volume III of *Geschichte Österreichs vom Ausgange des Wiener October-Aufstandes 1848.*), Prag, Verlag von F. Tempsky, 1872, p. 145.
16. Sforza, Carlo, *Gestalten und Gestalter des Heutigen Europa*, Berlin, S. Fischer Verlag, 1931, p. 30.
17. Tritsch, p. 698.

Chapter 6

1. Heller, p. 42, Redlich, J., p. 60.
2. Srbik, Heinrich Ritter von, *Aus Österreichs Vergangenheit*, Salzburg, Otto Müller Verlag, 1949, pp. 221-41.
3. *New York Times Magazine*, January 26, 1964, "Mayerling Remains a Mystery."
4. Chlumecky, Leopold von, *Erzherzog Franz Ferdinands Wirken und Wollen*, Berlin, Verlag für Kulturpolitik, 1929, p. 15. Sforza, p. 30.
5. Heller, p. 40.
6. *Ibid.*, pp. 40-41.
7. Srbik, p. 234.
8. Margutti, Albert Freiherr von, *Vom Alten Kaiser*, Leipzig und Wien, Leonhardt-Verlag, 4th edition, 1921, p. 52.
9. Tschuppik, p. 389.
10. Görlitz, Walter, *Franz Joseph und Elisabeth. Die Tragik einer Fürstenehe*, Stuttgart, Verlag Silberburg, 1938, p. 284. Redlich, J., p. 385. Corti, Egon Caesar Conte und Hans Sokol, *Der Alte Kaiser Franz Joseph I. vom Berliner Kongreß bis zu seinem Tode*, 2nd edition, Graz-Wien-Köln, Verlag Styria, 1955, p. 130.
11. Tschuppik, p. 389.
12. *Ibid.*, p. 486.
13. Hennings, Fred, *Ringstrassen Symphonie, 3. Satz: 1884 bis 1899. Mir Bleibt Nichts Erspart*, Wien-München, Verlag Herold, 1964, p. 64.
14. Klastersky, Cissy, *Der Alte Kaiser wie nur Einer ihn sah. Der wahrheitsgetreue Bericht seines Leibkammerdieners Eugen Ketterl*, Wien, Gerold & Co., Universitäts-Buchhandlung, 1929, p. 163.
15. Ernst, p. 13.
16. Redlich, J., p. 212.
17. Srbik, p. 227.
18. Schnürer, Dr. Franz, *Briefe Kaiser Franz Josephs I. an seine Mutter 1838-1872*, München, Verlag Jos. Kosel & Friedr. Pustet, 1930, p. 126.
19. Ernst, p. 151.
20. Corti, *Der Alte Kaiser*, p. 21.

Chapter 7

1. Corti, *Vom Kind zum Kaiser*, p. 276.
2. Margutti, p. 364.
3. Helfert, p. 392.
4. Tschuppik, p. 241.
5. Sforza, p. 31.

6. Corti, *Vom Kind zum Kaiser*, p. 286.
7. Schnürer, p. 88.
8. Margutti, p. 365.
9. Corti, *Mensch und Herrscher*, p. 537.
10. Franzel, Emil, *Sehnsucht nach den alten Gassen*, Wien-München, Verlag Herold, 1964, p. 40.
11. Ernst, p. 122.
12. Weckbecker, Part II, p. 173.
13. Heller, p. 27.
14. Corti, *Vom Kind zum Kaiser*, pp. 334 ff.
15. Schnürer, p. 117.
16. Glaise-Horstenau, Edmund von, *Franz Josephs Weggefährte. Das Leben des Generalstabschefs Grafen Beck*, Zürich-Leipzig-Wien, Amalthea-Verlag, 1930, pp. 474-83.
17. Redlich, J., p. 221.
18. Ernst, p. 97.
19. *Ibid.*, pp. 103-105.
20. Görlitz, p. 211.

Chapter 8

1. Redlich, J., p. 361.
2. Kray, Stefan Baron, *Im Dienste der Kabinettskanzlei während des Weltkrieges*, Budapest, Revai, 1937, p. 75.
3. Redlich, J., p. 360.
4. Klastersky, pp. 115-16.
5. Corti, *Der Alte Kaiser*, p. 260.
6. Görlitz, p. 242.
7. Hofkammer & Finanz Archiv, Vienna, Document 3504 11.1.
8. Klastersky, p. 169.

Chapter 9

1. Wandruszka, Adam, *Das Haus Habsburg*, 2nd edition, Wien, Verlag für Geschichte und Politik, 1959, p. 190.
2. Lhotsky, Alphons, "Apis Colonna. Fabeln und Theorien über die Abkunft der Habsburger . . ." *Mitteilungen des Instituts für Geschichtsforschung und Archivwissenschaften in Wien*, Volume LV., Innsbruck, Universitäts-Verlag Wagner, 1944, pp. 172-80.
3. *Ibid.*, pp. 182-201.
4. *Ibid.*, p. 220.
5. *Ibid.*, p. 231.
6. Haus, Hof, und Staatsarchiv, Vienna. *Erklärender Führer*, 2nd edition, Vienna, 1931, p. 11.
7. This section is based mostly on information obtained in February 1965 from Dr. Bruno Thomas, Director of the Arms Collection of the Museum of Art History in Vienna.
8. *Graz als Residenz Innerösterreich 1564-1619 Katalog der Ausstellung, Grazer Burg, 6. Mai bis 30. September 1964*, p. 104.
9. Wandruszka, p. 184.

Chapter 10

1. *Grätzer Zeitung*, Monday, August 23, 1830.
2. Corti, *Vom Kind zum Kaiser*, p. 140.
3. Redlich, J., p. 28.
4. Corti, *Vom Kind zum Kaiser*, pp. 41, 53-54.

5. Schnürer, pp. 7-8.
6. Metternich-Winneburg, Fürst Richard, *Aus Metternichs nachgelassenen Papieren. Dritter Theil, 1848-1849,* Wien, Wilhelm Braumüller, 1884. Letter of April 8, 1850, No. 1795.
7. Helfert, p. 370.
8. Tschuppik, p. 23.
9. Helfert, p. 372.
10. Corti, *Vom Kind zum Kaiser,* p. 195.
11. Tritsch, p. 657.
12. Corti, *Vom Kind zum Kaiser,* p. 120.
13. Heller, p. 15.
14. *Ibid.,* p. 17.
15. Helfert, pp. 373-74.
16. Corti, *Vom Kind zum Kaiser,* p. 152.

Chapter 11

1. This calculation is based on information contained in Corti, Egon Caesar Conte, *Elisabeth "Die Seltsame Frau,"* 33rd edition, Graz-Wien-Köln, Verlag Styria, 1950.
2. Bagger, Eugene, *Franz Joseph,* Zürich-Leipzig-Wien, Amalthea-Verlag, 1927.
3. Görlitz, pp. 171-72.
4. *Ibid.,* p. 236.
5. *Ibid.,* p. 161.
6. Corti, *Elisabeth,* p. 225.
7. Bourgoing, Jean de, *Briefe Kaiser Franz Josephs an Frau Katharina Schratt,* Wien, Ullstein Verlag, 1949, pp. 84-87.
8. Corti, *Elisabeth,* p. 234.
9. Tschuppik, p. 151.
10. Klastersky, p. 44.

Chapter 12

1. Corti, *Der Alte Kaiser,* p. 143.
2. *Ibid.,* p. 144.
3. Janetschek, Ottokar, *Kaiser Franz Joseph,* Zürich-Leipzig-Wien, Amalthea-Verlag, 1951, p. 409.
4. Gamillscheg, Felix, *Kaiseradler über Mexiko,* Granz-Wien-Köln, Verlag Styria, 1964, p. 40.
5. Corti, *Mensch und Herrscher,* pp. 314-15.
6. Heller, pp. 144-45.
7. Ernst, p. 85.
8. Gamillscheg, pp. 34, 94, *et passim.*
9. *Ibid.,* p. 299.
10. Görlitz, p. 210.
11. Tschuppik, p. 382.
12. Richter, Werner, *Kronprinz Rudolf von Österreich,* Erlenbach-Zürich und Leipzig, Eugen Rentsch Verlag, 1941, p. 306.
13. *New York Times Magazine,* January 26, 1964, "Mayerling Remains a Mystery."
14. Richter, p. 319.
15. Margutti, pp. 109 ff.

Chapter 13

1. Schnürer, Dr. Franz, *Habsburger-Anekdoten*, Stuttgart, Verlag von Robert Lutz, 1906, pp. 121-22.
2. Schnürer, *Briefe*, p. 166.
3. Kübeck, Max Freiherr von, *Tagebücher des Carl Friedrich Freiherrn Kübeck von Kübau*, 2 vols., Wien, Gerold & Co., 1909, Vol. II., p. 60.
4. Sieghart, Rudolf, *Die letzten Jahrzehnte einer Grossmacht*, Berlin, Im Verlag Ullstein, 1932, p. 374.
5. Schnürer, *Briefe*, p. 302.
6. Sieghart, p. 380.
7. Tschuppik, p. 133.
8. *Ibid.*, pp. 133-34.
9. Redlich, J., p. 276.
10. Sieghart, p. 382.
11. *Ibid.*, p. 386.
12. Tschuppik, p. 243.
13. *Ibid.*, p. 263.
14. Spitzmüller, p. 14.
15. Corti, *Mensch und Herrscher*, p. 334.
16. Taylor, A. J. P., *The Habsburg Monarchy 1809-1918*, Penguin Books Ltd., 1964, pp. 170-71.
17. Spitzmüller, p. 26.

Chapter 14

1. Redlich, J., p. 79.
2. Schnürer, *Briefe*, p. 292.
3. *Ibid.*, p. 320.
4. Corti, *Mensch und Herrscher*, p. 305.
5. *Ibid.*, p. 309.
6. *Ibid.*, p. 346.
7. *Ibid.*, p. 346.
8. Schnürer, *Briefe*, p. 355.
9. Corti, *Mensch und Herrscher*, p. 352.
10. *Ibid.*, p. 339.
11. Friedjung, Heinrich, *Benedeks Nachgelassene Papiere*, 3rd edition, Dresden, Verlag von Carl Reißner, 1904, pp. 427-28.
12. Margutti, p. 269; Heller, pp. 70-71.
13. Schnürer, *Briefe*, p. 358.
14. Friedjung, *Vorherrschaft*, Vol. II, pp. 370 ff.
15. Corti, *Mensch und Herrscher*, p. 423.
16. Tschuppik, pp. 272 ff.

Chapter 15

1. Tschuppik, pp. 130 ff.
2. Corti, *Elisabeth*, p. 443.
3. Corti, *Mensch und Herrscher*, p. 396.
4. *Ibid.*, p. 419.
5. Sforza, p. 75.
6. Taylor, p. 147.
7. Gopčević, pp. 239 ff.

Chapter 16

1. Regele, Oskar, "Die Donaumonarchie als Machtfaktor 1914," *Der*

Donauraum, Zeitschrift des Forschungsinstitutes für den Donauraum, 9. Jahrgang, 3. Heft, 1964.
2. Fischer, p. 130.
3. Tschuppik, p. 42.

Chapter 17

1. Benedikt, Heinrich, *Die wirtschaftliche Entwicklung in der Franz-Joseph-Zeit,* Wien-München, Verlag Herold, 1958, p. 181.
2. *Ibid.,* p. 160.
3. *Ibid.,* p. 23.
4. Pistor, Dr. Erich, *Die Volkswirtschaft Österreich-Ungarns und die Verständigung mit Deutschland,* Berlin, Verlag von Georg Reimer, 1915, p. 112.
5. Hennings, Fred, *Ringstrassen Symphonie, 1. Satz 1857-1870. Es ist mein Wille,* Wien-München, Verlag Herold, 1963, pp. 26-27.
6. Doderer, Heimito von, *Roman No. 7,* First Part, Munich, Biederstein, 1965.
7. Scheffer, Egon, *Das Bankwesen in Österreich,* Wien, 1924, p. 289. Brusatti, Alois, "Die wirtschaftliche Situation Österreich-Ungarns am Vorabend des Ersten Weltkrieges," *Österreich am Vorabend des Ersten Weltkrieges,* Graz-Wien, Stiasny Verlag, 1964, p. 71.
8. Mayer, Hans, editor, *Hundert Jahre Österreichischer Wirtschaftsentwicklung 1848-1948,* Wien, Springer-Verlag, 1949, pp. 127 ff.
9. Benedikt, p. 166.
10. Pistor, p. 40.
11. *Ibid.,* p. 54.
12. Brusatti, p. 71.

Chapter 18

1. Schnürer, *Briefe,* p. 232.
2. Friedjung, Heinrich, *Der Krimkrieg und die österreichische Politik,* 2nd edition, Stuttgart und Berlin, J. G. Cotta'sche Buchhandlung Nachfolger, 1911, pp. 122, 124.
3. Richter, p. 12.
4. Tschuppik, p. 521.
5. Heller, p. 124.
6. Tschuppik, p. 605.
7. *Ibid.,* p. 609.

Chapter 19

1. Tschuppik, p. 589.
2. Corti, *Der Alte Kaiser,* p. 363.
3. Srbik, Heinrich Ritter von, "Heinrich Friedjung," *Deutsches Biographisches Jahrbuch, 1917-1920,* Berlin, Deutsche Verlagsanstalt Stuttgart Berlin, 1920. Taylor, pp. 235-36.
4. Tschuppik, p. 562.
5. Editors of American Heritage, *The American Heritage History of World War I,* narrative by S. L. A. Marshall, New York, American Heritage Publishing Co., Inc., 1964, pp. 25-26.
6. Tschuppik, p. 609.
7. Spitzmüller, p. 32.
8. Kray, p. 65.
9. Klastersky, pp. 172-74.

Genealogical Table

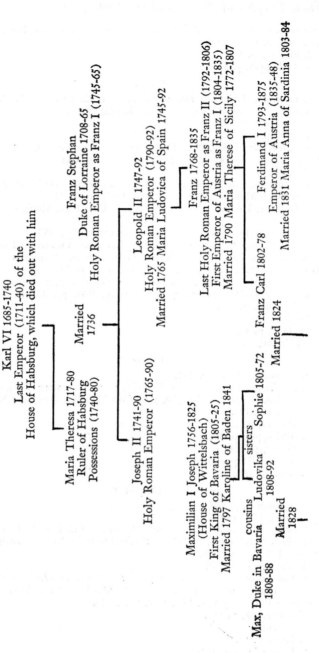

Karl VI 1685-1740
Last Emperor (1711-40) of the
House of Habsburg, which died out with him

Franz Stephan
Duke of Lorraine 1708-65
Holy Roman Emperor as Franz I (1745-65)

Married
1736

Maria Theresa 1717-80
Ruler of Habsburg
Possessions (1740-80)

Leopold II 1747-92
Holy Roman Emperor (1790-92)
Married 1765 Maria Ludovica of Spain 1745-92

Joseph II 1741-90
Holy Roman Emperor (1765-90)

Franz 1768-1835
Last Holy Roman Emperor as Franz II (1792-1806)
First Emperor of Austria as Franz I (1804-1835)
Married 1790 Maria Therese of Sicily 1772-1807

Ferdinand I 1793-1875
Emperor of Austria (1835-48)
Married 1831 Maria Anna of Sardinia 1803-84

Franz Carl 1802-78

Married 1824

Maximilian I Joseph 1756-1825
(House of Wittelsbach)
First King of Bavaria (1805-25)
Married 1797 Karoline of Baden 1841

sisters

Sophie 1805-72

cousins

Ludovika
1808-92

Married
1828

Max, Duke in Bavaria
1808-88

Elizabeth
1837-98

FRANZ JOSEPH I
1830-1916
Emperor of Austria
(1848-1916)

first cousins
Married
1854

Ferd. Maximilian
1832-67
Emperor of Mexico (1864-67)
Married 1857 Charlotte,
Princess of Belgium 1840-1927

Karl Ludwig
1833-96
Married 1862
Maria Annunziata
of Bourbon-Sicily
1843-71

Maria Anna
1835-40

Ludwig Viktor
1842-1919

Sophie
1855-57

Gisela 1856-1932
Married 1873
Leopold, Prince of
Bavaria 1846-1930

Rudolf, Crown Prince
1858-89
Married 1881 Stephanie,
Princess of Belgium
1864-1945

Elisabeth 1883-1963
Married 1902 Prince Otto
Windisch-Grätz
Divorced 1924. Married Leopold Petznek

Marie Valerie 1868-1924
Married 1890 Archduke
Franz Salvator 1866-1939

Franz Ferdinand d'Este
1863-1914
Married 1900 Sophie Countess
Chotek, Duchess of Hohenberg
1868-1914

Both murdered at Sarajevo

Otto 1865-1906
Married 1886
Maria Josepha of
Saxony 1867-1944

Karl I 1887-1922
Last Emperor of Austria
1916-18
Married 1911 Zita, Princess
of Bourbon-Parma 1892-

Otto 1912-
and 7 other children

Chronology

1830 August 18 Birth of Franz Joseph at Schönbrunn, Imperial summer palace in Vienna suburb.
1835 March 2 Death of Emperor Franz I, Franz Joseph's grandfather. Accession of Ferdinand "The Kindhearted."
1837 December 24 Birth of Elisabeth, first cousin and future wife of Franz Joseph.
1848 February Revolution in Hungary.
      March Revolution in Vienna, Prague, and Italian provinces. Metternich resigns March 13, flees to England. King Charles Albert of Sardinia "liberates" Milan. Austrians driven out of Venice.
      April Emperor Ferdinand accepts Bohemian demands, approves Hungarian independence.
      May Imperial army under Radetzky defeats Sardinian-Piedmontese army at Santa Lucia. Franz Joseph's baptism of fire. Flight of Imperial family from Vienna to Innsbruck.
      June 17 Prague revolution crushed by Imperial army under Windisch-Grätz.
      July A new Reichstag meets in Vienna to draft a constitution. Feudal obligations of peasants abolished.
      August Imperial family returns to Vienna.
      October Revolution flares up anew. Court flees to Olomouc with strong military escort. Windisch-Grätz takes Vienna.
      November Executions in Vienna. Reichstag moved to Kroměříz̆. Prince Felix Schwarzenberg named Minister-President.
      December 2 Abdication of Emperor Ferdinand. Accession of Franz Joseph.
1849 March Kroměříz̆ Reichstag dispersed by Imperial army. March Constitution promulgated by Franz Joseph. Sardinia-Piedmont resumes war against Austria. Italians decisively defeated at Novara by Radetzky.
      April Kossuth deposes Habsburg dynasty in Hungary. Franz Joseph dismisses Windisch-Grätz from supreme command of Imperial army.
      June Russian army invades Hungary to suppress revolution.
      August 13 General Görgei surrenders Hungarian army to Russians at Világos. End of Hungarian Revolution. Executions in Hungary and Italy.
1850 November 29 Olomouc Conference. Prussia yields to Franz Joseph's demands that it withdraw its troops from Hesse-Cassel.
1851 September 24 Metternich returns to Vienna.

December 31   Franz Joseph's "Sylvester Patent" rescinds March Constitution. Franz Joseph is absolute ruler.

1853   February 6   Storming of Milan Main Guard by Italian putschists.
February 18   Assassination attempt on Franz Joseph by János Libényi.
August 18   Engagement of Franz Joseph to Elisabeth.

1854   April 24   Wedding of Franz Joseph and Elisabeth in Vienna.
June 3   Franz Joseph issues ultimatum to Czar Nicholas I.

1855   March 5   Daughter Sophie born.
August 18   Concordat with Holy See gives Roman Catholic Church extensive powers, especially over education, in the Monarchy.

1856   July 15   Daughter Gisela born.

1857   December 29   Franz Joseph orders wall around Vienna razed in order to facilitate expansion of the city.

1858   August 21   Son Rudolf born.

1859   April 23   Franz Joseph issues ultimatum to Sardinia, demanding disarmament by that country.
April 29   Franz Joseph declares war against Sardinia.
June 24   Franz Joseph defeated by French and Italians at Solferino.
July 11   Preliminary peace signed at Villafranca. Franz Joseph surrenders Lombardy.

1860   March 25   Franz Joseph convenes Reichsrat (Empire Council) to draft a new constitution.
October 20   Franz Joseph's "October Diploma" approves new constitution which would make the Empire into a federation of national states dominated by aristocrats.
November   Elisabeth leaves for Madeira—the first of some 59 extensive voyages she made during the rest of her life.

1861   February 26   Franz Joseph's "February Patent" revokes the October Diploma and promulgates a new constitution making the Monarchy into a centralized and essentially German-dominated state.

1863   August   Franz Joseph convokes a meeting of the German Princes at Frankfort to propose a new constitution for Germany. King of Prussia refuses to attend.

1864   January 20   Austria and Prussia invade Denmark.
October 30   Peace between Denmark and the Allies (Prussia and Austria). Denmark surrenders Schleswig, Holstein, and Lauenburg to them.

1865   August 14   Gastein Agreement. Austria and Prussia agree to rule Schleswig-Holstein jointly.
September 20   Franz Joseph's Manifesto repeals constitution, restores absolutism.

1866   June 15   War between Austria and Prussia.
June 20   Italy declares war against Austria.
June 24   Austrians defeat Italians at Custoza.
July 3   Prussians defeat Austrians at Königgrätz (Sadowa).
July 20   Austrians defeat Italian navy near Lissa.
August 23   Peace treaty of Prague. Austria excluded from German confederation, surrenders Venetia and its rights in Schleswig-Holstein.

1867 February 18 Franz Joseph appoints Count Julius Andrássy Minister-President of the first independent Hungarian government.
March-April Hungarian Parliament approves "Settlement" with Franz Joseph. Hungary virtually independent.
June 8 Franz Joseph crowned King of Hungary at Budapest.
June 19 Emperor Maximilian of Mexico, brother of Franz Joseph, executed at Querétaro.
August 18 Franz Joseph and Elisabeth meet Emperor Napoleon III and Empress Eugénie at Salzburg. Hint of alliance against Prussia.
December 21 "December Constitution" promulgated. Applies only to non-Hungarian part of the Monarchy.

1868 March 21 Repeal of Concordat of August 18, 1855 with Holy See.
April 22 Daughter Marie Valerie born.

1871 January 18 Wilhelm I of Prussia proclaimed German Emperor. End of Franz Joseph's hopes to regain German hegemony.

1872 May 28 Death of Archduchess Sophie, Franz Joseph's mother.

1873 May 1 Opening of World Exposition at Vienna.
May 9 "Black Friday." Collapse of Vienna stock market, with world-wide financial repercussions.

1878 June-July Congress of Berlin.
August Occupation of Bosnia and Hercegovina by Austria-Hungary.

1879 March 8 Death of Archduke Franz Carl, Franz Joseph's father.
October 7 Alliance of Austria-Hungary with Germany.

1881 December 8 Ringstrassen Theater in Vienna burns. Hundreds of lives lost.

1883 December Italy joins alliance between Germany and Austria-Hungary. This "Triple Alliance" renewed several times until World War I.

1886 May 21 Beginning of Franz Joseph's thirty-year friendship with Katharina Schratt.

1889 January 30 Death of Crown Prince Rudolf, allegedly by suicide.

1893 October Direct popular vote introduced in Austria.

1898 September 10 Empress Elisabeth assassinated by Luigi Lucheni at Geneva.

1905 February 9 Hungarian Parliament dissolved by an army unit.

1908 October 5 Annexation of Bosnia and Hercegovina by Austria-Hungary.
November Relations between Austria-Hungary and Serbia near breaking point.

1913 October 18 Austria-Hungary sends ultimatum to Serbia, demanding withdrawal of Serbian troops from Albania. War narrowly averted by Serbia's compliance.

1914 June 28 Archduke Franz Ferdinand, Heir Presumptive to the Habsburg throne, and his consort, the Duchess of Hohenberg, assassinated by Bosnian nationalists at Sarajevo, the capital city of Bosnia.
July 7 Austro-Hungarian Council of Ministers decides on war against Serbia.
July 23 Franz Joseph's Minister in Belgrade hands ultimatum to Serbian government.

July 25   Austria-Hungary breaks off diplomatic relations with Serbia.
July 28   Franz Joseph declares war against Serbia. Beginning of
    World War I.
1915   May 23   Italy declares war against Austria-Hungary.
1916   November 21   Franz Joseph dies at Schönbrunn.

Selected Bibliography

Bibliographies

Dahlmann-Waitz. *Quellenkunde der Deutschen Geschichte*, 9th edition, edited by Hermann Haering, Leipzig, Verlag von K. F. Koehler, 1931. This is the principal guide to source material in German history.

Kertesz, Johann. *Bibliographie der Habsburgerliteratur, 1318-1934*, Budapest, Verlag Gergely, 1934. An extensive bibliography on Habsburg history.

Novotny, Alexander. "Austrian History from 1848 to 1938 as Seen by Austrian Historians Since 1945," *Austrian History News Letter*, No. 4 (1963), published by Rice University, under the Auspices of the United States Committee to promote Studies of the History of the Habsburg Monarchy, pp. 18-50. A useful survey by a leading Austrian historian.

Uhlirz, Karl. *Handbuch der Geschichte Österreichs und seiner Nachbarlander Böhmen und Ungarn*, II. Band, 2. Teil 1848-1914. Bearbeitet von Mathilde Uhlirz, Graz-Wien-Leipzig, Universitätsbuchhandlung Leuschner & Lubensky, 1941. Indispensable source book on Austrian history.

Letters, Papers, Diaries

Bourgoing, Jean de. *Briefe Kaiser Franz Josephs an Frau Katharina Schratt*, Wien, Ullstein Verlag, 1949. Franz Joseph's letters to his intimate friend over a period of three decades.

Ernst, Dr. Otto. *Franz Joseph I. in seinen Briefen*, Wien, Rikola Verlag, 1924. A selection of Franz Joseph's letters to various persons, topically arranged.

Friedjung, Heinrich. *Benedeks Nachgelassene Papiere*, 3rd edition, Dresden, Verlag von Carl Reißner, 1904. Papers of the defeated commander of the Austrian Army in the war against Prussia in 1866, edited by the great Austrian historian of the period.

Kübeck, Max Freiherr von. *Tagebücher des Carl Friedrich Freiherrn Kübeck von Kübau*, 2 vols., Wien, Gerold & Co., 1909. Diaries of one of the most fascinating Austrian statesmen of the period of Metternich and the first years of Franz Joseph's reign.

Metternich-Winneburg, Fürst Richard. *Aus Metternichs nachgelassenen Papieren, 1848-1859*, Wien, Wilhelm Braumüller, 1884.

Schnürer, Dr. Franz. *Briefe Kaiser Franz Josephs I an seine Mutter, 1838-1872*, München, Verlag Jos. Kösel & Friedr. Pustet, 1930. The revealing letters of Franz Joseph to his mother.

Newspapers and Documents (1830 and subsequent years)

Allgemeine Zeitung. Augsburg, Germany.

Grätzer Zeitung. Graz, Austria.

Wiener Zeitung. Vienna, Austria. (Official newspaper of the Austrian
government.)
Haus, Hof, und Staatsarchiv. Vienna, Austria.
Hofkammer & Finanz Archiv. Vienna, Austria.

Biographies and Reminiscences of Franz Joseph

Bagger, Eugene. *Franz Joseph*, Zürich-Leipzig-Wien, Amalthea-Verlag,
1927.
Corti, Egon Caesar Conte-Hans Sokol. *Der Alte Kaiser Franz Joseph I.
vom Berliner Kongress bis zu seinem Tode*, Graz-Wien-Köln, Verlag
Styria, 1955. This is the third volume (first: *Vom Kind zum Kaiser;*
second: *Mensch und Herrscher*, see below) of the most detailed and
complete chronicle of the life of Franz Joseph published thus far.
Though published as separate volumes, the three in fact constitute one
continuous work.
Corti, Egon Caesar Conte-Hans Sokol. *Kaiser Franz Joseph*, Graz-Wien-
Köln, Verlag Styria, 1960. A one-volume abridged edition of Corti's
trilogy.
Corti, Egon Caesar Conte. *Mensch und Herrscher. Wege und Schicksale
Kaiser Franz Joseph I. zwischen Thronbesteigung und Berliner Kon-
gress*, Graz-Wien-Altötting, Verlag Styria, 1952.
Corti, Egon Caesar Conte. *Vom Kind zum Kaiser. Kindheit und Erste
Jugend Kaiser Franz Josephs I. und seiner Geschwister*, Graz-Salzburg-
Wien, Verlag Anton Pustet, 1950.
Gopčević, Spiridion. *Österreichs Untergang-Die Folge von Franz Josefs
Missregierung*, Berlin, Verlag von Karl Siegismund, 1920. A critical
evaluation and condemnation of Franz Joseph's character and policies.
Görlitz, Walter. *Franz Joseph und Elisabeth. Die Tragik einer Fürstenehe*,
Stuttgart, Verlag Silberburg, 1938. Critical of Franz Joseph.
Harding, Bertita. *Golden Fleece. The Story of Franz Joseph and Elisabeth
of Austria*, New York, Halcyon House, 1939. (Copyright 1937 by
Bobbs-Merrill Company.) Quasi-fictionalized, unreliable, but entertain-
ing.
Heller, Dr. Eduard. *Kaiser Franz Joseph I. Ein Charakterbild*, Wien,
Militärwissenschaftlicher Verlag GM. Franz Schubert, 1934. A character
sketch of Franz Joseph by an admiring former army officer.
Janetschek, Ottokar. *Kaiser Franz Joseph. Schicksale und Tragödien aus
der guten alten Zeit*, 2nd edition, Zürich-Leipzig-Wien, Amalthea-
Verlag, 1951. Mainly a description of the private lives of Franz Joseph
and Elisabeth. Anecdotal. One of the more engaging of the many Franz
Joseph biographies.
Klastersky, Cissy. *Der alte Kaiser wie nur einer ihn sah. Der wahrheits-
getreue Bericht seines Leibkammerdieners Eugen Ketterl*, Wien, Gerold
& Co. Universitäts-Buchhandlung, 1929. An intimate view of Franz
Joseph as seen by his chief valet.
Kray, Baron Stefan. *Im Dienste der Kabinettskanzlei während des Welt-
krieges*, Budapest, Révai, 1937. Details the inner workings of Franz
Joseph's secretariat and describes the Emperor's daily routine of work.
Margutti, Albert Freiherr von. *Vom alten Kaiser*, Leipzig und Wien, Leon-

hardt-Verlag, 4th edition, 1921. Chatty reminiscences by one of Franz Joseph's military aides.

Portisch, Emil. *Eines Kaisers grosse Liebe. Das Geschick eines alten Herrscherhauses,* St. Pölten, Newag-Druckerei, 1952. A journalistic, anecdotal, entertaining account of the lives of Franz Joseph and Elisabeth. Many factual errors. No bibliography, no citations of sources.

Redlich, Joseph. *Kaiser Franz Joseph I. Eine Biographie,* Berlin, Verlag für Kulturpolitik, 1928. Up to the present, this is the most scholarly and complete critical account of Franz Joseph's life and reign.

Redlich, Oswald. "Kaiser Franz Joseph," in *Neue Österreichische Biographie 1815-1918,* geleitet von Anton Bettelheim, Erste Abteilung, Biographien, Wien, Wiener Drucke, 1923. A brief, but much-praised portrait and appraisal of Franz Joseph.

Rumbold, Sir Horace. *The Austrian Court in the Nineteenth Century,* London, Methuen & Co., 1909. A review of the principal episodes bearing on the lives and fates of Franz Joseph and his family, by a one-time British Ambassador to Vienna.

Tschuppik, Karl. *Franz Joseph I. Der Untergang eines Reiches,* Hellerau bei Dresden, Avalun-Verlag, 1928. One of the principal accounts of Franz Joseph's life and reign.

Other Works

Benedikt, Heinrich. *Monarchie der Gegensätze,* Wien, Ullstein Verlag, 1947. A study of the contradictions besetting the Monarchy.

Benedikt, Heinrich. *Die Wirtschaftliche Entwicklung in der Franz-Joseph-Zeit,* Wien, München, Verlag Herold, 1958. A valuable summary of economic development in the Monarchy of Franz Joseph, by an eminent historian.

Brusatti, Alois. "Die wirtschaftliche Situation Österreich-Ungarns am Vorabend des ersten Weltkriegs," *Österreich am Vorabend des ersten Weltkrieges,* edited by Hugo Hantsch, Graz-Wien, Stiasny Verlag, 1964. From a collection of essays portraying the situation in the Monarchy on the eve of World War. I.

Charmatz, Richard. *Lebensbilder aus der Geschichte Österreichs,* Wien, Danubia-Verlag, 1947. A series of brief sketches of men who played prominent parts in Austrian history.

Chlumecky, Leopold von. *Erzherzog Franz Ferdinands Wirken und Wollen,* Berlin, Verlag für Kulturpolitik, 1929. A revealing study of the heir to the Habsburg throne who was murdered at Sarajevo.

Clark, Chester Wells. *Franz Joseph and Bismarck,* Cambridge, Harvard University Press, 1934. An analysis of Austrian diplomacy in the years leading up to the war of 1866.

Corti, Egon Caesar Conte. *Elisabeth "Die seltsame Frau,"* 33rd edition, Graz-Wien-Köln, Verlag Styria, 1950. Like its monumental companion work on Franz Joseph, this chronicles the life of the Empress Elisabeth, Franz Joseph's wife.

Crankshaw, Edward. *The Fall of the House of Habsburg,* London, Longmans, Green and Co. Ltd., 1963. Contains too many errors to be useful.

Fischer, Ernst. *Österreich 1848. Probleme der demokratischen Revolution in*

Österreich, Wien, Stern-Verlag, 1946. A Socialist appraisal of the Revolution of 1848.

Franzel, Emil. *Sehnsucht nach den alten Gassen*, Wien-München, Verlag Herold, 1964. Nostalgic vignettes of old Austria.

Friedjung, Heinrich. *Der Ausgleich mit Ungarn*, 2nd edition, Leipzig, Verlag von Otto Wigand, 1877. Friedjung (1851-1920) was the foremost Austrian historian of the period. His works are a principal source of information for any study of the history of Austria during that period.

Friedjung, Heinrich. *Der Kampf um die Vorherrschaft in Deutschland 1859 bis 1866*, 2 vols., 6th edition, Stuttgart und Berlin, J. G. Cotta'sche Buchhandlung Nachfolger, 1904.

Friedjung, Heinrich. *Der Krimkrieg und die österreichische Politik*, 2nd edition, Stuttgart und Berlin, J. G. Cotta'sche Buchhandlung Nachfolger, 1911.

Friedjung, Heinrich. *Osterreich von 1848 bis 1860*, 2 vols., Stuttgart und Berlin, J. G. Cotta'sche Buchhandlung Nachfolger, 1908.

Gamillscheg, Felix. *Kaiseradler über Mexiko*, Graz-Wien-Köln, Verlag Styria, 1964. An account of Maximilian's Mexican adventure, based on the diaries and letters of one of his Austrian officers.

Glaise-Horstenau, Edmund von. *Franz Josephs Weggefährte. Das Leben des Generalstabschefs Grafen Beck*, Zürich-Leipzig-Wien, Amalthea-Verlag, 1930. The story of an officer, for many years chief of staff of the Austro-Hungarian Army, whose life was closely tied to Franz Joseph's.

Gratz, Dr. Gustav (Minister a. D.) and Dr. Richard Schüller (Sektionschef Prof.) *Der wirtschaftliche Zusammenbruch Österreich-Ungarns. Die Tragödie der Erschöpfung*, Wien, Holder-Pichler-Tempsky A. G., New Haven, Yale University Press, 1930. An analysis of the economic breakdown of the Monarchy in World War I.

Hantsch, Hugo. *Die Geschichte Österreichs*, Vol. I, 4th edition, 1959; Vol. II, 3rd edition, 1962, Graz-Wien-Köln, Styria Verlag. A history of Austria by one of its most eminent present-day historians.

Haslip, Joan. *The Lonely Empress*, Cleveland and New York, World Publishing Company, 1965. Stresses Empress Elisabeth's willfulness and neglect of her children. Good selection of pictures.

Helfert, Joseph Alexander Freiherr von. *Die Thronbesteigung des Kaisers Franz Joseph I.*, Vol. III of *Geschichte Österreichs vom Ausgange des Wiener October-Aufstandes 1848*, Prag, Verlag von F. Tempsky, 1872. A detailed account of Franz Joseph's accession.

Hennings, Fred. *Ringstrassen Symphonie. 1. Satz 1857-1870. Es ist mein Wille*, Wien-München, Verlag Herold, 1963. The first of three enchanting movements of the "Ring Symphony" picturing the Vienna of the second half of the nineteenth century, by a well-known Burgtheater actor.

Hennings, Fred. *Ringstrassen Symphonie. 2. Satz 1870-1884. Es war sehr schön es hat mich sehr gefreut*, Wien-München, Verlag Herold, 1963.

Hennings, Fred. *Ringstrassen Symphonie. 3. Satz 1884-1899. Mir bleibt nichts erspart*, Wien-München, Verlag Herold, 1964.

Historisch-ethnographisch-statistische Notizen über die Nationalitäten Österreichs, ihre Zahlen und Sprachverhältnisse. Nebst einer kurzen

Darstellung der politischen Angelegenheiten der Serben und ihrer Privilegien . . . Zusammengestellt von einem beschaulichen Reisenden, Wien, Verlag der Buchhandlung von Alber A. Wenedikt, 1849. A mine of factual information about the Austrian Empire in 1848.

Kann, Robert A. *The Habsburg Empire. A Study in Integration and Disintegration,* New York, Frederick A. Praeger, 1957. A scholarly appraisal of Habsburg Empire problems.

Kann, Robert A. *The Multinational Empire,* 2 vols., New York, Octagon Books, Inc., 1964. Vol. I analyzes the growth of nationalism among the Empire's nationalities. Vol. II deals with the many proposals for solution of the Empire's problems.

Kiszling, Rudolf. *Die Revolution im Kaisertum Österreich 1848-49,* 2 vols., Wien, Universum Verlagsges, m.b.H., 1948.

Kiszling, Rudolf. *Fürst Felix zu Schwarzenberg. Der politische Lehrmeister Kaiser Franz Josephs,* Graz-Köln, Hermann Böhlaus Nachf. Ges. m.b.H., 1952.

Knappich, Wilhelm. *Die Habsburger Chronik. Lebensbilder, Charaktere und Geschichte der Habsburger,* Salzburg/Stuttgart, Verlag "Das Berglandbuch," 1959. Brief sketches of Habsburg rulers from Rudolf I to the last Emperor, Karl I. Suffers from some inaccuracies.

Lhotsky, Alphons. "Apis Colonna. Fabeln und Theorien über die Abkunft der Habsburger . . ." *Mitteilungen des Instituts für Geschichtsforschung und Archivwissenschaften in Wien,* Vol. LV, Innsbruck, Universitäts-Verlag Wagner, 1944. A fascinating survey of fables and theories about the descent of the Habsburgs.

Mayer, Hans, editor. *Hundert Jahre österreichischer Wirtschaftsentwicklung 1848-1948,* Wien, Springer-Verlag, 1949. Various aspects of Austrian economic development analyzed in chapters by specialists in the respective fields.

Novotny, Dr. Alexander. *1848 Österreichs Ringen um Freiheit und Völkerfrieden vor Hundert Jahren,* Graz-Wien, "Styria" Steirische Verlagsanstalt, 1948. A centennial evaluation of the events of 1848, by an eminent Austrian historian.

Payne, Robert. "Mayerling Remains a Mystery," *New York Times Magazine,* January 26, 1964. Doubts the suicide theory of the death of Crown Prince Rudolf.

Pistor, Dr. Erich. *Die Volkswirtschaft Österreich-Ungarns und die Verständigung mit Deutschland,* Berlin, Druck und Verlag von Georg Reimer, 1915. An analysis of the economy of Austria-Hungary.

Pusztay, A. von. *Thronfolge und die pragmatische Sanction in Ungarn,* Pressburg, 1849. Analysis of legal and consitutional aspects of Franz Joseph's succession in Hungary.

Rath, R. John. *The Viennese Revolution of 1848,* Austin, University of Texas Press, 1957. A scholarly analysis of the Revolution. Excellent bibliography.

Regele, Oskar. "Die Donaumonarchie als Machtfaktor 1914," *Der Donauraum,* Zeitschrift des Forschungsinstitutes für den Donauraum, 9. Jahrgang, 3 Heft, 1964. This article by a well-known author and former director of the Austrian War Archives analyzes the Monarchy as a power factor in 1914.

Richter, Werner. *Kronprinz Rudolf von Österreich*, Erlenbach-Zürich und Leipzig, Eugen Rentsch Verlag, 1941.

Scheffer, Egon. *Das Bankwesen in Österreich*, Wien, 1924.

Schmitt, F. *Statistik des österreichischen Kaiserstaates*, Nach "Hains Handbuch der Statistik" für den Schulgebrauch bearbeitet, Wien, Verlag von Tendler & Comp., 1858.

Schmitt, F. *Statistik des österreichisch-ungarischen Kaiserstaates*, in vierter Auflage neu bearbeitet von Gustav Adolf Schimmer, Wien, Carl Gerold's Sohn, 1872.

Schnürer, Dr. Franz. *Habsburger-Anekdoten*, Stuttgart, Verlag von Robert Lutz, 1906.

Sforza, Carlo. *Gestalten und Gestalter des Heutigen Europa*, Berlin, S. Fischer Verlag, 1931. Reminiscences and reflexions by a former Italian Minister.

Shepherd, Gordon. *The Austrian Odyssey*, London, Macmillan & Co., Ltd., 1957. Argues the civilizing mission of the Habsburg Empire.

Sieghart, Rudolf. *Die letzten Jahrzehnte einer Grossmacht. Menschen, Völker, Probleme des Habsburger-Reichs*, Berlin, im Verlag Ullstein, 1932. The account of problems and pressures in the Monarchy, by the Governor of one of the principal Austrian banks.

Spitzmüller, Dr. Alexander Freiherr von. *Kaiser Franz Joseph als Staatsmann*, Wien, Manzsche Verlags- und Universitäts Buchhandlung, 1935. A panegyric to the Emperor as a statesman, by his last surviving minister.

Srbik, Heinrich Ritter von. *Aus Österreichs Vergangenheit*, Salzburg, Otto Müller Verlag, 1949. Essays by the famous Austrian historian (1878-1951).

Srbik, Heinrich Ritter von. "Heinrich Friedjung" in *Deutsches Biographisches Jahrbuch 1917-1920*, Berlin, Deutsche Verlags-Anstalt Stuttgart Berlin, 1920.

Statistische Rückblicke aus Österreich. Der XIV. Tagung des internationalen statistischen Institutes überreicht, Wien, K. k. Statistische Zentral Kommission, 1913.

Taylor, A. J. P. *The Habsburg Monarchy 1809-1918*, Penguin Books, Ltd., 1964. A well-known history by an Englishman. Some Austrian scholars regard it as not showing adequate understanding of Austrian problems.

Tritsch, Walther. *Metternich und sein Monarch. Biographie eines seltsamen Doppelgestirns*, Darmstadt, Holle Verlag, 1952. An account of the lives of Metternich and Emperor Franz I.

Wandruszka, Adam. *Das Haus Habsburg*, 2nd edition, Wien, Verlag für Geschichte und Politik, 1959. An absorbing brief history of the Habsburg dynasty.

Weckbecker, Wilhelm, editor. *Von Maria Theresia zu Franz Joseph*, Berlin, Verlag für Kulturpolitik, 1929. Contains material of interest for the pre-March era.

Zöllner, Erich. *Geschichte Österreichs von den Anfängen bis zur Gegenwart*, 2nd edition, Wien, Verlag für Geschichte und Politik, 1962. A history of present-day Austria from the earliest times. Extensive bibliography.

Index

Achilleion, Empress Elisabeth's villa in Corfu, 116
"Activist" policy, 216
Adam, 89
Adler, Friedrich, 218, 221
Adler, Dr. Viktor, 221
Aehrenthal, Alois, Count Lexa von, 207, 208, 214-215
Agriculture in Austrian Empire, 188, 198-199
Albania, 208
Albert, King of the Belgians, 64
Albert, King of Saxony, 56, 59, 64, 160
Albrecht I, German King, 87, 90
Albrecht II, German King, 90
Albrecht, Archduke, 29, 62, 77-78, 118-119, 159-160, 162, 166
Alexander I, King of Serbia, 207
Alliance between Austria and France, 166
Alliance between Austria and Germany, 167-168
Amnesties, 56-57, 172
Andrássy, Count Gyula (Julius), 38, 54, 112, 142, 147, 165, 167, 171-175, 180, 185, 186, 204-205, 207
Angerer, Fanny, 113
Arad, executions at, 38, 170
Arbor monarchica, 89
Archduke Trio, 58 *n*
Army, chief support of Habsburg throne, 65 *ff*, 68-70
Assassination attempt on Franz Joseph, 42, 42 *n*

Assassination of Archduke Franz Ferdinand and Duchess Sophie von Hohenberg, 209-210
Assassination of Count Karl Stürgkh, 218, 221
Assassination of Empress Elisabeth, 117
Austerlitz, battle of, 180
Austria, House of, 17, 85-95
Austria-Hungary, 17, 172
Austria, meaning of name, 87
Austrian parliament, advisory, 146
Autocracy of Franz Joseph, 131-134, 137-139

Babenberg, dukes of, 87
Bach, Baron Alexander, 41
Bach Hussars, 41
Bacquehem, Marquis Olivier, 127
Badeni, Count Casimir, 143, 145
Balkan wars, 208
Balls at court, 47, 47 *n*, 60
Batthyány, Count Lajos, 26, 38-39
Bazaine, Marshal Achille, 122-123
Beck, Baron Max Vladimir von, 144
Beck, General Count Friedrich, 68-69
Beethoven, Ludwig van, 58 *n*
Beet-sugar industry in Austria, 192 *ff*
Belcredi, Count Richard, 138, 171, 172
Bem, General Josef (Murad Pasha), 177
Benedek, General Louis von, 154, 160 *ff*

Berchtold, Count Leopold, 211, 213, 214, 216, 217 *n*, 220
Berlin Congress, *see:* Congress of Berlin, Treaty of Berlin
Bethlen, Gábor, Prince of Transylvania, 178
Bethmann-Hollweg, Theobald von, 211
Beust, Count Friedrich Ferdinand von, 55, 142, 161, 165, 167, 171-173, 176
Biliński, Leon von, 217
Billroth, Theodor, 4
Bismarck, Prince Otto von, 80, 154-157, 160-161, 165, 180, 185
Black Cabinet, 70
"Black Hand," 209
"Black Friday," 194
Blum, Robert, 31, 151
Bocskay, István, Prince of Transylvania, 178
Bohemia, Kingdom of, 27
Bombelles, Count Heinrich, 101, 103
Bosnia and Hercegovina, 18, 140, 167-168, 188, 195, 204-207
Bourgeois ministry, 141-142
Brahms, Johannes, 4
Breweries in Austro-Hungarian Monarchy, 193
Bruckner, Ánton, 4
Brussels, Treaty of, 92-93
Budapest city representatives conduct their discussions in German, 136
Burg, Ferdinand, *see:* Ferdinand Karl, Archduke
Burgtheater, 58
Burián, Count Stefan, 220

Cap Martin, 63
Carbonari, 35
Carols II, King of Spain, 93
Cartels in Austria-Hungary, 200
Casa de Austria, 93
Centralist government, aim of Schwarzenberg, 37, 171
Chapultepec Castle, 123
Charles IV, Holy Roman Emperor, 91

Charles V, Holy Roman Emperor, 51, 92-93
Charles VIII, King of France, 89
Charles Albert, King of Sardinia, 27-28, 34
Charlotte, Empress of Mexico, 121-126
Chotek, Countess, *see:* Hohenberg, Duchess Sophie von
Christian IX, King of Denmark, 156
Cisleithania, 139, 175
Civil list, 80
Civil war in Transylvania, 26
Colonna, Roman family of, 88
Colors and emblems of Habsburg family, 91-92
"Comrade" Franz Joseph, 145-146
Confederation, German, *see:* German Confederation
Congress of Berlin, 195, 205, 207
Congress of Vienna, 23, 93, 155
Congress, Slav, at Prague, 27
Conrad von Hoetzendorf, Field Marshal Count Franz, 196, 208, 214-216, 220
Constitution, ancient Hungarian, 35, 35 *n*; December, 140; in the reign of Franz Joseph, 130-148
Constitution, Kroměříž, 130-131; March, 131-132; of 1848 in Hungary, 139-140, 169, 171, 173; Paragraph 14 of Austrian, 81, 137, 145; Schmerling's, 135-138, 169
Corfu, 63, 80, 110, 116
Coronation of Franz Joseph and Elisabeth in Budapest, 112, 165, 173, 174
Coronini-Cronberg, Count Johann Baptist, 102-103
Corti, Egon Caesar Conte, 78, 104, 114
Council of Ministers of Austria-Hungary, 209
Counterrevolution, triumph of, 34 *ff*, 43
Court balls, 47, 47 *n*
Crash of 1873, 194
Creditanstalt, 193
Crenneville, General Count Franz, 174

Crimean War, 44, 49, 203-204
Croatian settlement with Hungary, 174
Crown of Saint Stephen, 174
Crown of Saint Wenceslaus, 174
Curias (electoral interest groups), 136, 140-141, 143
Currency of Austro-Hungarian Empire, 197
Custoza, battles of, 28, 160
Cyrenaica, 208

Danish War, 155
"Danube Monarchy," 181-182, 187
Dardanelles, 207-208
Deák, Ferencz, 112 112 *n*, 163, 165, 169, 171-172
December Constitution, 140 *ff*
"The Delegations," 140, 173, 179
Disorders in Austrian parliament, 145
Doderer, Heimito von, 192 *n*
Dual Monarchy, 139, 172, 179
Dürnkrut, battle of, 87
Dvořák, Anton, 4

"Eastern Half" (of the Dual Monarchy), *see:* Transleithania
Economic policy of Austro-Hungarian Empire, 201-202
Economy of Franz Joseph's Empire, 187-202, 221
Edward VII, King of England, 64, 76, 208
Elisabeth, Archduchess (granddaughter of Franz Joseph), 129
Elisabeth, Empress of Austria, 52, 53, 57, 63, 80, 83, 99-100, 105-117, 165-166, 170-172
Elizabeth I, Queen of England, 94 *n*
Emblems and colors of Habsburg family, 91-92
Emigration from Austria-Hungary, 198
"Empire of Seventy Millions," 151-155
Entailed estates, 136 *n*
Esterházy, Count Moritz, 138

Eticho, Duke of Alsatia, 90
Eugénie, Empress, 166
Eve, 89
Executions, at Arad, 38, 170; in Italy, 35; more wanted by Prince Schwarzenberg, 39; authorized by Franz Joseph, 40
External trade of Austria-Hungary, 200-201

February Patent, 135-138
Ferdinand I, Holy Roman Emperor, 92-93, 94 *n*, 183
Ferdinand II, Holy Roman Emperor, 21-22, 177, 182, 224
Ferdinand I, "The Kindhearted," Emperor of Austria, 6-8, 26-27, 29, 96, 98
Ferdinand Karl, Archduke (Ferdinand Burg), 120
Ferenczy, Ida von, 113
Festetics, Countess Marie, 113
Feudal obligations of peasants abolished, 189
Financial institutions in Austria-Hungary, 193
Flour mills in Budapest, 193
Foreign policy, Franz Joseph's, 215
France, alliance of Austria with, 166
Franco-Prussian War, 166-167
Frankfort, meeting of German Princes at, 155
Frankfort Parliament, 150-152
Franz, Duke of Reichstadt, "*l'Aiglon*," 101
Franz I, Emperor of Austria, 6, 6 *n*, 7, 17, 23, 58, 73, 75, 82, 93, 94, 96, 120, 130, 149, 188, 189, 224
Franz I, Holy Roman Emperor, 82, 149
Franz Carl, Archduke, 7-8, 96-97
Franz Ferdinand, Archduke, 50, 54, 55, 68-69, 78, 78 *n*, 120, 209, 209 *n*, 215-216
Franz Joseph I, absolute ruler, 1851-1859, 131-134; 1865-1867, 137-139; afraid of revolutions, 71; appeased Hungarians, 176-178; assassination of, attempted, 42; attains majority,

6; character and personality, 45-59; chief ministers, 226-228; Concordat with Pope, 22; his constitutions, 130-148; Crimean War policy, 203-204; dismisses Windisch-Grätz, 36-37; distrusts modern technology, 3; education, 101-104; extravagant sport, hunting, 76; father image, 4; frequent travels, 3; interest in him stirred by Austrian tourism promoters, 4; joins his army in Hungary, 37; joins Radetzky's army, 31-32; medieval ideas and values, 3; meets Napoleon III at Salzburg, 166; military uniform his habitual dress, 60; myth of his frugality and simplicity, 82-84; opposed to innovation, 3; parents, 96-101; the Peace Emperor, 212-222; pinnacle of his career, 205; plans for revenge against Prussia, 164 ff; popularity, 2; proclaims himself "constitutional" Emperor, 8; reaction to his accession, 8-9; receives baptism of fire, 32, 63-64; his reign a period of economic expansion, 187 ff; relations with Katharina Schratt, 115-116; troublesome relatives, 118-129; responsibility for terrorism, 40-41; retinue and personal attendants, 75; simplicity, 72-83; as a soldier, 60-71; symbol of good old days, 4; titles and territories, 10, 223-225; wealth and income, 80-82

Franz Salvator, Archduke, 75 n
Franz Stephan of Lorraine, see: Franz I, Holy Roman Emperor
Frederick II, Holy Roman Emperor, 88, 224
Free trade, 189
Freud, Sigmund, 4
Friedjung, Heinrich, 216
Friedrich III, German King, 90
Friedrich III, Holy Roman Emperor, 91, 149 n
Friedrich Wilhelm, Elector of Hesse-Cassel, 152
Friedrich Wilhelm IV, King of Prussia, 150-152

Gastein, Treaty of, 156-157
Gautsch, Baron Paul, 145
Geneva, 117
German Confederation, 150-151, 156-157, 161, 167, 189
German Customs Union, 150, 189
Germany hegemony, see: Hegemony in Germany
German princes meet at Frankfort, 155
Gisela, Archduchess, 108
Giesl, Baron Wladimir, 211
Glacis around Inner City of Vienna, 191
Gödöllö, royal castle near Budapest, 3, 74, 110, 113
Gold standard adopted by Austria-Hungary, 197
Golden Bull of King Andrew II of Hungary, 35 n
Golden Bull of Emperor Charles IV, 91
Gopčevič, Spiridion, viii
Görgei, General Arthur, 36, 38, 163, 177
Grant, Ulysses S., 64
Greater Germany, 150-151
Grey, Sir Edward, 211
Grillparzer, Franz, 4, 184
Grünne, General Count Karl, 33, 39, 57, 70, 108, 114, 154, 162
Gustav V, King of Sweden, 61
Gyulay, General Count Franz, 154

Habsburg dynasty, 7, 9, 17, 23, 88, 91-95, 149 ff
Habsburg Empire, a constant threat to its eastern and southern neighbors, 186; broken up by internal pressures, 65; economy of, 187-202; held together by army, 65 ff; liquidation of, considered by Napoleon I, 180; "mission" of, 180-186; naming of, 17; nationalism tabooed in, 16; no universal language spoken in, 16; racial, national, and language groups in, 11, 14-21; religions of peoples in, 21-22; territories included in, 11-13, 18-21

Habsburg-Lorraine dynasty, 86, 224
Habsburg rulers, 229-230
Hassenpflug, Hans, 152
Haynau, General Baron Julius von, 38, 39
Hegemony in Germany, 37, 135, 138, 149-168
Helene, Duchess in Bavaria, *see:* Nené
Heller, Colonel Eduard, 40-41, 132
Hentzi, Colonel Heinrich, 177
Hercegovina, *see:* Bosnia
Hirsch, Baron Moritz, 196
Hofmannsthal, Hugo von, 4
Hofburg, Imperial residence in Vienna, 3, 29, 73, 74, 76, 145, 192
Hog industry in Serbia, hurt in interests of Hungary, 207
"Hog war," 201
Hohenberg, Duchess Sophie von (Countess Chotek), 50, 54, 55, 120, 121, 209
Hohenembs, Countess von (incognito of Empress Elisabeth), 117
Hohenwart, Count Karl Siegmund von, 142-143
Holstein, 155-157, 161
Holy Alliance, 23
Holy Roman Emperors, 149, 223-224
Hradschin, 74
Hungarian constitution, *see:* Constitution
Hungarian parliament, dispersed by army, 148
Hungarian ruling class, opposed to universal suffrage and Czech nationalism, 143
Hungarian Settlement, *see:* Settlement
Hungary, clamors for national independence, 24; entire monarchy ruled by, 176 *ff;* Franz Joseph resented in, 9; gift of Czar to Franz Joseph, 43-44; Habsburg dynasty deposed in, 9; invaded by Imperial army, 35 *ff;* in War of 1866, 170-171; Kingdom of, 18; "March laws," approved in, 26; Revolution of 1848 in, 25-26; ruled from Vienna, 169-170; under Turkish rule, 183
Hunger riots in Vienna, 221
Hyena of Brescia, *see:* Haynau

Independence, demanded by national minorities in Habsburg Monarchy, 24; meaning of, in Habsburg Monarchy, 24 *n*
Industry in Franz Joseph's Empire, 199
Innsbruck, temporary residence of Imperial family, 7, 30, 33
Insanity, in Wittelsbach family, 110-111; alleged, of Crown Prince Rudolf, 127
Interregnum, 87
Ischl, Franz Joseph's summer residence, 3, 73, 76, 78, 97, 106, 110, 114
Izvolski, Alexander Petrovich, 207-208

Jelačić, General Count Josip, 26, 31
Jellinek, Hermann, 30
Johann, Archduke, 9, 73, 120, 150
Johann II, Prince of Liechtenstein, 1
Johann Salvator, Archduke (Johann Orth), 119-120
John, General Baron Franz, 162
John III, Sobieski, king of Poland, 183
Joint ministries of Dual Monarchy, 139-140, 173
Joseph II, Holy Roman Emperor, 6, 25, 58, 61, 62, 82, 188
Juárez, Benito, 122-124

Kafka, Franz, 4
Karl, Archduke, defeated Napoleon I, 159
Karl, Archduke, intended to be married to Queen Elizabeth I, 94 *n*
Karl I, Emperor of Austria, 115-116
Karl VI, Holy Roman Emperor, 86, 93, 188
Karl Ludwig, Archduke, 101
Karoline Augusta, Empress of Austria, 98, 99

Károlyi, Countess, 39
Kaspar, Mizzi, 128
Kempen, General Baron Johann, 39, 57, 70, 133
Kerzl, Dr. Joseph von, 57
Ketterl, Eugen, 61, 77, 79, 83-84, 117 *n*, 218, 219
Klapka, General Georg, 171
Koerber, Ernest von, 190
Königgrätz, battle of (Sadowa), 160, 163, 166, 169, 171, 196
Kossuth, Lajos (Louis), 24-26, 36, 38, 170, 172, 178
Kraus, General Baron Alfred von, 143
Krauss, Baron Philipp von, 133
Kray, Baron Stefan, 74, 218
Krobatin, General Baron Alexander, 217
Kroměříž (Kremsier), 8
Kroměříž Constitution, 130-131
Kübeck, Baron Karl Friedrich, 133
Kudlich, Hans, 30

Ladislaus II, King of Hungary, 183
"Lady in Black," 105
Lamberg, General Count Franz, 26
Landsteiner, Professor Dr. Karl, 4
Language, national, and racial groups in Habsburg Empire, 11, 14-21
Language, no universally spoken, in Habsburg Empire, 16
Language order, Count Badeni's, 145
Larisch, Countess Marie, 128
Latour, General Count Theodor, 26, 31
Laxenburg, castle near Vienna, 74
"le beau pendu" (Count Andrássy), 172
Lebrun, General Bartholomé, 166
Leopold I, Holy Roman Emperor, 58, 193
Leopold II, Holy Roman Emperor, 188
Leopold II, King of the Belgians, 129
Lexa von Aehrenthal, *see:* Aehrenthal
Libényi, János, 42

Liberalism, trend toward, in Austria, 189
Liechtenstein, Prince Johann II, 1
Lipizza horses, 77
Lissa, battle of, 160
Lombardy, invaded by Sardinians, 28
Lónyay, Prince Elemer, 129
Lorraine, exchanged for Tuscany, 86
Louis XIV, King of France, 1 *n*, 93
Lucheni, Luigi, 117
Ludovika, Duchess in Bavaria, 106, 107
Ludwig, Archduke, 67
Ludwig IX, of Hesse-Darmstadt, 110
Ludwig II, King of Bavaria, 111
Ludwig Viktor, Archduke, 101 *n*, 119
Luxemburg, House of, 90

Madeira, 109-110
Magenta, battle of, 204
Magyarization, in Hungary, 20, 21 *n*
Mahler, Gustav, 4
Manufacturing in Franz Joseph's Empire, 188 *ff*
March Constitution, 131-132
"March laws," 26
Maria Anna, Empress of Austria, 32, 133
Maria Theresa, Empress, 82, 86, 149, 181, 188
Marie Louise, Archduchess, 23
Marie Valeria, Archduchess, 75 *n*, 76, 113, 173
Marx, Karl, 30
Masaryk, Thomas Garrigue, 185
Master race, 18, 18 *n*, 20, 175
Max, Duke in Bavaria, 106
Maximilian, Archduke, Emperor of Mexico, 70, 101, 121-125, 164, 165
Maximilian I, Holy Roman Emperor, 49, 51, 89, 92, 183
Maximilian I, Joseph, King of Bavaria, 98
Mayerling, 127
Mazzini, Giuseppe, 35
Mejía, General Tomás, 124
Mensdorff-Pouilly, Count Alexander, 67, 159

Metternich era, 23-24
Metternich, Prince Klemens Lothar, 7, 23-24, 29, 43-44, 93, 101, 103, 134
Metternich, Prince Richard, 161
Mexico, 121-124
Milan, King of Serbia, 207
Milan main guard stormed, 35
Ministers of Franz Joseph, 226-228
Miramar, castle, 124, 125 *n*
Miramón, General Miguel, 124
"Mission" of the Habsburg Empire, 180-186
Mississippi Bubble, 194
Mohács, battle of, 92
Moldavia, 204
Montenuovo, Prince Alfred, 50 *n*, 57, 115
Murad Pasha (General Josef Bem), 177

Napoleon I, 23, 180, 191, 224
Napoleon III, 122-124, 134, 153, 154, 158, 159, 161, 165, 166, 167, 169, 204
National, racial, and language groups in Habsburg Empire, 11, 14-21
Nationalism tabooed in Habsburg Empire, 16, 175
Nationalities problem, sharpened by Hungarian Settlement, 174-176
Nené, Duchess in Bavaria, 106, 110
Nicholas I, Czar of Russia, 33-34, 49, 56, 152, 203, 204
Nikolsburg, Peace of, 161
Noah, 89
Novara, battle of, 34

October Diploma, 134-135, 138
O'Donnell, Count Maximilian, 42
Olomouc (Olmütz), 6, 9, 29, 33, 153
Orth, Johann, *see:* Johann Salvator
Osiris, 89
Otto, King of Bavaria, 111
Ottokar II, King of Bohemia, 87, 88

Palacký, František, 27, 180, 185
Panslavism, 206-207
Paragraph 14 of Austrian Constitution, 81, 137, 145
Parliament at Frankfort, 150-152

Parliament, Austrian, advisory, 146
Parliament, Hungarian, dispersed by army, 148
Parliamentary cabinets, 142
Parliamentary reform, 143 *ff*
Parliamentary rule and national conflict, 144-148
Pašić, Nikola, 211
Paskevich, General Prince Ivan Feodorovich, 38, 43
Payne, Robert, 47, 128-129
Peace, in 19th century, 195-196
"Personal union," 171-172
Peter I, Karageorgevich, King of Serbia, 207
Petznek, Leopold, 129
Pierleoni, Roman family of, 88-89
Pius, Duke in Bavaria, 110
Pius IX, Pope, 28
Plochl, Anna, morganatic wife of Archduke Johann, 120
Pollet, Sergeant Johann, 29
Postal Savings Bank in Austria, 193
Potocki, Count Alfred, 142
Potiorek, General Oskar, 217, 219
Prado, 2
Pragmatic Sanction, 86
Prague, Peace of, 161
Princip, Gavrilo, 209
Privilegium maius, 90-91
Privilegium minus, 91
Profits, war a source of, 197
Property interests, dominant in Franz Joseph's Empire, 189 *ff*

Querétaro, Emperor Maximilian executed at, 124

Racial, national, and language groups in Habsburg Empire, 11, 14-21
Radetzky, Field Marshal Count Johann Josef, 27, 28, 34, 39, 63, 67
Railroads, Austrian, 190 *ff*
Rákóczy, Ferencz, 177, 178
Rampolla, Mariano Cardinal, 127 *n*
Rastatt, Peace of, 93
Rauscher, Joseph Othmar Cardianal von, 98, 102, 108
"Real union," 172
Redlich, Joseph, 74, 130

Reichstag, 130-131
Reichsrat, 131, 134, 136, 139
Religions of peoples in Habsburg Empire, 21-22
Revolution of 1848, 23-33, 66
Rilke, Rainer Maria, 4
Ringstrassentheater, 56
Ringstrasse, 191-192
Roosevelt, Theodore, 2
Rothschild, Salomon, 29, 196
Rudolf, Archduke, 58 *n*
Rudolf, Crown Prince, 53-54, 59, 65, 97, 108, 125-129, 164
Rudolf I, German King, 87, 88, 149, 159
Rudolf IV, "The Founder," Duke of Austria, 90-91
Russo-Japanese War, 207

Sacher, Hotel-Restaurant in Vienna, 118
Sadowa, *see:* Königgrätz
Salzburg, meeting of Franz Joseph with Napoleon III at, 166
San Stefano, Treaty of, 205
Santa Lucia, battle of, 28, 32, 63
Sarajevo, 206, 209
Schäffle, Albert, 142-143
Schleswig, 155-157, 161
Schmerling, Anton von, 135-138, 154-155, 169-172
"Schmerling theater," 137
Schnitzler, Arthur, 4
Schnürer, Dr. Franz, 100 *n*
Schönbrunn, summer palace of Habsburg Emperors, 1-3, 73-74, 76, 96, 101, 111, 221, 222
Schratt, Katharina, 58, 59, 73, 76, 79, 114-116
Schwarzenberg, Prince Felix, 33, 34, 36, 37, 39, 41, 44-46, 132, 133, 151-153, 171, 172, 204
Serbian nationalism, 206-207
Serfdom in Austria, 188-189
Settlement with Hungary, 17, 19-20, 112, 138-141, 169-179, 180
Sevastopol, 203
Sisi, *see:* Elisabeth, Empress
Slav Congress at Prague, 27
Smaller Germany, 150-151

Smetana, Bedřich, 4
Sobieski, King John III of Poland, 183
Social Democrats enter Austrian parliament, 143
Solferino, battle of, 62, 64, 154, 204
Soliman "The Magnificent," Turkish Sultan, 183
Sophie, Archduchess, daughter of Franz Joseph, 108
Sophie, Archduchess, "Empress-Mother," 7-9, 22, 31, 33, 38, 62, 67, 96-102, 105, 107-109, 112, 113, 124, 132, 138, 156, 162, 166
Sophie, Duchess of Alençon, 110
Sophie, wife of Archduke Franz Ferdinand, *see:* Hohenberg
South Sea Bubble, 194
South Tirol, 220
Spanish-American War, 196
Spanish etiquette, 51-52
Spanish Riding School, 77
Spanish Succession, War of the, 93
Spitzmüller, Baron Alexander von, viii, 147-148, 218
Srbik, Heinrich von, 57-58 *n*
Stadion, Count Franz, 131
State Conference, 97
State railways in Austria, 190 *ff*
Steinbach, Emil, 143-144, 147
Stephanie, Crown Princess, 126-129
Stephen, Saint, Crown of, 174
Stifter, Adalbert, 4
Straus, Oscar, 4
Strauss, Johann, 4
Strauss, Richard, 4
Stürgkh, Count Karl, 57, 217-218, 220, 221
Sturmfeder, Baroness Louise von, 101, 103
Succession states, 182-183
Swiss Confederation, 184
Sylvester Patent, 131-133
Szécsen, Count Anton, 134-135
Szeps, Moritz, 126
Sztáray, Countess Irma, 117

Taaffe, Count Eduard, 128-129, 147, 184

Talleyrand, Prince Charles Maurice de, 180
Tariff wars, 201
Tegetthoff, Admiral Wilhelm von, 160
Temesvár, *see:* Timisoara
Territories included in Habsburg Empire, 11-13, 18-21
Textile industry in Austrian Empire, 193
Timisoara (Temesvár), Hungarians defeated near, 38
Tisza, Count István, 210, 210 *n,* 217, 220
Todesco, Baron Eduard, 196
Tököly, Imre, 177, 178
Trade, external, of Austria-Hungary, 200-201
Transleithania, 139, 175
Transylvania, civil war in, 26
Treaty of Berlin, 208
Trialism, 209 *n*
Tripoli, 208
Tschuppik, Karl, 210 *n,* 217

Ultimatum, 204, 209-211
Universal suffrage, 143 *n*

Valerie, Archduchess, *see:* Marie Valerie
Venice, 28, 34, 161
Venetia, 158
Versailles, 73, 167
Vetsera, Baroness Mary, 127-128
Victor Emanuel I, King of Sardinia, 134
Victoria, Queen of England, 109
Vienna, besieged by Turks, 183; Congress of, 23, 93, 155; expansion of, 191-192; Inner City of, 191; Parliament, 173; Revolution of 1848 in, 28-31; World Exposition, 194

Világos, Hungarians surrender at, 38

Wagner-Jauregg, Professor Dr. Julius von, 4
Walachia, 204
Wallenstein, General Albrecht, Duke of Friedland, 177
War hawks around Franz Joseph, 214
War of 1859 with France and Sardinia, 153-154
War of 1866 with Prussia, 157 *ff*
Washington, George, 178
Weckbecker, Baron Hugo von, 66
Welden, General Baron Ludwig, 37
Wenceslaus, Saint, Crown of, 174
Wessenberg, Baron Johann Philipp von, 40
"Western Half" of the Dual Monarchy, *see:* Cisleithania
Weygand, General Maxime, 125 *n*
Wilhelm I, German Emperor, 80, 157, 167
Wilhelm II, German Emperor, 61, 196, 208, 211, 215
Windisch-Grätz, Field Marshal Prince Alfred, 27, 31-32, 36-37, 39, 43, 151
Windisch-Grätz, Prince Otto, 129
Wittelsbach, House of, 98, 106 *n*
Wolf, Hugo, 4
Wölfling, Leopold (Archduke Leopold Ferdinand), 118
World War I, 203-211, 218, 219-221
World War II, bombing of Vienna, 192

Young Czechs, 143

Zápolya, John, King of Hungary, 178, 183

DATE DUE

FEB 11 '72			
MAR 20 75			
MAR 11 '76			
MAR 23 '76			
AP 21 '77			
OC 12 '77			
MR 7 '79			
MR 29 '79			
FE 27 '83			
MR 1 '84			
NOV 15 '??			
GAYLORD			PRINTED IN U.S.A.